JOURNAL FOR THE STUDY OF THE OLD TESTAMENT
SUPPLEMENT SERIES
110

Editors
David J.A. Clines
Philip R. Davies

Sheffield Academic Press

The Canaanites
and Their Land

The Tradition of the Canaanites

Niels Peter Lemche

Journal for the Study of the Old Testament
Supplement Series 110

First published by JSOT Press 1991
Reprinted 1999

Copyright © 1991, 1999 Sheffield Academic Press

Published by
Sheffield Academic Press Ltd
Mansion House
19 Kingfield Road
Sheffield S11 9AS
England

Typeset by e.l. arab-text, Gurre, Denmark
and
Printed on acid-free paper in Great Britain
by Bookcraft Ltd
Midsomer Norton, Bath

British Library Cataloguing in Publication Data

A catalogue record for this book is available
from the British Library

ISSN 0309-0787
ISBN 1-85075-310-5

CONTENTS

ACKNOWLEDGMENTS

It is an interesting consquence of the new reconstructions of the early history of Israel that the Israelites must originally have been Canaanites. Nevertheless, an outspoken hatred against the Canaanites permeates the Old Testament. It is my aim in this study to present a new way of explaining the anti-Canaanite sentiments of the Old Testament historians. I hope, at the same time, to disclose some of the aims and ideas which governed Old Testament history writing.

Many friends have been greatly helpful and have contributed to the completion of this book, notably my colleagues at the University of Copenhagen, Niels Hyldahl and Eduard Nielsen, who critically revised an early Danish version of the manuscript and thus prevented a number of errors from being perpetuated. I should also like to thank Gösta Ahlström of Chicago. Without his interest the book may never have appeared. Finally, the English style of my manuscript was revised by Mr Charles Blair, MA, of Chicago, whose contribution, however, by far surpasses the duties of a revisor of language. He especially pointed out several blurred arguments which have been corrected. However, the argument and theses of this book are solely mine, and I am the only person to blame, should factual errors or errors of judgment have survived.

Gurre, 28th December 1990

PREFACE

It would be a mistake to say that students of the ancient Near East have in any fundamental way changed their ideas about the Canaanites because of this little book. Most scholars continue to use the term 'Canaanite' in the same manner as before. According to this majority, Canaan is still a geographical entity of the Late Bronze Age, is populated by Canaanites, and its culture is Canaanite. Some scholars may think that by applying this term in such a careless way they are excused because Canaan is a traditional and well-defined name of the ancient Southern Levant. They are not excused. They are playing the usual game: they are implanting foreign ideas and notions into a region that did not necessarily conform to our expectations, mostly coined by biblical tradition and beliefs.

Two recent studies by Keith W. Whitelam[1] and Michael Prior[2] have told us how precarious it can be to disregard the evidence of the ancients and substitute their ideas with modern sentiments. The thesis is in both cases that the eurocentric concentration on the evidence of the Bible has made scholars blind. By applying biblical terms such as 'Canaan' scholars have—in Keith Whitelam's words—'silenced Palestinian History', i.e., they have in practice wiped this history out as if the biblical history of ancient Israel is the real history of ancient Palestine. This view of the Near East only leaves room for the evidence of the Bible. The Bible establishes a filter through which all other information has to be sifted. The result is a distortion of facts not preserved in the Bible. When the filter of biblical readings combines with colonialism, the dynamism of the biblical hatred against the Canaanites turns into a political program for the suppression of other nations also in modern times.

1. Keith W. Whitelam, *The Invention of Ancient Israel. The Silencing of Palestinian History* (London and New York: Routledge, 1996).
2. Michael Prior, *The Bible and Colonialism* (Sheffield: Sheffield Academic Press, 1997).

A few rejoinders have been published to the argument developed in this volume. The two most notable critical reviews are those by Nadav Na'aman and Anson F. Rainey.[3] Apart from including a few other texts of dubious value to the general argument, Na'aman and Rainey concentrate on the interpretation of the text EA 151:49-67 presented in this book.[4] In my view this text indicates that the King of Tyre did not realize that he was himself an inhabitant of Canaan. When asked about news from Canaan, Abi-Milku answers with a survey of incidents covering most of Western Asia. Na'aman attacked this reading as being 'twisted', while Rainey considered it to be absurd and argued for a different interpretation: Abi-Milku has been asked to provide information *from within Canaan*. All kinds of evidence are cited in favour of this translation. Rainey, however, forgot the closest parallel to this passage, EA 147:66-69. These lines are part of another letter from Abi-Milku of Tyre. This time Abi-Milku does not bring news from Canaan; he refers to Zimrida of Sidon who is sending news from Egypt to Aziru of Amurru. Apart from the names, the two phrases are exactly the same, meaning that if Sidon is not placed in Egypt (which it is of course not), then Tyre is according to Abi-Milku's estimation not placed in Canaan. I shall not deal with these rejoinders in detail. Detailed answers to Na'aman and Rainey have already been published in other places.[5]

Both Na'aman and Rainey are right as far as the importance of EA 151 goes. If a king could be in doubt about his own ethnic affiliation although he was ruling a city like Tyre that should by all means be considered a part of Canaan, who *would* in those days have realized that he or she was a Canaanite? Undoubtedly Tyre would have belonged to Canaan if there ever was a political or geographical locality of this name. EA 151 shows—as well as the vague indications in other ancient documents—that Canaan was never a well defined and identifiable territory and that the term 'Canaanite' meant little to the people that lived in the Southern Levant in Antiquity. In a recent contribution to the

3. Nadav Na'aman, 'The Canaanites and Their Land. A Rejoinder', *UF* 26 (1994), pp. 397-418; Anson F. Rainey, 'Who Is a Canaanite? A Review of the Textual Evidence', *BASOR* 304 (1996), pp. 1-15.
4. Pp. 30-31.
5. Niels Peter Lemche, 'Where Should We Look for Canaan? A Reply to Nadav Na'aman', *UF* 28 (1996), pp. 767-72; Niels Peter Lemche, 'Greater Canaan: The Implications of a Correct Reading of EA 151:49-67', *BASOR* 310 (1998), pp. 19-24.

discussion, Robert Drews argues that Canaan was in the first millennium BCE seen as identical with Phoenicia. This is probably true. He is, however, hardly right when he assumes that we have evidence from this period of the inhabitants of Phoenicia calling themselves 'Canaanites'.[6]

Developments within Old Testament studies have been more promising. The main thesis of this book is that the 'Canaanites' of the Old Testament are not a real nation but an imagined nation placed in opposition to the Israelites. The Canaanites of the Old Testament are the 'bad guys', hated by God and the world, doomed, and to be replaced by the Israelites. Nothing has so far appeared that in a serious way questions the validity of this thesis.

On the contrary, several studies have probed further into this. One conclusion I did not reach in 1991, when this book first appeared, was that the party of 'bad guys' needs another consisting of the 'good guys'. Any literary plot must have its heroes and villains—otherwise something would be missing. The Canaanites certainly play the role of the 'bad guys' but who are the 'good guys'? This question was settled in two studies by Philip R. Davies and Thomas L. Thompson that appeared already in 1992.[7] Both authors argue that the Israel of the Old Testament is an invention of the mind of later Judaism of the Persian Period. It is not the Israel of the Iron Age that appears on the pages of the Old Testament. It is an imaginative Israel with a literary rather than historical role to play. While this study placed the tradition of the Canaanites among the many tales told by the authors of the literature of the Old Testament, Davies and Thompson elaborated further on this and created the foundation for subsequent developments within the study of 'ancient Israel'.

In order to place these studies in the right perspective, all three of them contributed immensely to the liberation of the Old Testament from the burden of having to provide exact historical information about the past. As long as Israel and the Israelites of the Old Testament were

6. Robert Drews, 'Canaanites and Philistines', *JSOT* 81 (1998), pp. 39-61, pp. 48-49. As evidence he refers to a lexicon article by Otto Eissfeldt. With all respect, Eissfeldt was hardly a 'Canaanite'.

7. Philip R. Davies, *In Search of 'Ancient Israel'* (JSOTS, 148; Sheffield: Sheffield Academic Press, 1992); Thomas L. Thompson, *Early History of the Israelite People. From the Written and Archaeological Sources* (SHANE, 4; Leiden: E.J. Brill, 1992).

still believed to represent a nation that once existed, a proper appraisal of the intentions of the historical narrative in the Old Testament was hardly possible. It turned out that the main characters of the drama created by the historiographers of the Old Testament were parts of a narrative and not active in 'real' history—whatever this meant. It also became possible in a hitherto unforeseen way to present a radically new analysis of the historical narrative in the Old Testament. It is by now obvious that this historical narrative is governed by the need for an explanation of their own situation current among Jews of the late first millennium BCE.

Instead of a continuous wrestling with historical and literary information that cannot be joined together into a coherent picture of ancient Palestine and its history, modern studies of the historical parts of the Old Testament have turned to the motives behind the historical narrative and the techniques employed by the historiographers as they construct their past. Gone are the days of happy and irresponsible historical reconstruction. What remains is the unmolested text of the Old Testament that has in no way been harmed by recent developments within biblical historical studies. It is only the ego of modern western humankind that has been hit, by showing its understanding of the world to be a mirage. It is the modern world's obsession with history that is here being challenged and shown to be idiosyncratic to Western civilization. This obsession does not involve the world of the Old Testament that followed quite different rules.[8]

8. Important examples of this development within Old Testament studies are— apart from the already quoted literature—the studies by Niels Peter Lemche, *The Israelites in History and Tradition* (Library of Ancient Israel; Louisville: Westminster/John Knox; London: SPCK, 1998), and Thomas L. Thompson, *The Bible in History. How Writers Create a Past* (London: Jonathan Cape, 1999).

ABBREVIATIONS

AB	Anchor Bible
AHw	*Akkadisches Handwörterbuch*, I-III, ed. W. von Soden
AIUON	*Annali dell'Istituto Universitario Orientale di Napoli*
*ANET*³	*Ancient Near Eastern Texts Relating to the Old Testament*, ed. J.B. Pritchard, 3rd edn
AOAT	Alter Orient und Altes Testament
ASTI	*Annual of the Swedish Theological Institute*
AT	Alalaḫ Tablets
ATD	Altes Testament Deutsch
AThANT	Abhandlungen zur Theologie des Alten und Neuen Testaments
BASOR	*Bulletin of the American Schools of Oriental Research*
BHH	*Biblisch-Historisches Handwörterbuch*, I-IV
BHS	*Biblia Hebraica Stuttgartensia*
BHTh	Beiträge zur historischen Theologie
BIFAO	*Bulletin d'Institut français d'archéologie orientale*
BKAT	Biblischer Kommentar. Altes Testament
BN	*Biblische Notizen*
BO	*Bibliotheca Orientalis*
BWANT	Beiträge zur Wissenschaft vom Alten und Neuen Testament
BZAW	Beihefte zur Zeitschrift für die alttestamentliche Wissenschaft
CAH	*Cambridge Ancient History*
CBO	Coniectanea Biblica. Old Testament Series
CBQMS	Catholic Biblical Quarterly Monograph Series
DBAT	*Dielheimer Blätter zum Alten Testament*
DTT	*Dansk Teologisk Tidsskrift*

EA	El-Amarna letter
FRLANT	Forschungen zur Religion und Literatur des Alten und Neuen Testaments
GHKAT	Göttinger Handkommentar zum Alten Testament
HALAT	*Hebräisches und aramäisches Lexikon zum Alten Testament*, ed. W. Baumgartner *et al.*
HAT	Handbuch zum Alten Testament
HSM	Harvard Semitic Monographs
IEJ	*Israel Exploration Journal*
IDB	*Interpreter's Dictionary of the Bible*
IDBS	*Interpreter's Dictionary of the Bible. Supplementary Volume*
JAOS	*Journal of the American Oriental Society*
JBL	*Journal of Biblical Literature*
JEA	*Journal of Egyptian Archaeology*
JNES	*Journal of Near Eastern Studies*
JSOTSup	Journal for the Study of the Old Testament Supplement Series
KAI	Kanaanäische und aramäische Inschriften, ed. H. Donner and W. Röllig
KAT	Kommentar zum Alten Testament
KHCAT	Kurzer Hand-Commentar zum Alten Testament
KTU	*Die Keilalphabetischen Texte aus Ugarit, Band 1. Transkription*, ed. M. Dietrich, O. Loretz, J. Sanmartín
KUB	*Keilschrifturkunde aus Boghazköy*
MIO	*Mitteilungen des Instituts für Orientforschung*
NEB	*New English Bible*
OA	*Oriens Antiquus*
Or	*Orientalia*
OTL	Old Testament Library
OTS	*Oudtestamentische Studiën*
RA	*Revue d'assyriologie et d'archéologie orientale*
RLA	*Reallexikon der Assyriologie*
REB	*Revised English Bible*
RGG	*Die Religion in Geschichte und Gegenwart*
SJOT	*Scandinavian Journal of the Old Testament*
SVT	Supplements to Vetus Testamentum
TWAT	*Theologisches Wörterbuch zum Alten Testament*, ed. G. Botterweck *et al.*

VT	*Vetus Testamentum*
WMANT	Wissenschaftliche Monographien zum Alten und Neuen Testament
WO	*Die Welt des Orients*
ZA	*Zeitschrift für Assyriologie*
ZAW	*Zeitschrift für die alttestamentliche Wissenschaft*
ZDPV	*Zeitschrift des Deutschen Palästina-Vereins*

Chapter 1

THE CANAANITES AND OLD TESTAMENT STUDY.
INTRODUCTION

Upon reading a number of lexicographical articles dealing with the
Canaanites, one is left with the impression that although these
Canaanites created problems for the ancient Israelites, they themselves
are not considered problematic by current Old Testament scholarship.
In such general descriptions of the Canaanites, the evaluation is
generally fair and neutral, sometimes also instructive; however, viewpoints which do not conform with the age-old notions about the
Canaanites, or which question the validity of the accepted opinions,
are normally not represented in such literature.[1]

Not all descriptions of the life and culture of the ancient
Canaanites can, however, be described as neutral. Sometimes the
wording used about the Canaanites seems to have been borrowed
from the description of their idolatry employed by some of the old
Israelite prophets. Characteristic of this attitude towards Canaanite
culture is the famous evaluation of the extremely low standard of
Canaanite religious beliefs published by William Foxwell Albright,
who considered Canaanite religion to have been absolutely abomin-
able, containing a mythology almost devoid of ethical content.[2]

---

1 Cf. such articles as J. Hempel, 'Kanaan' and 'Kanaaniter', *BHH*, II, pp.
   926-30; A. Alt, 'Kanaan–II. Geschichtlich', *RGG*, III, cols. 1109-11, and M.
   Weippert, 'Canaan, Conquest and Settlement of', *IDBS*, pp. 125-30. Weippert
   has also written the equally instructive article about Canaan in *RLA*, V, pp.
   352-55.
2 We can refer to Albright's description of Canaanite religion in his 'The Role
   of the Canaanites in the History of Civilization', which appeared in 1942, and
   which was reprinted in *The Bible and the Ancient Near East* (ed. G.E.
   Wright; London, 1961), pp. 328-62 (338).

Furthermore, it is not unusual for such characterizations of Canaanite culture to be embedded in scholarly descriptions of the history of Israelite religion, which are often paraphrases of Old Testament texts rather than independent scholarly accounts of the Israelite religion. In such contexts it is easy to recognize that some modern authors operate with an idea that early Israelite society was from an ethnic point of view, 'pure', and in possession of religious beliefs and standards which were equally untouched by the religion of the Canaanites, that is, that the early Israelite religion was the pure Yahwistic faith which originated in 'the desert'. After their settlement the Israelites as well as their Yahwistic religion became 'contaminated' because of the Canaanite presence. The result was that the ethnic unity of the Israelites was lost, while Israelite religion became infested with Canaanite religious beliefs and practices. This development is usually termed *syncretistic*.[3]

A more elegant method for describing the 'Canaanization' of Israelite society is to consider the historical development as a reflection of the continuous struggle between Israelite and Canaanite cultural phenomena.[4]

A fine example of such an understanding of the history of Israel is presented by Walther Dietrich, according to whom we may speak of an ongoing battle between two contrasting cultures, on one hand the culture of the Israelites and on the other the culture of the Canaanites. In his study devoted to this subject, the history of Israel is divided into a number of succeeding phases in accordance with the periodization of this history as present in the Old Testament. However, each phase is characterized according to the relations between the Canaanites and the Israelites which prevailed at the time. Thus Dietrich's study begins with the period of the Israelite settlement, which is called *disposition*, later to be followed by the period of the judges and the early monarchy, a period of *confrontation*. David's empire represents the period of the *integration* of

3 To cite but one example of a pronounced use of this concept of syncretism, cf. W.H. Schmidt, *Alttestamentlicher Glaube und seine Umwelt* (Neukirchen, 1968; in later editions nothing has changed).
4 Only two titles will be mentioned in this connection: with emphasis on the historical development, W. Dietrich, *Israel und Kanaan. Vom Ringen zweier Gesellschaftssysteme* (Stuttgarter Bibelstudien, 94; Stuttgart, 1979); stressing religious matters, W.F. Albright, *Yahweh and the Gods of Canaan. A Historical Analysis of Two Contrasting Faiths* (London, 1968).

Israelites and Canaanites into a single nation, and accordingly Solomon's reign can be called the era of *cooperation*. This situation was to change over the next century, following the death of Solomon, when the amalgamation of the two cultures became so evident that any difference between the two *ethne*, the Israelites and the Canaanites, seemed a matter of the past. The period in question is considered a *digression* by Dietrich. The further limit of this digression was reached during the reign of the Omrides in the 9th century BCE, and from then on we may reckon with a regular Canaanite *infiltration* of the Israelite nation. The consequences of this infiltration are easy to trace in the *reaction* against Canaanite influence in the time of Jehu and his successors. However, the religio-revolutionary zeal of this renewed Israelite reaction towards the Canaanite culture did not last forever, but at the end of the independent history of the kingdom of Israel a regular *assimilation* between Israelite and Canaanite elements was obvious to everybody; it was a development which was evidently furthered by the influence of the Assyrian culture in the same period. After the sack of Samaria in 722 BCE, the history of the struggle between the Canaanites and the Israelites continued, now, however, in the southern kingdom of Judah. Here we find, in the days of king Manasseh, a regular *repression* of genuine Israelite cultural elements, but this situation was reversed after Manasseh's death and the departure of the Assyrian imperial power at the end of the 7th century BCE, when Judaean society reacted in a forceful way against the syncretistic influence of the Canaanite culture. This reaction was clearly anti-Canaanite and anti-Assyrian, but nevertheless, not as bloodthirsty as the one in the days of Jehu of Israel. Nonetheless, the result was indisputable, since the period represents an Israelite (or Judaean) *revision*, that is, a renewed interest in the genuine Israelite cultural and religious heritage.

Such an interpretation of the relations between the Israelites and the Canaanites may look deceptively promising, not least because it seems so obvious in light of the biblical historical narratives. We may of course ask whether Dietrich, in order to make the Israelite history conform with his own interpretation, does not go too far, especially as concerns the later parts of the pre-exilic period. Nevertheless, his description of the history of Israel conforms well with the portrait of this history which is handed down to us by the Old Testament itself.

However, although we may consider Dietrich's monograph a

sympathetic treatment of the vexed history of Israelite and Canaanite interrelationships, and so far beyond Albright's understanding of Canaanite culture, as exemplified by the rejection of Canaan in his works, the Canaanites are still viewed in the light of the Old Testament description. We may therefore ask whether scholars have not too easily accepted the role of spokesmen for the basically anti-Canaanite attitude of the biblical writers, thereby preventing themselves from forming their own unprejudiced opinions of Canaanite life and culture. Still the Canaanite world—understood as the antithesis of Israelite culture—seems to be a rather unattractive place for most Old Testament scholars, although we should not overlook that Albright has in other respects contributed substantially to our knowledge of the Canaanites and their culture.[5]

Thus it is only fair to describe the attitude of biblical scholars towards Canaanite culture as ambiguous. Only a few Old Testament scholars doubt the essential superiority of Israelite culture, especially as concerns the content of Israel's religious beliefs as compared to those of its neighbours, while at the same time the same scholars are attracted by the fascination of the ancient oriental cultures—including the culture of the Canaanites.[6] This concern with the cultures of Western Asia has, over the years, led to quite a number of fine studies of Canaanite culture written by Old Testament scholars.

A remarkable example of this has been the involvement of biblical scholars in the deciphering and interpretation of the Ugaritic epic literature, the first indigenous texts from the ancient Near East on which to base the study of West Semitic religion. Since the discovery of the Ugaritic texts beginning in 1929 the contribution of Old Testament scholars in the field of Ugaritic studies has been impressive.[7]

---

5   Cf. my *Early Israel. Anthropological and Historical Studies on the Israelite Society before the Monarchy* (SVT, 37; Leiden, 1985), p. 60 n. 92, with comments on Albright's many contributions to our knowledge of pre-Israelite Palestinian culture.

6   Thus we should not miss the important role played by biblical scholars in the development of oriental studies—not least at the universities of northern Europe.

7   It is impossible here to enumerate all these scholars. Surveys of the impact of Ugaritic studies on the field of Old Testament study between 1930 and c. 1960 may be found in A.S. Kapelrud, *The Ras Shamra Discoveries and the Old Testament* (Oxford, 1965), or in E. Jacob, *Ras Shamra et l'Ancien Testament* (Neuchâtel, 1960). Among the more recent English translations of the texts we

The interest of the Old Testament scholar in the exploration of the literary treasure from Ugarit was well-founded, especially because it was obvious to everybody that the interpretation of the Ugaritic texts would be enormously important for Old Testament studies; after all, it is virtually impossible to overrate the importance of these texts for our understanding of ancient Israelite culture and religion. A substantial number of biblical scholars have, since the 1930s, published valuable studies on Ugaritic matters, and they have invested much energy in demonstrating parallels between the religions of the Ugarites and of the Israelites.

The study of the Ugaritic religious texts was carried on regardless of the warnings of some scholars against the tendency too easily to identify Israelite and Ugaritic religious features. After all, Ugarit differed in many respect from Israel. First of all, the ethnic composition of the Ugaritic state was very different from that found in the land of Israel. Secondly, the Ugaritic texts which were reduced to writing in the 13th century BCE were perhaps more than 500 years older than their biblical counterparts. And finally, we may ask whether Ugarit was a Canaanite state at all, since the area in which the Ugaritic state was situated, northern Syria, did not form part of the Canaan of the Old Testament, nor is it included in Canaan as described by other ancient texts.

It is at the same time characteristic of the general scholarly climate that the titles of a number of studies of Ugaritic religion and culture since the 1930s already indicate that scholarly interest focused on biblical issues rather than on strictly Ugaritic matters.

In order to illustrate this situation I may quote the title of a well-known study by the Danish Old Testament scholar Flemming Friis Hvidberg, who had in 1938 already published an important monograph on the Ugaritic religion and its relations to the Israelite religion, *Weeping and Laughter in the Old Testament. A Study of Canaanite-Israelite Religion.*[8] It is characteristic that the title is *Weeping and Laughter in the* Old Testament, not *Weeping and Laughter in the Ugaritic Epic Literature*, although the most important contribu-

---

may mention J.C.L. Gibson, *Canaanite Myths and Legends* (Edinburgh, 1978), and J.C. de Moor, *An Anthology of Religious Texts from Ugarit* (Religious Texts Translation Series Niṣaba, 16; Leiden, 1987).

8   The Danish original, *Graad og Latter i Det gamle Testamente. En Studie i kanaanæisk-israelitisk Religion*, appeared in 1938. The posthumous English edition was published by Frede Løkkegaard in 1962.

tion of this book is perhaps Hvidberg's interpretation of Ugaritic texts. This tendency is still noticeable in some more recent titles, for example by J.C. de Moor, F.M. Cross, E.T. Mullen, J. Day and C. Kloos, just to mention some of the more important recent treatments of Ugaritic literature in connection with biblical issues.[9] The efforts of biblical scholars have generally been invested in the study of the Ugaritic epic literature, whereas other manifestations of ancient Ugaritic society have been more or less neglected or left in the hands of specialists—and this development has perhaps been more pronounced in later years than it was at the beginning of Ugaritic studies. The result has been that the Ugaritic epic literature—and especially the cycle of Baal—has been decisive for the interpretation of Canaanite culture. Therefore, when the content of this literature—not least the description of the brutal and abnormal behaviour of the Ugaritic gods—has been compared to the supposed content of the pre-exilic Israelite religion, the fertility elements which evidently played a dominant part in the Ugaritic texts have also decided the interpretation of the Canaanite religion to the neglect of other aspects of Canaanite culture. Moreover, the way for such an understanding of Ugaritic religion was more or less paved by certain circles of Old Testament scholarship, such as the history of religions school, the myth-and-ritual school, as well as the writings of the famous Norwegian scholar Sigmund Mowinckel.[10]

We may, accordingly, find reason to question this scholarly concentration on the fertility elements of the Canaanite religion, which may be out of proportion with the actual content of the religious beliefs of the Canaanites. This concentration on fertility may have caused other aspects of the Canaanite religion to have been overlooked, among which we may mention such vital questions as the relationship between 'life and death' understood as an ethical problem rather than a question about fertility, or the question of 'good and evil', which may also fall inside the scope of the Ugaritic

---

9 Cf. F.M. Cross, *Canaanite Myth and Hebrew Epic* (Cambridge, Mass., 1973); J.C. de Moor, *New Year with Canaanites and Israelites*, I-II (Kampen, 1972); E.T. Mullen, *The Assembly of the Gods. The Divine Council in Canaanite and Early Hebrew Literature* (HSM, 24; Chico, 1980); J. Day, *God's Conflict with the Dragon and the Sea. Echoes of a Canaanite Myth in the Old Testament* (Cambridge, 1985), and C. Kloos, *Yhwh's Combat with the Sea. A Canaanite Tradition in the Religion of Ancient Israel* (Leiden, 1986).
10 Cf. especially S. Mowinckel, *Psalmenstudien*. II. *Das Thronbesteigungsfest Jahwäs und der Ursprung der Eschatologie* (Oslo, 1922).

epic literature.[11] Although no cosmogonic myths are known from ancient Ugarit, we are, nevertheless, entitled to ask how the religion of the Canaanites could manage without any sense of an ordered cosmos created by the gods.

Without doubt the ancient citizens of Ugarit—like all other inhabitants of the fertile crescent—wished to be informed about such questions, and we can be certain that they also tried to find the answers in their religious beliefs. We can therefore be absolutely sure that the fertility aspects of the Ugaritic religion were supplemented by other—ethical—aspects. But it is all too easy to show that such aspects, which are perhaps more pronounced in the poem of Kirtu and Aqhat than in the the cycle of Baal, are underplayed by many modern historians of the Ugaritic/Canaanite religion. As a result it is possible to speak about a certain unwillingness to acknowledge that also in the case of its ethical standards, Israel was indebted to its predecessors in Western Asia.[12]

We may safely say that although the critical studies of the ancient Canaanite religion published by Old Testament scholars have certainly contributed to our knowledge of this ancient Near Eastern religion, they have also—because of the presence of a number of anti-Canaanite polemical passages in the Old Testament itself—to some degree blocked the road to a true understanding of the civilization of the Canaanites. In this study it is not, however, my aim to concentrate on the supposed similarities and the divergences between Israelite and

---

11 Cf., for example, the discussion of 'life' and 'death' in a study on the Baal cycle from Ugarit by B. Margalit, *A Matter of 'Life' and 'Death'. A Study of the Baal-Mot Epic (CTA 4-5-6)* (AOAT, 206; Kevelaer/Neukirchen, 1980), p. 203.

12 Of course it is easy to point to exceptions to this. I shall only mention a few older studies here, such as E. Hammershaimb's comparison between the ethics of the Hebrew prophets and ethical ideas of the ancient Near East, in his 'On the Ethics of the Prophets' (1959), reprinted in E. Hammershaimb, *Some Aspects of Old Testament Prophecy from Isaiah to Malachi* (Copenhagen, 1966), pp. 63-90. See also the important study by B. Albrektson devoted to the clarification of the concept of 'God who acts in history' in Israelite belief as well as in ancient oriental religion, *History and the Gods. An Essay on the Idea of Historical Events as Divine Manifestations in the Ancient Near East and in Israel* (CBO, 1; Lund, 1967), and finally, H.H. Schmid's study on the idea of justice and cosmos in the Near East in antiquity, *Gerechtigkeit als Weltordnung. Hintergrund und Geschichte des alttestamentlichen Gerechtigkeitsbegriffes* (BHTh, 40; Tübingen, 1968).

Canaanite religion.[13] Instead the argument is here devoted to another problem, that is, the supposed difference between what may be termed genuine Israelite and genuine Canaanite society and culture.

The basis of the scholarly notion that Canaanite civilization must be viewed as the antithesis of Israelite society can be found in the narratives about the oldest Israelite history contained in the historical literature in the Old Testament. However, as long as modern descriptions of this Israelite history were almost paraphrases of the biblical narratives, nobody thought it worthwhile to question the fundamental *ethnic* difference between the Israelite and the Canaanite population of Palestine.

Now we can, of course, distinguish between several levels of scholarly paraphrases of the Old Testament historical narratives. One reason for this divergence among modern scholars may be that scholars often demonstrate a definite lack of understanding of the important question of *ethnicity*, the result of which is the occasionally confused discussion about the characteristics of a 'people', an 'ethnos', which is sometimes present in the works of Old Testament scholars.[14] Thus we may distinguish between scholars who consider the Israelite nation to be founded on the basis of ties of blood and common descent, and scholars who believe that the presence of a special Israelite religion (the Yahwistic faith) formed the constitutive element of the early Israelite nation.[15] According to the first

13 See the short review of Israelite religious history in my *Ancient Israel. A New History of Israelite Society* (The Biblical Seminar, 5; Sheffield, 1988), pp. 197-257.
14 Cf., for example, the comprehensive but not very clear review of the classical definition of a nation in C.H.J. de Geus, *The Tribes of Israel* (Studia Neerlandica Semitica, 18; Assen, 1976), pp. 156-64, where we find the longstanding misinterpretation of ethnic identity exposed. This misinterpretation, that ethnic unity is based on common blood, common language and common religion, goes back to Herodotus. Cf. also on the concept of *ethnicity* below, pp. 51-52.
15 The first group includes the advocates of the two classical positions on the origin of Israel, the hypothesis of the Israelite conquest of Canaan (mainly Albright and his disciples and some of the more conservative Israeli scholars like Y. Kaufmann; cf. Y. Kaufmann, *The Biblical Account of the Conquest of Palestine* [Jerusalem, 1953]), and the so-called infiltration hypothesis, which goes back to the German school of Old Testament research, especially to A. Alt and M. Noth. The important difference between these two theories on the emergence of Israel really concerns the speed with which the Israelites penetrated the Canaanite areas, one school believing in a massive, forceful invasion, the other speculating about an originally peaceful infiltration of

mentioned group the Israelites were ethnically of another stock than the Canaanites, whereas the second group believe the Israelites originally to have been Canaanites, although from an ideological (religious) point of view removed from the other Canaanites' offspring. Thus, according to the last mentioned group of scholars, Israelite religion formed the important dividing line between Israelites and Canaanites.

We may, on the other hand, question the views of this group, among whom we find the adherents of the so-called 'revolution hypothesis'. After all, the description of the origin of Israel and its religion presented by older scholars like Albrecht Alt and Martin Noth, as well as by scholars of the younger generation, who follow Manfred Weippert in his defence of Alt's and Noth's theories, is more consistent than the one presented by, say, George E. Mendenhall and Norman K. Gottwald. In their reconstruction of the early history of Israel, Alt and Noth presented a sketch of this development which is generally in line with their understanding of early Israelite religious development. Mendenhall and Gottwald realize that the historical foundation of the biblical historical narratives is more uncertain than older scholars believed it to be. Therefore they have largely given up this historical picture of the Old Testament, although Mendenhall especially still believes in the basic truth of the origin of the Israelite religion as described by the Old Testament. Somehow Mendenhall has tried, so to speak, to 'save' the religion of Israel at the cost of losing its history. To Mendenhall religion is seemingly more important than history.[16]

A more adequate procedure would be to consider the Old Testament description of the history of the Israelite nation and the origin of the Israelite religion as two parts of one and the same narrative. Only if we find indications—not, however, included in the historical narratives in the historical books—which definitely point in another direction and say that the religion of Israel originated in the 'desert' in the 13th century BCE, the distinction made by Mendenhall

Israelite sheep- and goat-nomads. On this subject cf. my *Early Israel*, pp. 48-61. The second group consists of advocates of the revolution hypothesis, especially G.E. Mendenhall, N.K. Gottwald, and their disciples. According to this group of scholars the only foreign element was the 'group of Moses', who brought the Yahwistic faith to Canaan.

16 I have tried to comment on this problem in the final section of *Early Israel*, ('Future Perspectives: Israelite Religion'), pp. 432-35.

and Gottwald between the sacred history and the profane history of Israel may, after all, be tenable. Until such a distinction is proved, the correct scholarly procedure will, however, be to base the reconstruction of the early history of the Israelite religion on one of the current historical interpretations of Israelite history presented by Old Testament scholars. Thus, if the Israelite nation originated in the desert and settled in Palestine as a foreign *ethnos*, then it would of course be reasonable to consider the religion of these immigrants also to be foreign to the traditional Palestinian society and the content of this Israelite religion to be distinguishable from the religious beliefs of the Canaanite population. On the other hand, if it is maintained that Israel originated as the result of social and demographic upheavals in Palestine in the Late Bronze Age—and this is certainly the opinion of this writer—then it is more natural to consider early Israelite religion to have been at least in its main features 'Canaanite'. The point of departure in the study of early Israelite religion cannot be the religious divergences which were in existence in the Land of Israel around the middle of the 1st millennium BCE. In the last case there is far more reason to stress the importance of the similarities between Israelite religion and other religions of the area. This does, not, however, mean that the opinion of Mendenhall and Gottwald as to the original content of the Israelite religion must necessarily be wrong, but such an opinion can only be the result of a complete analysis of the available historical material; it cannot form the basis on which to analyse the extant sources.[17]

In order to maintain the biblical notion of two contrasting cultures, on one hand the Israelite, and on the other the Canaanite, it is necessary to operate with two different nations or *ethne*. According to this opinion the Canaanites were an ethnos quite distinguishable from the Israelite nation. Thus in the scholarly literature we find references to the Canaanites, Canaanite culture and Canaanite religion

---

17 It is relevant in this connection to mention the religious movements which have appeared in the Near East up until modern times. The argument that such a comparison may contribute to a better understanding of religious development in early Israel cannot simply be ignored. Thus it is easy to see J.W. Flanagan's fascination with the movement of the Wahhabites in Arabia and his interest in the role this movement played in the formation of the Saudi Arabian state; his enterprise is certainly legitimate. See his *David's Social Drama. A Hologram of Israel's Early Iron Age* (The Social World of Biblical Antiquity, 7/JSOTS, 73; Sheffield, 1988), pp. 325-41.

more or less in the same fashion as the Old Testament itself refers to the Canaanites and the Canaanite religion and country. Both the Old Testament and traditional biblical scholarship presuppose that the Canaanites formed a distinctive people or nation in the ancient world.

It is the aim of this study to investigate this question and to ask whether such an understanding of the Canaanites is as self-evident as is often presupposed. In this study we shall try to present an analysis of the source material contained in the Bible, as well as in written documents from the ancient Near East. Archaeological material from Palestine or Phoenicia will not, however, be considered, because such material is mostly silent about its ethnic background. Furthermore, studies of the material culture as evidenced by the archaeological excavations already exist, although they may to some degree be used to illustrate my point in this introduction, that ethnic divergences along the lines laid down by the biblical writers between various parts of the population in Palestine have been decisive for the archaeologists' interpretation of their findings.

A well-known example of this is Kathleen M. Kenyon's study of the supposed differences between Amorite and Canaanite culture.[18] It is characteristic of this attitude of the archaeologists that Kenyon, when drawing the dividing line between two different material cultures which should have existed at the same time in the Syro-Palestinian area, actually refers to ethnic divisions set out by the Old Testament writers. In fact she found the basis for attaching ethnic tags to the two types of material culture in Num. 13.29:

עמלק יושב בארץ הנגב והחתי והיבוסי והאמרי יושב בהר והכנעני
ישב על־הים ועל יד הירדן

Amalekites who live in the Negev, Hittites, Jebusites, and Amorites who live in the hill-country, and the Canaanites who live by the sea and along the Jordan.[19]

Since such opinions are actually founded on literary evidence, it will, of course, from an analytical point of view, be correct to give precedence to the written sources. Only after the written sources have been properly studied will it be possible to compare the results of

---

18 *Amorites and Canaanites* (The Schweich Lectures, 1963; London, 1966).
19 Biblical quotations all follow the *Revised English Bible* (REB, 1989).

this analysis with the likewise independent evaluation of the non-written archaeological remains.[20]

---

20 Accordingly archaeological arguments will not be used in this study. I see no reason to comment on Miss Kenyon's ethnic interpretations since they rely on opinions which are not based in fact, since they presuppose that the Amorites were a distinct nation or ethnos which migrated to the Syro-Palestinian area at the end of the Early Bronze Age. Cf. M. Liverani, 'The Amorites', in D.J. Wiseman (ed.), *Peoples of Old Testament Times* (Oxford, 1973), pp. 100-33, as well as his 'Per una considerazione storica del problemo Amorreo', *OA* 9 (1970), pp. 5-27, which includes a review of Kenyon's book.

Chapter 2

THE CANAANITES AND THEIR LAND IN ANCIENT NEAR
EASTERN DOCUMENTS: THE 2ND MILLENNIUM BCE

Many scholars consider the Canaanites to be unproblematic from a
historical point of view, although we do not know when they arrived
in the Syro-Palestinian area nor where their original homeland was. It
is traditional among orientalists to view the Canaanite immigration
into Palestine as having occurred around the beginning of the
historical age in the Middle East, that is c. 3000 BCE. Most scholars
readily admit that this date is more conventional than based on real
knowledge, and that it is also a scholarly convention for modern
authors to call the people in question 'Canaanites'.[1] In recent times
scholars have been more cautious when speculating about great
migratory movements of Semitic peoples, all having their original
home somewhere on the dry steppes along the border areas between
the arable land and the Syro-Arabian Desert.[2] The result is, however,
that describing the Palestinian population as being 'Canaanite' already
in the third millennium is mostly maintained for practical reasons; the
name has nothing to do with any imagined origin of the 'Canaanite'
population, about which we are totally in the dark.

Another enigmatic part of the problem of the Canaanites is the
name *Canaan* itself, although several different proposals have been

1 It is interesting to note that the evaluation of this situation is very much the
   same, whether it be E. Meyer's description of the ethnic composition of the
   Palestinian population c. 3000 BCE. (*Geschichte des Altertums*, I.2 [3rd edn;
   Berlin, 1913; repr. Darmstadt, 1965], p. 419), or R. de Vaux's in *CAH*[3], I, 2
   (Cambridge, 1971), in his chapter, 'Palestine in the Early Bronze Age', pp.
   208-37; see p. 234.
2 Cf. on this question the excursus, 'The Desert as the Semitic Place of Origin',
   in *Early Israel*, pp. 148-52.

put forward over the last hundred years or so.[3] Normally two different explanations of the etymology of the name are considered by
modern scholars. (1) The name Canaan, Hebrew כנען, derives from
the Semitic verbal root *kn*ᶜ, which is well represented in Hebrew with
a meaning like 'to be humble', 'to be depressed'.[4] A derivative
meaning of the same root could be 'to be low', and if this is correct
Canaan may well mean 'the low country' or just 'lowland'.[5] (2) The
word Canaan comes from Hurrian *Kinaḫḫu*, which is attested by the
documents from Nuzi (15th century BCE) and which is supposed to be
a Hurrian word for the colour of purple. Canaan may, accordingly,
mean 'the Land of Purple'.[6]

It is easy to explain why many scholars have subscribed to the last-
mentioned explanation of the name Canaan. In spite of the fact that
Nuzi was removed by more than 600 miles from the Mediterranean
coast, Hurrians were present all over ancient Western Asia, and it is
highly feasible that the Hurrian version of Canaan, *Kinaḫḫu*, was
transmitted by Hurrians from Syria or Phoenicia to their fellow
Hurrians in Mesopotamia. It is also a remarkable coincidence that this
explanation of *Canaan/Kinaḫḫu* is very similar to the traditional
interpretation of the Greek designation of the Levantine coast as
Φοινίκη, Phoenicia, since the name Phoenicia is normally explained
as the Greek translation of a Phoenician word meaning 'purple'. Thus
the Greek rendering could reflect the common knowledge that the
production of purple-coloured textiles, which were the famous
merchandise of the Phoenician traders all over the Mediterranean,
were in fact produced in Phoenicia. However, serious philological
objections have been raised against this seemingly obvious explanation

3 Eduard Meyer's commentary, *Geschichte des Altertums*, I.2, p. 419, '. . . die
   Bedeutung des Namens ist völlig dunkel', is just as valid today as it was fifty
   years ago. Cf. also Manfred Weippert, *RLA*, V, p. 352: '. . . so daß die Etymo-
   logie und Wortbedeutung von 'K.' als noch ungeklärt gelten müssen'.
4 Cf. *HALAT*, p. 461.
5 Cf. on this M.C. Astour, 'The Origin of the Terms 'Canaan', 'Phoenician', and
   'purple' ', *JNES* 24 (1965), pp. 346-50.
6 Thus W.F. Albright, 'The Role of the Canaanites in the History of Civilization'
   (1942). However, he partly abandoned this position in the reprint of this work
   in G.E. Wright (ed.), *The Bible and the Ancient Near East*, pp. 328-62, p. 356
   n. 50. Here Albright claims that Hurrian *Kinaḫḫu* must be derived from a
   West Semitic word meaning 'snail', a word which is, however, unattested in
   West Semitic literature. Of course this is more a hypothesis than an argument.

of the name.[7] Thus both Michael Astour and Roland de Vaux refer to the old idea of Ephraim A. Speiser, that Hurrian *Kinaḫḫu* was actually no more than the Hurrian rendering of the Semitic geographical name *Canaan*.[8] Finally, to conclude the discussion about the name of Canaan, it may be necessary to refer to the proposal of de Vaux, who maintained that Canaan could be a very old geographical name for which no obvious etymological explanation can be offered—irrespective of the fact that the name is itself certainly Semitic.[9]

The region where we should look for this Canaan is, on the other hand, not considered to be problematic. Most sources from the 2nd millennium BCE point to Western Asia as the homeland of the Canaanites, and especially to the coastal area along the Mediterranean.[10] However, all but one of the references belong to the second half of the 2nd millennium BCE, the one exception being the mention of some Canaanites in a document from Mari from the 18th century BCE. In this document we find a reference to ᴸᵁ*ḫabbātum* ù ᴸᵁ*Ki-na-aḫ-num*ᵐᵉˢ.[11] The wording of this passage creates some problems as to the identity of these 'Canaanites', because of the parallelism between ᴸᵁ*Ki-na-aḫ-num*ᵐᵉˢ and ᴸᵁ*ḫabbatum*, which is unexpected. The Akkadian word *ḫabbatum*, the meaning of which is actually 'brigands', is sometimes used to translate the Sumerian expression SA.GAZ, which is normally thought to be a logogram for *ḫabiru*, 'Hebrews'.[12]

---

7   See Astour, 'The Origin of the Terms 'Canaan'', p. 346. Compare R. de Vaux, 'Le pays de Canaan', *JAOS* 88 (1968), pp. 23-30, pp. 23ff.

8   E.A. Speiser, 'The Name *Phoinikes*', *Language* 12 (1936), pp. 121-26.

9   See de Vaux, 'Le pays de Canaan', p. 25. An exhaustive discussion about the various etymological proposals (including some which are not mentioned here) can be found in H.-J. Zobel, 'כְּנַעַן, כְּנַעֲנִי', *TWAT*, IV, cols. 224-43, cols. 227ff.

10 A divine name is known from Ebla which may be of interest in this connection, ᵈBE *Ga-na-na-i/um* , which may be translated as 'the Canaanite Dagan'. The precise meaning of this name must await further confirmation as to the correct rendering of the name itself. Moreover, this is the only reference of the kind coming from Ebla, and the exact meaning of this 'Canaan', should it at all be Canaan, is not clear. K.A. Tångberg has recently written on this divine name, in 'Eblaite. An Introduction to the State of Research on the Cuneiform Tablets of Ebla', *SJOT* 1/1 (1987), pp. 110-20; see p. 120.

11 Cf. G. Dossin, 'Une mention de Cananéens dans une lettre de Mari', *Syria* 50 (1973), pp. 277-82.

12 On SA.GAZ (and the scribal variants as well as translations) see especially J. Bottéro, *Le problème des ḫabiru à la 4ᵉ rencontre assyriologique internationale* (Cahiers de la Société asiatique, 12; Paris, 1954), pp. 144-49.

Thus there is some reason to question the identity of the 'Canaanites' who appear in this text from Mari. We may ask whether these people were called 'Canaanites' because they were ethnically of another stock than the ordinary population of Mari, or whether it was because they came from a specific geographical area, the land of Canaan. However, because of the parallelism in this text between LÚ*ḫabbatum* and LÚ*Ki-na-aḫ-num*ᵐᵉˢ, we cannot exclude the possibility that the expression 'Canaanites' was used here with a sociological meaning. It could be that the word 'Canaanites' was in this case understood as a sociological designation of some sort which shared at least some connotations with the sociological term *ḫabiru*. Should this be the case, the Canaanites of Mari may well have been refugees or outlaws rather than ordinary foreigners from a certain country (from Canaan). Worth considering is also Manfred Weippert's interpretation of the passage LÚ*ḫabbātum* ù LÚ*Ki-na-aḫ-num*ᵐᵉˢ—literally 'Canaanites and brigands'—as 'Canaanite brigands', which may well mean 'highwaymen of foreign origin', whether or not they were actually Canaanites coming from Phoenicia.[13]

The references to Canaan dating from the second millennium BCE are rather numerous, and are included in documents which originate in the Syro-Palestinian area as well as in other parts of the Near East. Furthermore, these sources are found in several different kinds of documents from the period between c. 1500 and 1200 BCE and appear in textual evidence reaching from the Hittite Empire in Asia Minor and the state of Arrapḫa (Nuzi) in northeastern Mesopotamia in the north to Egypt in the south. From Syria and Palestine proper there are quite a number of references included in the el-Amarna correspondence of the early 14th century BCE, which may be compared to contemporary evidence from Ugarit and Alalaḫ.[14]

Canaan and the Canaanites in the el-Amarna Letters

Among the most important evidence must be reckoned the references to Canaan in the el-Amarna letters. After all, most of these documents were written in Syria, Phoenicia and Palestine, that is, in the

---

13 *RLA*, V, p. 352.
14 The material has never been completely surveyed. In order to get a preliminary idea of the sources, cf. Weippert, in *RLA*, V, pp. 352-55.

area where we generally believe Canaan to have been situated. These letters must, therefore, irrespective of the fact that they belonged to an Egyptian state archive, be considered reliable sources bearing on the problem of the identification of the Canaanites and their land.[15] However, as is often the case when we try to obtain precise informations from an ancient source, the actual information which can be extracted from these letters is sometimes rather disappointing.

On the basis of a number of Egyptian references to Canaan and the Canaanites from the time of the 19th and 20th dynasties (from the late 14th century until well into the 12th century BCE) it has often been assumed that Canaan was the official name of the southwestern Egyptian imperial province in Western Asia. This assumption seems more or less to be based on a passage in one of the el-Amarna letters from the king of Alašia to Pharaoh, where the following reconstruction of the wording of the text has been proposed:[16] [*p*]*li-ḫa-ti ša Ki-na-ḫi*, 'the province of Canaan'.[17] As one might realize, the passage in question is severely mutilated and the emendations proposed by modern scholars might be less certain than is often assumed. Thus the correctness of the transcription *Ki-na-ḫi* cannot be proved. Not only is the context broken, but the reconstruction of the second important

---

15 Summaries of these letters and their historical background can be found in *CAH*[3], II, 2 (Cambridge, 1975), pp. 98-116 (by W.F. Albright). A less traditional evaluation of the content of the letters and of the historical situation during the el-Amarna period is contained in a series of studies by M. Liverani, a few of which have been translated into English; cf. *Three Amarna Essays* (Sources and Monographs on the Ancient Near East. Monographs, 1/5; Malibu, 1979). The standard edition of the greater part of the corpus of letters, which was unearthed quite unexpectedly in Egypt in 1888, is still J.A. Knudtzon, *Die el-Amarna Tafeln*, I-II (Vorderasiatische Bibliothek, 2, 1-2; Leipzig, 1915). Letters which were unknown to Knudtzon, but which have been edited in various places since 1915, are collected by A.F. Rainey, in *El Amarna Tablets* 359-379 (AOAT, 8; Neukirchen-Kevelaer, 1970). It seems unlikely that a new text edition will ever appear to substitute the edition of Knudtzon; cf. the introduction to the new and complete translation of the letters into French by W.L. Moran, *Les lettres d'el-Amarna. Correspondance diplomatique du pharaon* (Littératures ancienne du Proche-Orient, 13; Paris, 1987), pp. 9ff., with a description of the deplorable state in which several of the tablets are preserved; a small number of letters are now seemingly lost.
16 EA 36:15.
17 Thus at least since Knudtzon, *Die el-Amarna Tafeln*, pp. 288-89. Cf. also, for example, de Vaux, 'Le pays de Canaan', p. 27, Y. Aharoni, *The Land of the Bible* (2nd edn; London, 1979), p. 68, and Weippert, *RLA*, V, p. 353.

word in the passage is equally uncertain, although most scholars seem
to be satisfied with the proposed emendation, which is the Akkadian
word *pīḫātum*, 'province'.[18] It cannot, therefore, be excluded that the
scholarly reconstruction of the text has been influenced by the
decision to *read* 'Canaan' in the same line.[19] I shall later refer to the
Egyptian sources which have been called upon in support of this
reading of the text because they are believed to inform us that
Canaan was actually the name of an Egyptian administrative district
already in the 18th dynasty. However, we must in this place maintain
that only if such Egyptian evidence for an administrative province in
Palestine or Phoenicia called Canaan can actually be presented, then
the emendation of this passage in the el-Amarna letters ought, after
all, to be sustained. However, other sources must be taken into
consideration, although they may at least cast some doubts whether
such a province existed at all in the el-Amarna period.

First I shall quote a passage from a letter written by Abi-Milku of
Tyre:

> My Lord, the king, has written to me: 'Write to me what you have
> heard from Canaan'. The king of Danuna has died, his brother has
> become king after him and his country is safe. A fire has destroyed the
> palace at Ugarit; it has destroyed half of it and the other half has
> disappeared. There are no Hittite troops in the area. Etakkama is
> prince of Qidšu, and Aziru is at war with Biriawaza.[20]

In the opinion of the Tyrian monarch, Abi-Milku, Canaan embraced
practically the whole of Western Asia, from Damascus in the south to
the Hittite border in the north. His description of what had happened
in Canaan includes events which took place in eastern Cilicia
(Danuna), in Ugarit in northern Syria, as well as in Qidšu (Qadeš),
Amurru and Damascus in inner Syria. Some scholars, however, dispute

18 Cf. W. von Soden, *AHw*, II, p. 862: 'Verantwortungs(bereich)', but also
    (marked as representing a special Middle and Late Babylonian understanding
    of the word) 'Amtsbezirk, Provinz'.
19 On the problems of this passage see W.L. Moran, *Les Lettres d'el-Amarna*, p.
    204 n.
20 EA 151:49ff. As to the translations of the passages from the el-Amarna letters,
    I to a large degree follow Moran's proposal in his *Les lettres d'el-Amarna*.
    The only comments here will concern the relevant passages, the interpretation
    of which is less than certain. On EA 151:49ff. see Moran, *Les lettres d'el-
    Amarna*, p. 386. On the translation of this passage, which does not conform to
    Moran's translation, cf. the discussion in M. Liverani, *Storia di Ugarit nell'età
    degli archivi politici* (Studi Semitici, 6; Roma, 1962), pp. 29-30.

this interpretation of the content of Abi-Milku's letter. Thus Anson F.
Rainey remarks that Abi-Milku's letter only refers to a demand from
Pharaoh that this Phoenician prince should report to the Egyptian
court what he has heard *in* Canaan, that is, in his own city and
country, Tyre, which was, of course, situated in Canaan.[21] Rainey's
interpretation of the decisive line of this letter is perhaps not very
precise. First of all, his rendering of the passage is from a philological
angle not the most obvious.[22] Secondly, his translation may be based
on an argument in another article of his, according to which Canaan
and Ugarit must be two different places. In the text in question a
foreign merchant visiting Ugarit is described as being a 'Canaanite'.[23]

In light of the conflicting evidence of this letter written by the
king of Tyre we are forced to review all occurrences of 'Canaan' and
'Canaanite' in the el-Amarna letters in order to clarify what was
considered to be Canaan in the Late Bronze Age. This would seem to
be the best procedure if we are to gauge with any certainty the extent
of this Canaan. In addition, such a review may also contribute to a
better understanding of the identity of the Canaanites.[24]

Canaan or the Canaanites are mentioned twelve times by the el-
Amarna letters. Eleven times the territory is intended; only once do
we find a reference to its population, in a letter from the Cassite king
Burra-Burriaš of Karduniaš, Babylonia, to Pharaoh:[25]

---

21 Cf. A.F. Rainey, 'Ugarit and the Canaanites Again', *IEJ* 14 (1964), p. 101.
Rainey is followed by several scholars, for example by de Vaux, 'Le pays de
Canaan', p. 27.

22 EA 151:50: *ša ta-aš-me iš-tu* KUR*ki-na-aḫ-na*, 'What you hear *from* Canaan' (cf.
Knudtzon: 'Was du hörst von Kinaḫna', *EA-Tafeln*, I, p. 625). The preposition
ištu in such contexts normally indicates from which territory a certain person,
thing or information comes; it is not normally used to indicate where something has been heard, or exists.

23 More on this below, pp. 50-51.

24 Short summaries can be found in the indices of Knudtzon, *Die el-Amarna
Tafeln*, II, p. 1577, and Moran, *Les lettres d'el-Amarna*, p. 596. The major part
of the material has been reviewed by Horst Klengel, *Geschichte Syriens im 2.
Jahrtausend v.u.Z.* II. *Mittel- und Südsyrien* (Deutsche Akademie der Wissenschaften zu Berlin. Institut für Orientforschung. Veröffentlichung 70; Berlin,
1969), *passim*, without, however, reaching any conclusion.

25 EA 9:19ff. Burra-Buriaš (or perhaps more commonly, Burnaburiaš) reigned
from c. 1375 to 1347. In this chapter we normally follow the dates in *CAH*,
II, 1-2 (3rd edn; Cambridge, 1973-1975) without thereby excluding the possibility that the chronological estimates of this work may be partly outdated. The
question of chronology, however, is unimportant for the argument in this
book.

> In the days of Kurigalzu, my predecessor, all the Canaanites[26] wrote to
> him and said: 'Come to the border of the country, and we will revolt
> and become your allies . . .'[27]

According to this letter, the 'Canaanites' once communicated with the
Babylonian king Kurigalzu (c. 1400 BCE) in order to persuade him to
enter an anti-Egyptian alliance. Burra-Burriaš, however, makes it clear
to Pharaoh that this entreaty was unsuccessful. It is very likely an
exaggeration in the literary style of the period when Burra-Burriaš
speaks of 'all the Canaanites'. By this he most likely intends to say
that a rebellious group of West Asiatic princes investigated the
feasibility of an open revolt against their Egyptian overlord and for
this purpose they sent envoys to the Babylonian king. In that case,
however, the letter hardly contributes to a better understanding of the
identity of the Canaanites, except that the Babylonian king must have
considered the petty kings mentioned by the letter to be the subjects
of Pharaoh,[28] and must have considered their territory, 'Canaan', to
be part of the Egyptian Empire already in the days of Burra-Burriaš's
predecessor and most likely also in his own time (or else the inten-

26 *ki-na-ḫa-a-a-ú ga-ab-bi-šu-nu*, actually 'the Canaanites in their totality'.
27 On the translation and problems of line 20, cf. Moran, *Les lettres d'el-Amarna*,
    p. 81 n.
28 On the general political situation of the territory in this period (both the
    foreign policy and the domestic one), cf. my *Ancient Israel*, pp. 77-88. The
    description in that book of the political conditions is dependent on some
    recent work by, especially, Michael Heltzer and Mario Liverani, but also on
    G. Buccellati, *Cities and Nations of Ancient Syria* (Studi Semitici, 26; Rome,
    1967). The older descriptions of international political affairs in this period,
    for example, those published by C. Aldred and W.F. Albright in *CAH*³, II, 1
    (Cambridge, 1975), in their chapters 'Egypt: The Amarna Period and the End
    of the Eighteenth Dynasty' (Aldred), pp. 49-97, and 'The Amarna Letters from
    Palestine' (Albright), pp. 98-116, must be considered to be outdated. In contrast
    to the opinion of older scholars, the el-Amarna Period did not represent a
    special period of dissolution of the Egyptian Asiatic empire nor were the
    Egyptians negligent in exercising control over their provinces in Western Asia.
    The evidence of the el-Amarna letters instead describes a situation which some
    may call *normal* in the history of this troublesome area in the Late Bronze
    Age as long as Palestine and Syria were ruled by the Egyptians. On the
    internal causes of the permanent crisis in Syrian and Palestinian society in this
    period—a crisis which was to some degree ideologically motivated—see es-
    pecially M. Liverani, 'Contrasti e confluenze di concezioni politiche nell'età di
    El-Amarna', *RA* 61 (1967), pp. 1-18, and the summary in his 'Political Lexicon
    and Political Ideologies in the Amarna Letters', *Berytus* 31 (1983), pp. 41-56.

tion of the letter—to stress the loyalty of the Babylonian king towards his fellow king, Pharaoh—would have been meaningless).

Another letter from the same king of Babylon, Burra-Burias, however, shows that the Babylonian king could express himself more precisely when he wrote about the Canaanite territory. Thus in this letter he complains about the maltreatment of some of his merchants in the land of Canaan. These merchants was robbed and killed. Now Burra-Burias asks Pharaoh to act and to punish the criminals. The passage of interest to us says:

> Now my merchants who left together with Aḥutabu have been delayed because of business. After Aḥutabu continued his journey to my brother [i.e. Pharaoh], in the city of Ḥinnatuni in Canaan Šum-Adda, the son of Balume, and Šutatna, the son of Šaratum, from Acca, sent their men and killed my merchants and stole their money . . . Canaan is your country and its kings are your servants. In your country I have been robbed . . .[29]

In this letter the information about Canaan is rather precise, because two cities belonging to the Canaanite territory are mentioned by Burra-Burias, one of them being of course Acre, the Acca of this letter, the other Ḥinnatuni, which must be the same town as the Hannaton of the Old Testament. It may be uncertain where exactly this Ḥinnatuni/Hannaton was situated; however, according to the Old Testament, it was on the Zebulonite border, and since the next frontier station mentioned in the biblical text is the valley of Jiphtah-El, today better known as *Sahl el-Baṭṭōf* or *Naḥal Bet Natofa* in the central part of Galilee, Ḥinnatuni must have been a Galilean town.[30]

The deplorable events which this letter describes happened in Canaan, which in this case embraced Galilee. Furthermore, the letter informs us that this Canaan was part of Pharaoh's realm and was ruled by a number of local 'Canaanite kings'.[31] Now, since we may safely assume that Burra-Burias never visited Canaan and therefore

29 EA 8:25. The context is broken but scholars generally agree on its restoration.
30 Josh. 19.14. Cf. M. Noth, *Das Buch Josua* (HAT, I, 7; 2nd edn; Tübingen, 1953), p. 115, who follows a proposal by A. Alt to locate Hannathon on *Tell el-Bedēwīye* (174 243) at the western end of *Sahl el-Baṭṭōf*. This location is now considered to be the official one by modern Israeli authorities, and the modern name of the place is now Tel Ḥannathon.
31 The scribe has used the Sumerogram LUGAL to represent the Akkadian word for 'king', *šarrum* (here in the plural *šarrānum*). This is clearly in conflict with the usage of the Egyptians, who normally titled the petty kings of their empire LÙ, a Sumerogram meaning 'man'.

only had a second-hand knowledge of the country and its situation,[32] he evidently cites the reports of other persons, perhaps from his envoys at the Egyptian court or from—which may be more likely— colleagues of the unfortunate Babylonian merchants. His information as to the exact extent of this Canaan may therefore, after all, be less precise than the very firm wording of the letter makes us believe. Therefore, before a final decision as to the delimitation of ancient Canaan in the Late Bronze Age can be made, we have also to investigate the other references to Canaan in the el-Amarna letters.

Among the limited number of letters sent by Pharaoh to his vassals in Syria and Palestine only two references to Canaan are included.[33] One of these is contained in a letter from an angry Pharaoh to the prince of Amurru, the notorious Aziru, who is thus reprimanded by his master:

> Subject yourself to the king, your lord, and you shall live. You know best yourself that the king does not wish furiously to deal with the whole of Canaan.[34]

Now, in the light of the information in Burra-Burias's letters (especially in EA 108), we may be induced into believing that it was no concern of Aziru of Amurru whether or not Pharaoh planned to destroy Canaan. Aziru was, after all, the master of Amurru, not Canaan, and this Amurru was situated farther to the north in Syria, and not in Palestine or Phoenicia. According to the testimony of his Syrian and Phoenician colleagues, Aziru's only aspiration was to create as much discord as possible among Pharaoh's Asiatic vassals, in order

32 At least he did not realize the violation of etiquette which his reference to 'the kings of Canaan' represented. Cf. also the preceding note.

33 Actually the name shows up a third time, in EA 14 ii 26, in a list of deliveries from Egypt to Burra-Burias, among which a product of Canaan is included. The passage is, however, broken, and not much information can be derived from this text.

34 EA 162:41. In Moran's translation the text reads: 'Accomplis donc ton service pour le roi, ton seigneur, et tu vivras. Toi-même tu sais que le roi *n'échoue* pas lorsqu'il se met en rage contre tout Canaan'. This translation is, however, to some degree problematic. Line 41, especially, presents some difficulties to the translator. *Échouer* in French means something like to 'fail' or 'miscarry'. It is, on the other hand, difficult to find support for Moran's translation. On Akkadian *ḫašāḫu*, cf. *AHw*, p. 322, 'brauchen, begehren', or (secondary meaning) 'wünschen'. The conclusion must be that Knudtzon's old translation is still to be preferred: 'Unterwirf dich denn dem König, deinem Herrn! Dann lebst du. / Du weißt ja, daß der König nicht begehrt, das ganze Land Kinaḫḫi *heftig anzufahren'*.

to maintain a practical independence for his own kingdom.[35] Therefore, should Pharaoh's warning carry any weight, the Egyptian administration must have included Amurru among the Canaanite kingdoms,[36] and Canaan was in this way understood by the Egyptians to comprise much more than Palestine proper, especially the Syrian coast to the north, where Amurru was situated.[37] We have, on the other hand, no reason to believe the Egyptian officials to have been so ignorant that they would have considered the most northern part of their empire to belong to Canaan if Canaan was simply a well-defined administrative province of limited extent in the southern part of the Egyptian Empire. We may perhaps conclude that, according to the testimony of these Egyptian officials, Canaan comprised a territory of greater extent than the one allotted to Canaan in the letters from the Babylonian king. This view seems to be corroborated by the career of Aziru, since this king of Amurru evidently never stopped to cause trouble for his Syrian and Phoenician neighbours.

A concept of Canaan which can be compared to the one expressed by Burra-Burias may appear in a letter from Pharaoh to Indaruta of Aksapa, a city situated near Acre:

> Now: The king has sent to you Hanni, the supervisor of the king's stables in Canaan . . .[38]

Indaruta's city, Aksapa—without doubt to be identified with the Aksaph of the Old Testament, was situated in the later tribal area of Asher, that is, in northern Galilee,[39] and Aksapa would thus be

---

35 The literature on this problematic character of the el-Amarna Age and the dubious role he and other kings of Amurru played according to the el-Amarna Letters is relatively comprehensive. On Aziru I shall refer only to H. Klengel, 'Aziru von Amurru und seine Rolle in der Geschichte der Amārnazeit', *MIO* 10 (1964), pp. 57-83, his *Geschichte Syriens*, II, pp. 264-99, and, as the most recent study, M. Liverani, 'Aziru, servitore di due padroni', Studia Mediterranea, 4 (*Studi Orientalistici in Ricordo di Franco Pintore*, ed. O. Carruba, M. Liverani and C. Zaccagnini; Pavia, 1983), pp. 93-121.

36 Cf. also Klengel, *Geschichte Syriens*, II, p. 259 n. 6: 'Vgl. etwa in EA 162:39ff. die Bezeichnung Amurrus als Kanaᶜan'.

37 On the territory of the state of Amurru, cf. the map in G.D. Young (ed.), *Ugarit in Retrospect* (Winona Lake, 1981), opposite p. 8. According to this map Amurru was located between Ugarit to the north and Byblus to the south, and between the Mediterranean to the west and Nuḫašše, Qatna and Kinza (Qadeš) to the east.

38 EA 367:6-8.

39 Josh. 19.25.

situated in the same territory that was considered to be Canaan by
Burra-Burias̆. The Egyptian official who is mentioned in this letter
was evidently a very high-ranking person,[40] but we have no
knowledge of any particular connection between the title 'the supervisor of the king's stables in Canaan' and an Egyptian administrative
district called Canaan, the more so because the letter does not say
whether there existed a specific relationship between Ḫanni's mission
to Indaruta and his position as 'supervisor'. He might have been
appointed to act as the Egyptian emissary to Indaruta in order to
make preparations for an Egyptian military expedition towards the
north.[41] Whether the Canaan of this letter only comprised Galilee or
whether it was a name of the Egyptian province of Palestine and
perhaps southern Syria is uncertain.

In order to obtain a more precise delimitation of the area of
Canaan, the information contained in the letters from the princes who
ruled over the city-states of Syria, Phoenicia and Palestine must be
taken into consideration. The references to Canaan are, however, only
found in letters from two of these princes. Both of them ruled over
small kingdoms in present-day Lebanon, Rib-Adda over Byblus and
Abi-Milku over Tyre. One of Abi-Milku's letters has already been
quoted.[42] However, once more Abi-Milku mentions Canaan:[43]

> The king of Ḫaṣura[44] has abandoned his city and has joined the *ḫabiru*
> (LÚ.MEŠ.SA.GAZ). The king must realize . . .[45] The land of the king

40 Cf. Moran, *Les lettres d'el-Amarna*, p. 563, A.F. Rainey, *El-Amarna Tablets
   359-379*, p. 56, *s.v. akil tarbasi*, and W. Helck, *Die Beziehungen Ägyptens zu
   Vorderasien im 3. und 2. Jahrtausend v. Chr.* (Ägyptologische Abhandlungen,
   5; Wiesbaden, 1962), p. 263.
41 The letter evidently concerns some preparations to be made in the light of an
   impending Egyptian campaign in Asia: Indaruta was supposed to procure
   provisions for the Egyptian troops on the way to the north.
42 EA 151. The understanding of Canaanite territory as expressed by the author
   of this letter formed the point of departure for the discussion in this section.
43 EA 148:41-47.
44 Biblical Ḥazor.
45 The succeeding line contains a number of serious problems: Moran (p. 381)
   translates: 'Que le roi se sent concerné au sujet des *serviteurs du palais*. . .',
   but at the same time in a note to his translation he remarks that LÚ.GÌR,
   which he translates as *serviteurs du palais*, is likely to be the same as ÉRIN
   (MEŠ) GÌR (MEŠ), that is *ṣābū šēpi*[MEŠ], in *AHw*, p. 1215, translated as 'Infan-
   teristen (?)'; see also EA 149:62. Knudtzon translates (p. 615), 'Es wisse der
   König: dem . . . . -Mann *sind* [j]ene feindlich', without, however, being able to
   make sense of the passage.

has joined the *habiru.*[46] May the king ask his supervisor, who knows
Canaan!

In his letter Abi-Milku reports about problems with his neighbour
king, the king of Sidon, whom he—in the language of the period—
describes as Pharaoh's enemy,[47] and he informs Pharaoh about the
treacherous acts of the king of Hazor: this king has become the ally
of the *habiru.*[48] The geographical horizon of this letter is again confined to Galilee. It would therefore be reasonable—on the basis of this
letter—to maintain that Canaan was considered by the Tyrian king to
embrace the territory of Galilee as well as the adjacent territories to
the north, although the northern border is not defined by Abi-Milku
in this letter. How precise this evaluation is, is uncertain because of
Abi-Milku's second letter in which he presented quite a different
picture of the extent of Canaan.

In the correspondence of Rib-Adda of Byblus, who was beyond
doubt the most diligent letter-writer of his age, Canaan is mentioned
four times:

. . . However, when seeing the man from Egypt, the kings of Canaan
will fly before him . . .[49]

. . . no armed ships are allowed to leave Canaan.[50]

He [Pharaoh] must not be indifferent as to his city [Byblus]. If he does
not send [troops] to them, to Byblus, they [the enemies] shall conquer it,
and . . . the lands of Canaan shall not belong to the king.[51]

46 On the expression *nēpešu ana habiri,* cf. Liverani, 'Farsi habiru', *Vicino Oriente* 2 (1979), pp. 65-77. See esp. pp. 70-77, and on EA 148:45 p. 75.
47 We can be assured that Zimrida of Sidon, 'the enemy of Pharaoh', would have
described Abi-Milku of Tyre in exactly the same manner, as 'the enemy'
(although the two letters from Zimrida which have survived [EA 144-145] do
not mention Abi-Milku personally).
48 This cannot be understood as evidence of an alliance between a Canaanite
king and the early Israelites. As has been noted, the frequent allusions to
alliances between *habiru* and city-states in the el-Amarna letters do not
necessarily mean that this troublesome social element was actually present.
Often such references may better be understood as a kind of formulaic
language applied by a king in order to characterize his neighbouring king—
and enemy—as rebelling against the rule of Pharaoh. In this point see especially G.E. Mendenhall, *The Tenth Generation* (Baltimore, 1973), pp. 122-41,
and M. Liverani, 'Farsi Habiru', pp. 65-77.
49 EA 109:46. The context is somewhat fragmentary.
50 EA 110:49. This is the first legible passage of an almost totally destroyed
tablet.
51 EA 131:57-62. Very fragmentary.

If the king is indifferent as to the city [Byblus], all the cities of Canaan shall not belong to him.[52]

Rib-Adda's talk about the countries and the kings of Canaan must be viewed in light of his comprehensive correspondence, which comprises a long litany covering more than ten years during which Rib-Adda complains about his ill fate, the bad world in general and the defection of the god (Pharaoh), stressing at the same time his own loyalty.[53] However interesting his correspondence is from an ideological point of view, these elements do not fall within the scope of this study. Of interest in this connection is his often diffuse language, which permits Rib-Adda to speak to Pharaoh like this: 'If the king, my Lord, does not listen carefully to the words of his servant, Byblus shall be his (Abdi-Aširta of Amurru, 'the enemy's') ally, and all the lands of the king as far as Egypt will join the *habiru*;[54] 'if the archers will not arrive, all the lands will join the *habiru*'.[55] The only difference between such general warnings and the citation from Rib-Adda's correspondence already quoted is that Rib-Adda is sometimes more specific when he mentions the cities of Canaan or the countries of Canaan.[56] In another letter Rib-Adda does not refer to Canaan as

52 EA 137:76.
53 Even Pharaoh sometimes became tired of listening to the complaints of Rib-Adda. An inquiry from Pharaoh to Rib-Adda has survived, in which a bored Pharaoh asks: 'Why do you write all that much to me? You write more than all the other *hazānu*' (EA 124:35-40. *Hazānu* is the normal title in the el-Amarna letters for the petty kings of Western Asia). On the character of Rib-Adda's correspondence see especially the studies of M. Liverani, 'Rib-Adda, giusto sofferente', *Altorientalische Forschungen* 1 (1974), pp. 175-205, and 'Le lettere del Faraone a Rib-Adda', *OA* 10 (1971), pp. 253-68 (English trans. 'Pharaoh's Letters to Rib-Adda', in M. Liverani, *Three Amarna Essays*, pp. 3-13). In a recent study, 'Rib-Adda: Job at Byblos?' (in Ann Kort and S. Morschalker (eds.), *Biblical and Related Studies Presented to Samuel Iwry*; Winona Lake, 1985), pp. 173-81, W.L. Moran tries to modify the thesis of Liverani, without, however, changing the fundamental content of Liverani's interpretation of Rib-Adda's letters.
54 EA 88:28ff., in a letter mostly concerned with trifles, such as Rib-Adda's envoy not being received at the court of Pharaoh in a manner fully comparable to that of the envoy from Acre. As to the rendering of *habiru* in Rib-Adda's letters, it must be noted that they always use the logogram SA.GAZ (or some variant form of this Sumerian word).
55 EA 79:18ff.
56 'Cities' and 'countries' are here used as synonyms. A state of ancient Western Asia was normally named after the city where the king's residence was situated. For that reason it is quite common to see the two words 'city' and 'country' used indiscriminately to indicate states.

the country to benefit from Pharaoh's reaction. Instead he mentions Amurru: 'Besides, do you not know that the land of Amurru day and night expects the archers?'[57] This last quotation must be viewed in the light of the role usually attributed to Amurru in the majority of Rib-Adda's letters. Here Amurru remains the notorious enemy of Egypt (and Byblus) and thus the root of all evil which befalls Byblus. We may, therefore, conclude that Rib-Adda's use of geographical names is rather diffuse and vague. In this respect there was no great difference between Rib-Adda and his Tyrian colleague to the south, Abi-Milku, or for that matter the majority of the other Syro-Palestinian princes in the el-Amarna period.

In conclusion, it must be maintained that nowhere in the el-Amarna correspondence is a precise indication of the exact territory of Canaan to be found. In these letters, most of them written by the petty rulers of Syria, Phoenicia and Palestine, the references to Canaan are usually rather general or imprecise. Evidently the inhabitants of the supposed Canaanite territory in Western Asia had no clear idea of the actual size of this Canaan, nor did they know exactly where Canaan was situated. This conclusion is by no means new and revolutionary. Thus nearly thirty years ago Wolfgang Helck concluded: 'In den Amarnabriefen ist Kinaḫḫi, Kinaḫni, Kinaḫna deutlich eine allgemeine Bezeichnung für alle syrisch-palästinischen Gebiete'.[58] We may say, the problem of Canaan is not as simple as believed by Albrecht Alt, when he—in his article in *RGG*—maintained that Canaan was originally from the middle of the 2nd millennium BCE the name of the Phoenician coast and Canaanites the name of the inhabitants of this territory. If we were to settle the matter on the basis of the few letters in which specific place names are mentioned—apart from, of course, the description of Canaan in one of Abi-Milku's letters (EA 151)—Canaan must be looked for in Northern Palestine. Nowhere do we find definite evidence that Phoenicia belonged to this limited Canaan.[59]

It is, accordingly, impossible to agree with Yohanan Aharoni who, on the basis of the not too precise use of the geographical name Canaan in the el-Amarna letters, claimed that these letters prove that

57 EA 82:47ff.
58 W. Helck, *Die Beziehungen Ägyptens zu Vorderasien*, pp. 279-80 (see also his short summary in *LÄ*, V [1977], col. 310, s.v. 'Kanaan').
59 See *RGG*, III, col. 1109. Hempel's evaluation in *BHH*, II, col. 926, tallies almost exactly with Alt's understanding.

Canaan was already in the days of the 18th dynasty the official name of the Egyptian Empire in Western Asia, and that Canaan had thus been transformed into a political concept and had become the official name of the Egyptian province which included Palestine and Southern Syria.[60] Exactly the opposite conclusion is reached here on the basis of the el-Amarna correspondence. When Abi-Milku reckoned Danuna in Cilicia, that is, a territory never ruled by Egyptians, as part of Canaan, that indicates how uncertain any fixing of the territory of Canaan, understood as a political and geographical entity, must be in light of the evidence of the el-Amarna letters.

Canaan and the Canaanites in other Documents from Western Asia and Asia Minor

The analysis of the references to Canaan in the el-Amarna correspondence was unable to produce a definite result as to the actual territory covered by the geographical term 'Canaan'. It is therefore necessary to include the evidence from documents which come from other parts of the ancient Near East in the Late Bronze Age. It is only natural that sources from Western Asia be considered before evidence from the neighbouring cultures is drawn into the discussion.

From Alalaḫ in Northern Syria one document has survived which presents an idea as to the location of Canaan. This document, the autobiographical text of King Idrimi of Alalaḫ (15th century BCE),[61] describes· how in his youth King Idrimi left his asylum at Emar in order to travel through the desert to the city of Ammiah in 'the land of Canaan'. Here Idrimi joined the *ḫabiru* who had fled from his own homeland Aleppo and acknowledged him to be the son of their former king, and 'seven years' later Idrimi was able to return to Northern Syria where he became king, not over Aleppo proper but

---

60 *Land of the Bible*, pp. 68-69.

61 This inscription, which must be considered one of the most interesting ever found in Syria and Palestine from this period, was published by S. Smith, *The Statue of Idri-mi* (Occasional Publications of the British Institute of Archaeology in Ankara, 1; London, 1949). More recent studies of the text are published in *Ugarit Forschungen* 13 (1981), pp. 199-290 (especially by M. Dietrich, O. Loretz, 'Die Inschrift der Statue des Königs Idrimi von Alalaḫ', pp. 199-269). The text has also been translated in *ANET*³, pp. 557-58. We also have to refer to the very important study of the character of the narrative in this inscription by M. Liverani, 'Partire sul carro per il deserto', *AIUON* ns 22 (1972), pp. 403-15.

over its neighbouring state Alalaḫ.[62] The city of Ammiah, which is also mentioned by the el-Amarna letters, may be identified with modern Amjūn near Tripolis in Northern Lebanon. Thus, according to Idrimi, Canaan was a country farther south than Alalaḫ proper and situated along the Mediterranean coast.

The three other documents from Alalaḫ which mention Canaan[63] have nothing really important to contribute to the discussion. All three references to Canaan are found in lists enumerating among other persons individuals from Canaan. One of them was a soldier, another a *ḫabiru*, a 'refugee'.[64] Nowhere do the scribes who drafted these lists demonstrate any particular interest in the origins of the three persons from Canaan.

The same evaluation applies to the Ugaritic mention of a person from Canaan, a merchant named 'Yaʿel the Canaanite'.[65] This text, which belongs to the 13th century BCE, thus belongs roughly to the same period as a letter from the king of Ugarit to an Egyptian Pharaoh (Ramses II?), in which circumstances of interest to Ugarit as well as people living in 'the land of Canaan' are mentioned.[66] The letter to Pharaoh is interesting in that it has the king of Ugarit, who in this period was no longer an Egyptian subject but a vassal of the king of Ḫatti, describing Canaan as belonging to the Egyptian sphere of interest.[67]

62 The relevant part of the text, Idrimi line 18, reads: *u a-na ma-at ki-in-a-nim*[KI] *a-li-ik*, 'and I travelled to the land of Canaan'. On the variations of the spelling of Canaan in these documents (the examples from Alalaḫ never transliterate the West-Semitic ʿayin as a 'ḫ'), cf. Weippert, *RLA*, V, p. 352.

63 AT 48:4 (text in D.J. Wiseman, *The Alalakh Tablets* [Occasional Publications of the British Institute of Archaeology at Ankara, 2; London, 1953], pl. XIII), 154:24 (not published) and 181:9 (text in D.J. Wiseman, 'Supplementary Copies of Alalakh Tablets' *JCS* 8 [1954], pp. 1-30, p. 11).

64 In AT 48:4 the person in question comes from [uru]*Ki-in-a-nim* [KI], literally 'the city of Canaan', and in AT 181:9 another person is described as DUMU KUR *Ke-en-a-ni*, literally 'a son of the land of Canaan' (that is, as indicated by C. Blair, simply 'Canaanite'; DUMU = *māru* used here to indicate a member of a group, people or class like the Hebrew *ben*, 'son').

65 RŠ 11.840 = *KTU* 4.96. Cf. on this A.F. Rainey, 'A Canaanite at Ugarit', *IEJ* 13 (1963), pp. 43-45.

66 RŠ 20.182 = *Ugaritica*, V (1969), pp. 112. At p. 389 n. 36 the Canaanites are called DUMU.MEŠ KUR *Ki-na-ḫi*, 'the sons of the land of Canaan' (i. e. 'Canaanites'. See n. 64 above).

67 On international political affairs in general, cf. R.O. Faulkner, 'Egypt: From the Inception of the Nineteenth Dynasty to the Death of Ramesses III', *CAH*[3], II, 2 (Cambridge, 1975), pp. 217-51, and A. Goetze, 'The Hittites and Syria (1300-1200 B.C.)', *ibid.*, pp. 252-73.

Most other sources from Western Asia, from Assyria or Ḫatti, are rather uninteresting and do not contribute in any substantial way to the elucidation of the problem of Canaan in the Late Bronze Age.

A single text from Ḫattušaš, the Hittite capital, must, however, be included among the texts being discussed in this section. This text contains an incantion in which some gods are looked for in various countries:

> . . .wherever ye may be, O Cedar-Gods, whether in heaven or earth, whether on mountains or in rivers, whether in the Mitanni country or in the country of Kinza, the country of Tunip, the country of Ugarit, the country of Zinzara, the country of Dunapapa, the country of Idarukatta, the country of Gatanna, the country of Alalḫa, the country of Kinaḫḫi, the country of Amurru, the country of Sidon, the country of Tyre, the country of Nuḫašši, the country of Ugulzit, the country of Arrapḫa, the country of Zunzurḫi.[68]

This text evidently enumerates as many foreign countries as the scribe was able to remember, among which also Canaan was included. The scribe distinguishes between Canaan and Ugarit, Sidon and Tyre on one hand, while on the other he combines Canaan with the coastal states along the Mediterranean, indicating that according to his understanding of Canaan this country was also situated along the Mediterranean coast. This clear evidence must be compared to the fact that there is an obvious dividing line between the coastal area and inner Syrian states like Kinza (Qadeš), Nuḫašše, etc. However, we should not place too much weight on the geographical systematization of this text, since the reason for the arrangement of the various countries is not always absolutely evident. First, the two Syrian states of Qadeš and Nuḫašše are separated by the coastal states, although they were almost neighbours in Syria proper. Secondly, the arrangement of the coastal states is somewhat confusing, since Canaan is placed immediately after Alalaḫ farthest to the north, while Alalaḫ's southern neighbour, Ugarit, was already listed before the document mentioned the Mediterranean states. Furthermore, Ugarit's southern neighbour, Amurru, is mentioned only after Canaan. Finally, the text enumerates a number of entities the geographical placement of which is uncertain, for example, Ugulzit. However, despite such problems the geographical outlook of this document is quite clear, at least as concerns Canaan, which according to this Hittite document was

---

68 *KUB*, XV, p. 34, lines 50ff. The translation is from *ANET*[3], p. 353.

supposed to be a political and administrative geographical unit placed somewhere along the Mediterranean coast.

Canaan and the Canaanites according to Egyptian Sources

The references to Canaan found in documents which originate in Western Asia outside the Egyptian sphere of influence generally agree on one point, that Canaan belonged to the Egyptian empire. Thus we should expect the Egyptian sources to contain more precise information as to the delimitation of Canaan. After all, the Egyptians were the masters of what is traditionally believed to be 'the land of Canaan' from around 1550 BCE until at least 1150 BCE. The first Egyptian reference to the Canaanites and Canaan dates from the 18th dynasty while the last one—apart from a single reference from the 22nd dynasty (late 10th or early 9th century BCE)—belongs to the Ramesside era (20th dynasty).[69]

The oldest Egyptian document which mentions the Canaanites is a report composed by Pharaoh Amenophis II (c. 1450-1425 BCE) in memory of his campaign in Western Asia. In this document a list of prisoners from Asia is included:

> List of this booty: maryannu: 550; their wives: 240; Canaanites: 640; princes' children: 232; princes' children, female: 323; favorites of the princes of every foreign country: 270 women, in addition to their paraphernalia for entertaining the heart, of silver and gold, (at) their shoulders; total 2,214; horses: 820; chariots: 730, in addition to all their weapons of warfare.[70]

The first impression this list gives is that the Canaanites are placed in a rather distinguished environment. The other groups mentioned are persons of high rank, the *maryannu*, that is, the professional class of charioteers, who in some areas—if not everywhere—in the course of the Late Bronze Age obtained a position almost comparable to the one held by the knights of the Middle Ages,[71] as well as children of

---

69 The complete list is in M. Görg, 'Der Name 'Kanaan' in ägyptischer Wiedergabe', *BN* 18 (1982), pp. 26-27, and S. Aḥituv, *Canaanite Toponyms in Ancient Egyptian Documents* (Jerusalem-Leiden, 1984), pp. 83-84.

70 Following J.A. Wilson's translation in *ANET*[3], p. 246. On this text cf. the comprehensive study by E. Edel, 'Die Stelen Amenophis' II. aus Karnak und Memphis', *ZDPV* 69 (1953), pp. 97-176. On this passage see Edel, pp. 170-73.

71 The usual understanding of the *maryannu*, in itself an Indo-European word meaning 'young man, hero', more or less follows the definition of M. Mayer-

princely families and women belonging to the Syrian and Palestinian courts. According to Elmar Edel the Canaanites in this list, however, were not noble persons but representatives of the common population. In his opinion the Canaanites comprised not only individuals of Palestinian origin but also others from all of the Asiatic territory which had been the victim of Pharaoh's attack.[72]

This list may, however, be compared to a different list of Pharaoh's prisoners found in the same document. Here no Canaanites are mentioned; instead we find princes from Retenu,[73] *ḫabiru*, *šaśu*-nomads, Hurrians, etc. In this second list the ordinary population of Western Asia is mentioned, the refugees (*ᶜpr.w*[74]), the nomads (*š3św*[75]), the Hurrians, which in this case must be the term used for the settled population in Western Asia, as well as the ruling class.

It is, however, difficult to compare the two lists, since they seem to fulfil two different purposes in the report of Amenophis II. Edel's

hofer, *Or* 34 (1965), p. 336 n., 'wagenbesitzender Lehensadel', 'Junker' (here cited according to M. Dietrich and O. Loretz, 'Die soziale Struktur von Alalaḫ und Ugarit', *WO* 5, 1 [1969], pp. 56-93, p. 93 note); cf. also A.F. Rainey, *The Social Stratification of Ugarit* (Diss. Brandeis University, 1962), p. 134, 'man, hero, youth'. In the palatine society of the Syrian States of the Late Bronze Age these *maryannu* were also included among the 'king's men' who were employed by the palace. They at any rate belonged to the upper class of the society and exercised an important measure of economic control, not least because of the extensive amount of landed property which they received from the palace administration. Cf. also in general M.S. Drower, 'Syria c. 1550-1400 B.C.', *CAH* [3], II, 1 (Cambridge, 1973), pp. 421ff. (she simply describes the *maryannu* as the 'aristocracy').

72 'Die Stelen Amenophis' II.', p. 172.

73 General designation for the Egyptian province of Western Asia, in this period also encompassing most of Syria; cf. Edel, *ibid.*

74 The Egyptian rendering of *ḫabiru*.

75 Cf. on these chiefly the comprehensive survey of the material in R. Giveon, *Les bedouins Shosou des documents égyptiens* (Documenta et monumenta Orientis Antiqui 18; Leiden, 1971). See also M. Weippert, 'Semitische Nomaden des zweiten Jahrtausends. Über die *š3św* der ägyptischen Quellen', *Biblica* 55 (1974), pp. 265-80, 427-33. In spite of L.E. Stager's protests against the usual interpretation of the *š3św* as nomads (see L.E. Stager, 'Merneptah, Israel and the Sea Peoples', *Eretz Israel* 18 [1985], pp. 56*-64*, p. 59*), it is likely that the Egyptians, because of their insufficient knowledge of the sociological composition of the population of Western Asia, operated with stereotypes, just as was the case in the later European tradition, according to which the inhabitants of Western Asia during the Bronze Age should be subdivided into three different social categories: nomads, peasants, and city-dwellers. In the Egyptian version, however, this was refugees, nomads, and peasants/settled persons.

interpretation of the Canaanites as ordinary people is therefore hardly the most obvious one. It is easy to provide several arguments showing what kind of problems are posed by the two very different lists. First of all, the number of Canaanites in the first list is proportionally in line with the numbers of the various noble groups enumerated by the same list (550 *maryannu* and 555 princely children [males and females] as compared to 640 Canaanites). This may indicate that the Canaanites mentioned here were, after all, people of some standing. Secondly, the difference of number between the Canaanites in the first list and the common people mentioned in the second list is remarkable (640 Canaanites as compared to 3,600 *ḫabiru*, 15,200 *šasu*-nomads and 36,300 Ḥurrians). We are, accordingly, led to believe that there was a marked social difference between the Canaanites of the first list and the common men mentioned by the second.[76] It cannot be maintained that the reason for this difference is that the second list generally operates with greater numbers than the first one, since the second enumeration of noble persons is proportionally the same as the number mentioned in the first list (the second list includes only 127 princes and 179 members of princely families). Finally, J.A. Wilson refers in his translation to a textual problem connected with the reading of the word 'Canaanites' in this document: another version of the same report does not read 'Canaanites' but an Egyptian word

76 This was already acknowledged by B. Maisler (Mazar), 'Canaan and the Canaanites', *BASOR* 102 (1946), pp. 7-12; cf. p. 9. More dubious is Maisler's interpretation here of the 'Canaanites' as 'plutocrats', i. e. rich merchants. That such a plutocracy already existed in Syria and Palestine in the Late Bronze Age does not seem very likely, and if it did appear at some point, then it would have been at the end of the Late Bronze Age rather than at the beginning, where this text is to be placed. A common way of describing the political system of Syria and Palestine in this period is to see the whole area divided among a number of so-called city-states, or, perhaps better, palatine states, since the 'palace' formed the centre of the agricultural, industrial and trading complex which constituted the state of the Late Bronze Age; the king was 'general director' of the 'house'. The literature on this is quite extensive. Among the various studies, I would like to draw attention to Paul Garelli (ed.), *Le palais et la royauté* (XIXe rencontre assyriologique internationale; Paris, 1974), especially the article by M. Liverani, 'La royauté syrienne de l'âge du bronze récent', pp. 329-56. We should not, however, forget Liverani's description of the economic conditions; see 'Il modo di produzione' in S. Moscati (ed.), *L'alba della civiltà*, II (Torino, 1976), pp. 1-126, and his 'Economia delle fattorie palatine ugaritiche', *Dialoghi di Archeologia* n.s. 1 (1979), pp. 57-72.

which—although very similar to the Egyptian spelling of Canaanites—may be translated as 'baggage, pack'.[77]

It must be maintained—irrespective of how we are to interpret this Egyptian text in detail—that the only certain information which this report presents is that the Canaanites (if the reading is correct) were individuals of Asiatic origin. We do not know exactly to which part of Western Asia they belonged; the report is absolutely silent as to their precise provenience.

The report of Amenophis II is the only Egyptian text from the period of the 18th dynasty which mentions the Canaanites. During the next century the Egyptian sources are silent, although they occasionally mention Canaan itself.[78] Only during the 19th dynasty do the references to Canaan become a little more frequent, although it would be an exaggeration to claim that Canaan was in this era a general Egyptian designation of its province in Asia.[79] As to the Canaanites themselves the Egyptian texts have nothing more to tell. The nearest we come to a reference to the Canaanites is a mentioning of 'slaves of Canaan from Hurri'.[80]

In his descriptions of his Asiatic campaigns Sethos I (1318-1304 BCE) of the 19th dynasty describes the effect of an Egyptian attack on 'the city of Canaan', perhaps better translated as 'the city Canaan':

77 *ANET*[3], p. 246 n. 29, in Wilson's transcription *kin^canu*, the 'Canaanites' in contrast to **kena^cah*, 'baggage, pack'. On the problems connected with the different listings of the spoil in the two versions of the inscription, cf. Edel, 'Die Stelen Amenophis' II.', pp. 167ff.; on Wilson's textual problem, *ibid.*, p. 168 and n. 103 (including a categorical rejection of Wilson's argument).

78 The exceptions are generally not very informative; there is, for example, a list of toponyms from the time of Amenophis III (1417-1379 BCE), in which *Knn^cn* is placed next to *Bbr*, Raphia (*Rpwh*, a town to the south of Gaza) and Šaruhen (*šrhn*, cf. Josh. 19.6), and thus placing it together with a number of localities which were definitely situated in southwest Palestine (indicating that Canaan is here another name for Gaza) (R. Giveon, 'Toponymes ouest-asiatiques à Soleb', *VT* 14 [1964], pp. 239-55, p. 247, A.2., proposes to understand *Bbr* as 'Babel', although he qualifies this with a '?').

79 According to the listing in Aḥituv, *Canaanite Toponyms*, p. 84, there are eight references to Canaan and the Canaanites from the time of the 19th and 20th dynasties.

80 Pap. Anastasi IV 16, 4 (comp. Pap. Anastasi III A 5f.), translated in R.A. Caminos, *Late Egyptian Miscellanies* (Oxford, 1954), p. 117; cf. also Helck, *Beziehungen*, p. 279, and Weippert, *RLA*, V, p. 353. Ḥurri (or in Egyptian *H3rw*) was the usual Egyptian name for its provinces in Asia under the 18th and 19th dynasties; cf. Helck, *Beziehungen*, p. 275.

The desolation which the mighty arm of Pharaoh . . . made among the foe belonging to the Shasu from the fortress of Sile to the (fortress/city of) Canaan.[81]

In this period the Egyptian spelling of the word 'Canaan' was generally *p3 k3n^cn3* (although the spelling may vary), *p3* being the Egyptian definite article which here prefaces the name itself.[82] *P3 k3n^cn3* is generally believed to have been used by the Egyptian administration in order to signify that the city of Gaza in Southern Palestine was in this period the centre of Canaan, because the pharaohs had, since the early days of their sway over Asia, used Gaza as their most important base in Palestine. Moreover, in the course of the history of Palestine in the Late Bronze Age, Gaza may have been made the administrative centre of the southern province of Egypt's Asiatic empire.[83]

That southern Palestine is intended by this designation becomes obvious because of the description of Canaan in the famous Papyrus Anastasi I. Here an Egyptian scholar evidently blames a colleague because of his ignorance of the situation in Asia.[84] This text contains a fair amount of information about the geography of Palestine, and the survey seems to follow a path though the country from the north to the south. The scholar's 'route' through the country starts in the north at the coast of Lebanon and in Syria and continues towards the border of Egypt. After having bypassed Megiddo, the 'author' (or rather his victim, the pretended receiver of this literary letter) continues his journey over the coastal plain to Joppa (Japha) and finally reaches 'the end of the land of Canaan'. Here a certain change of direction is evident, because the next reference point mentioned is situated on the Egyptian border proper, more specifically, at the 'fortress of the way of Horus',[85] which may be identified with the Egyptian border fortress of Sile near modern el-Kantara on the Suez

---

81 Following the translation of Wilson in *ANET*[3], p. 254 (I have supplied the words in parentheses). For the text itself cf. K.A. Kitchen, *Ramesside Inscriptions Historical and Biographical*, I (Oxford, 1968-75), pp. 8, 16.

82 It must be noted that the Egyptian determinative for 'foreign nations' is used of Canaan only from the 19th dynasty on.

83 Helck, *Beziehungen*, p. 313.

84 Translated in *ANET*[3], pp. 477-79; the relevant passages are on p. 478.

85 Actually the border station on the official Egyptian route ('the Way of Horus') from Minieh in Middle Egypt to the border of Palestine, where it is continued by the *Via Maris*, along the Mediterranean Sea to the north. On the Way of Horus, cf. Helck, *Beziehungen*, pp. 323-27.

Canal.[86] From here the author makes his way back towards the Palestinian border and his final ironic question concerns the distance to be covered from Raphia to Gaza. We are, most likely, back at 'the end of the land of Canaan'.

It is highly feasible that the same narrow understanding of Canaan is intended on Merneptah's famous 'Israel-stela' from ca. 1200 BCE:

> The princes are prostrate, saying: 'Mercy!'
> Not one raises his head among the Nine Bows.
> Desolation is for Tehenu; Hatti is pacified;
> Plundered is the Canaan[87] with every evil;
> Carried off is Ashkelon; seized upon is Gezer;
> Yanoam is made as that which does not exist;
> Israel is laid waste, his seed is not;
> Hurru is become a widow for Egypt!
> All lands together, they are pacified;
> Everyone who was restless, he has been bound . . .[88]

The impact of this text on the discussion of the origin of Israel may be left aside in this connection; here we are only concerned with the interpretation of 'the Canaan' in this text.[89] The notion that this Canaan must be understood as a common name for the whole of Palestine is hardly to be maintained in light of the final sections of the text, especially in light of the sentence 'Hurru is become a widow for Egypt', which may be viewed as a kind of summary of the whole passage quoted. The geographical horizon of Merneptah's inscription points in the same direction, because—as far as Palestine is intended— the direction of Pharaoh's 'attack' is from the southwest towards the northeast.

We cannot, however, be absolutely certain as to the precise interpretation of 'the Canaan' in this inscription, since all Egyptian references to 'the Canaan' are rather imprecise and leave many

---

86 Cf. Helck, *Beziehungen*, pp. 323-24; Wilson, *ANET*[3], p. 478 n. 47.
87 In Egyptian: *p3 K3n^{c}n^c*.
88 Translation in *ANET*[3], p. 378.
89 On this text cf. E. Otto, *Jakob in Sichem* (BWANT, 110; Stuttgart, 1979), pp. 200-205, and H. Engel, 'Die Siegesstele des Merenptah', *Biblica* 60 (1979), pp. 373-99. See also the divergent interpretation of the text by G.W. Ahlström, *Who Were the Israelites?* (Winona Lake, 1986), p. 39 (cf. also G.W. Ahlström and D. Edelman, 'Merneptah's Israel', *JNES* 44 [1985], pp. 59-61), who thinks that Canaan in this text stands in parallel to the more comprehensive entities, Ḥatti and Ḥurru (Kharu or *ḫ3rw*). In the same vein is Stager, 'Merneptah's Campaign'.

problems to be solved. Thus Ramses III (1198-1166 BCE) describes a
foundation of a temple in 'the (city of) Canaan' in this manner:

> I built for thee a mysterious house in the land of Djahi, like the
> horizon of heaven which is in the sky, (named) 'the House of Ramses-
> Ruler-of-Heliopolis–life, prosperity, health!–in the Canaan'. . .[90]

Again, we are entitled to suppose that the city in question must be
Gaza,[91] whereas Djahi, which is otherwise the common Egyptian name
for Phoenicia (or a part of Phoenicia), is here used to indicate the
whole of Asia.[92]

Finally, as part of a survey of the Egyptian evidence, we cannot
fail to mention the references to Canaan in the correspondence
between Ramses II and his Hittite colleague Ḫattušiliš III. The letters
in question have been studied in great detail by Elmar Edel.[93] In one
of his letters Ramses describes the first days of his famous campaign
against the Hittites, when he travelled to 'the land of Canaan' in
order to join his army before advancing against the Hittite army
amassed around Qadeš in Syria.[94] He does not, however, give any
details as to the territory which he understood to be 'the land of
Canaan'.

The second letter, which is included in the 'marriage correspondence' between the Egyptian and the Hittite royal courts, may once

90 From Pap. Harris I, ix 1ff. The translation is according to Wilson, *ANET*[3], p.
   260; cf. on this text quite recently C. Uehlinger, 'Der Amun-Tempel Ramses'
   III. in *p3-Knᶜn*, seine südpalästinischen Tempelgüter und der Übergang von
   der Ägypter- zur Philisterherrschaft: ein Hinweis auf einige wenig beachtete
   Skarabäen', *ZDPV* 104 (1989), pp. 6-25.
91 Cf. on this text and its implications already A. Alt, 'Ägyptische Tempel in
   Palästina und die Landnahme der Philister' (1944), *Kleine Schriften zur
   Geschichte des Volkes Israel*, I (München, 1953), pp. 216-30. Uehlinger also
   accepts the identification with Gaza (*ZDPV* 104 [1989], p. 8).
92 It would take us too far afield to present here a survey of the application of
   such Egyptian geographical-political names as Djahi. Furthermore, such an
   enterprise would hardly do more than confirm the result of the investigation
   of the Egyptian use of Canaan here, namely that the Egyptians used such
   geographical and political terms in a rather imprecise manner. On Djahi cf.
   Helck, *Beziehungen*, p. 274, *s.v. ṣa-hi.*
93 Of interest in this connection are two articles by Edel, 'KBo I 15 + 19, ein
   Brief Ramses' II. mit einer Schilderung der Ḳadešschlacht', *ZA* 49 (1950), pp.
   195-212, and 'Weitere Briefe aus der Heiratskorrespondenz Ramses' II.: KUB
   III 37', *Geschichte und Altes Testament. Festschrift Alt* (Tübingen, 1953), pp.
   29-63.
94 The passage of interest runs (line 29): *ù ki-i* LUGAL *i[l-li]-ka ana* ᴷᵁᴿ*Ki-na-
   aḫ-ḫi* . . ., 'and as the king came to Canaan. . .'

have contained more detailed information. According to Edel, the various Egyptian administrative centres are enumerated in this letter, first Upe (the name of the Egyptian province of Syria), then Canaan. However, despite this opinion of Edel, the passage in question is mutilated to such a degree[95] that it is hardly advisable to base any argument as to the actual meaning of Canaan in this period upon this letter. Moreover, the passage which supposedly mentions Upe has survived in such a fragmentary state that even this part of Edel's interpretation may be looked upon with some suspicion. Sadly, therefore, that we cannot rely very much on the evidence of this letter.

This is not the place to discuss on the basis of existing documents why Egyptian officials displayed such a remarkable lack of interest and did not present any detailed description of their provinces in Asia, and especially of Canaan. Neither is their seeming geographical ignorance easy to explain. The reason, of course, could be that Asia was looked upon as a barbarian country and therefore uninviting and uninteresting in the eyes of the Egyptians.[96]

In this connection it is more interesting to note the correspondence between the imprecise and ambiguous Egyptian use of the geographical name Canaan and the likewise imprecise understanding of Canaan displayed by the inhabitants of Western Asia themselves. We should therefore rather look for a more general reason why people in this period were accustomed to using geographical terms in such imprecise ways.

An illustration of the problematic nature of applying modern ideas to the examination of ancient documents is Anson F. Rainey's denial that Ugarit could ever have been part of Canaanite territory. He bases this opinion on an Ugaritic administrative document which refers to a foreign merchant as coming from Canaan.[97] Rainey's argument may seem evident to the modern scholar, although it is based on a definite

---

95 Cf. 'Weitere Briefe', p. 50. Cf. also the reconstructed text (D' 12), p. 32: [(ša)] *i-na* ŠÀ-*bi* KU[R *Ki-na-aḫ-ḫi a-na ma-ḫa-ri*], which Edel translates (p. 34): '. . . die] in [Kanaan liegt]'.

96 It is exactly this lack of interest which is reflected by a great number of the el-Amarna letters, where the vassal kings of the Egyptians complain because of Pharaoh's lack of interest in the well-being of his Syrian subjects. Cf. on this the inspiring analysis by Liverani, 'Contrasti e confluenze', *RA* 61 (1967), pp. 1ff., and 'Rib-Adda, giusto sofferente', *Altorientalische Forschungen* 1 (1974), pp. 175ff.

97 Cf. above p. 31 and n. 22.

and preconceived 'modern' understanding of such subjects as Canaan
and the Canaanites according to which Canaan must be a specific
country or territory and the Canaanites the people who lived in this
territory. Moreover, Rainey regards his own conception of nationality
as being the same as that of the ancient writers.

However, it is very likely that the Ugaritic reference to a foreign
merchant makes sense even if Ugarit was in some quarters considered
to be part of Canaan itself, and even if it conflicts with the evidence
from the Tyrian king who included Ugarit among the countries which
belonged to his 'Canaan' (EA 151), which embraced most of Northern
Syria. Thus, according to this interpretation of Canaan in Abi-Milku's
letter, Idrimi of Alalaḫ should have started his journey towards
Canaan in Canaan itself.

The answer to this seemingly confusing use of geographical names
in the ancient sources from the 2nd millennium BCE should probably
be looked for in the notion of 'ethnicity', which was already
mentioned above. It is especially important to consider the current
discussion among social anthropologists about the criteria which can
be used to distinguish between different social and ethnic groups. I
have already dealt with this issue in another context and am not
going to repeat the argument here.[98] However, this much can be said:
social anthropologists have during the last decades become increas-
ingly aware of the great distance between the ethnographer's ideas
about traditional society and the ones prevailing in that society
itself.[99] The classic example of the importance of the issue of ethnicity
is the case of the African Nuer, who did not know that they were
themselves Nuer. 'Nuer' was an ethnic tag attached to the members
of the society in question by the ethnographer who studied their
society in the 1930s. However, as was shown by later investigators,
this name was in fact only the name for it which was current among
its neighbouring tribes.[100]

If we apply a scientific social-anthropological notion of 'ethnicity'

98   Cf. *Early Israel*, pp. 241f., with more bibliographical references.
99   In the jargon of some social-anthropological circles we may speak of the
     difference between the 'emic' (the concepts alive in the person who is the
     object of study) and the 'etic' (the concepts of the investigator, i.e. the social-
     anthropologist or the sociologist).
100 We refer here to one of the most important ethnographical studies which
     appeared between the two world wars, E.E. Evans-Pritchard's well-known
     monograph, *The Nuer* (Oxford, 1940).

to the ancient oriental world in the 2nd millennium BCE, one would argue that everybody in that period knew about Canaan and the Canaanites. To the scribe of ancient Western Asia 'Canaanite' always designated a person who did not belong to the scribe's own society or state, while Canaan was considered to be a country different from his own. In this way Abi-Milku was able to include Ugarit in his Canaan, although the citizens of ancient Ugarit never considered themselves to be Canaanites. It might well have been the case that conversely, in the eyes of the Ugaritic administration, Abi-Milku's city was situated in Canaan, although Abi-Milku himself never says so.

An obvious reason for this confusion, which arises because of the difference between the modern notion of ethnicity and the one current in ancient societies, is that we today possess very definite ideas about the identity of peoples and nations which accord well with the division of our world into nation-states. In the ancient world—and this at least is applicable to Western Asia—no such nation-states existed and no nationalistic ideology had yet arisen. The inhabitants of this area never considered themselves to be citizens of nations or nation-states and they never thought of themselves as belonging to a definite *ethnos* in contrast to other *ethne*.[101]

---

101 Here we must refer to the study of G. Buccellati, *Cities and Nations* (Rome, 1967). In his study Buccellati introduces the two concepts of a 'territorial state' and a 'national state'. Whereas states were originally only territorial, national states emerged in the 1st millennium BCE, or so Buccellati maintains. The city-states of Syria in the Bronze Age were all territorial states, whereas the later Israelite kingdom was, according to Buccellati, a national state. Maybe this last result is not as evident as Buccellati himself believed!

Chapter 3

THE CANAANITES AND THEIR LAND IN ANCIENT
NEAR EASTERN DOCUMENTS:
THE 1ST MILLENNIUM BCE AND LATER

In the preceding chapter the general impression was that Canaan—according to the testimony of the ancient sources—must be placed somewhere in Western Asia, most likely along the Mediterranean coast. However, a decision as to the precise location of Canaan cannot easily be reached in light of the sometimes rather contradictory evidence. In any case, the firm conviction expressed by some modern authors about where to look for Canaan seems hardly to be supported by the testimony of the sources from the 2nd millennium BCE. The only certain topographical information about Canaan in these documents indicates a location in Galilee, but this location is based mainly on a single source which, furthermore, comes from Babylonia and not from the territory understood by the Babylonian king to be Canaan. The 'local' writers expressed their opinion about where Canaan was far more ambiguously.

However, it would be wrong to assume that when we approach the sources from the 1st millennium BCE, a more definite indication of the geographical extent of Canaan can be reached. First and foremost, it must be noted that there exist only a very few references to Canaan in the 1st millennium BCE—apart, of course, from the ample evidence furnished by the Old Testament. Furthermore, it is clear that, limited as it is, the documentary material from the 1st millennium BCE does not contribute much towards solving the problem of Canaan.

The oldest text in which Canaan is mentioned is at the same time the only Egyptian reference to its former province.[1] Unfortunately, the interpretation of this text is problematic. The evidence consists of a short inscription on the burial statuette of an Egyptian official, who introduces himself as being 'Pateese, the envoy to Canaan in Palestine'.[2] Whether this Pateese was an Asiatic by birth and therefore an Asiatic envoy to the Egyptian court or whether he had served as the ambassador of Pharaoh to Palestine has been the usual subject of discussion in connection with this text.[3] Although this question may at first seem rather unimportant, the decision as to Pateese's birthplace may, nevertheless, have some bearing on the problems discussed in this chapter. If Pateese had been the Egyptian envoy to 'Canaan', this does not mean that Canaan was necessarily considered an actually existing political entity: 'Canaan' could have been used in this inscription as a literary device going back to the heyday of the Egyptian empire some centuries earlier. Should this be the case, the real political entity would have been Palestine, that is the land of the Philistines only. However, if Pateese was born in Western Asia, we would have reason to believe that he was the representative in Egypt of an Asiatic state called Canaan. If so, the expression 'Canaan in Palestine' would probably mean 'Canaan, that is Palestine'. Finally, the possibility cannot be excluded—irrespective of how one is to translate the inscription—that $p3\ kn^{cc}n$ was just another name for the Philistine city of Gaza, reflecting the earlier status of this city as an Egyptian administrative centre.

After Pateese's inscription there follows a gap of another five hundred years before another Near Eastern document mentions Canaan. Thus no Egyptian document—neither an official report nor a private document—mentions Canaan. No Assyrian or Babylonian writer ever uses this geographical name, and no reference to Canaan

1 The 22nd dynasty is the date usually proposed for this text, that is, the period between the 10th and 8th centuries BCE.
2 The text was studied for the first time by É. Chassinat, 'Un interprète égyptien pour les pays chananéens', *BIFAO* 1 (1901), pp. 98-100, although most references only mention G. Steindorff's edition, 'The Statuette of an Egyptian Commissioner in Syria', *JEA* 25 (1939), pp. 30-33 and pl. VII.
3 It is a problem whether the Egyptian $wpwṯi\ n\ p3\ Kn^{cc}n\ n\ P\text{-}r\text{-}š3\text{-}\underline{t}$ should be translated 'envoy from Canaan in Philistia' (thus Albrecht Alt, 'Ein Gesandter aus Philistäa in Ägypten', *BO* 9 [1952], pp. 163-64, followed by Edel, 'Weitere Briefe', p. 56) or 'envoy in Canaan in Philistia' (the normal interpretation; cf. on this M. Weippert, 'Semitische Nomaden', p. 429, where a more complete bibliography can be found).

is found in Syrian or Palestinian inscriptions belonging to the 1st millennium BCE.[4] Greek authors from Homer to the Hellenistic period never indicate that they had ever heard of Canaan or the Canaanites. Not before Hellenistic times does the name show up again in any connection, and even then the material is rather unimpressive.

The only real, exact information about Canaan which belongs to the Hellenistic period is found on coins from the Seleucid city of Laodicea in Phoenicia, which was actually a new city built on the ruins of ancient Berytus (Beirut). These coins, which belong to the last centuries before the birth of Christ, bear a monogram in Greek, ΛΑ ΦΟ (representing the Greek name of the city, Λα[οδικεῖς] Φο[ι-νίκης]), but also a Phoenician rendering of the Greek, *L'dk' 'š b-kn'n*, literally 'Laodicea in Canaan'. This translation is interesting because it proves that the authorities of this Hellenistic city identified Phoenicia with Canaan which was thus, according to their testimony, situated on the coast of modern Lebanon. The information is, however, restricted to these very short inscriptions, and the coins therefore have no bearing on the problem of the exact extent of this Canaan.[5]

The general direction of our quest for Canaan in the Hellenistic period is clear, on the other hand, and is confirmed by a number of other sources from the Hellenistic and Roman periods. In this connection we have to draw attention to the evidence from a fragment of the Phoenician History of Philo of Byblus, which has been transmitted by Eusebius, in his *Praeparatio Evangelica*. The fragment, which is supposed to go back to the Phoenician priest Sanchuniathon, also supports the identity between Canaan and Phoenicia, although the identification is contained in a mythological context only:

ὧν ἦν καὶ Εἰσίριος, <ὁ> τῶν τριῶν γραμμάτων εὑρετής, ἀδελφὸς
Χνᾶ τοῦ πρώτου μετονομασθέντος Φοίνικος.

---

4 Most scholars see no problem in the fact that the inscriptions from Syria, Phoenicia and Palestine are absolutely silent about Canaan during most of the 1st millennium BCE (Weippert may be quoted as expressing the general opinion on the matter, *RLA*, V, p. 354: 'Aufgrund der Quellenlage erscheint der Name K. bei Phöniziern und Puniern erst in hell.-röm. Zeit'). It is absolutely correct to say that only a very few texts from this area in the 1st millennium BCE have been handed down to us, but this cannot be used as an argument *for* the presence of the geographical term 'Canaan' in the 1st millennium BCE.
5 The fundamental study on these inscriptions is P. Roussel, 'Laodicée de Phénicie', *Bulletin de Correspondance Hellénique* 35 (1911), pp. 433-40. Bibliographical notes on the coins are presented by Weippert, *RLA*, V, p. 354.

... one of whom was Eisirios, inventor of the three scripts, brother of Chna, the first to change his name to Phoenix.[6]

I see no reason here to reopen the discussion about the reliability of Philo's source, Sanchuniathon, because, after Otto Eissfeldt wrote his defense of the trustworthiness of Sanchuniathon nearly thirty years ago, the historical value of these fragments, which are supposed to belong to the work of this ancient Phoenician priest, is generally believed to be high.[7] On the mythic—or perhaps better 'ideological'— level, where this specific fragment is to be placed, the question of historicity is unimportant. The important thing, however, is that the fragment considers the two eponymous heroes Χνᾶ and Φοῖνιξ to be one and the same person, and this may be used as evidence of a more popular and widespread identification of Canaan with Phoenicia going back to the 1st millennium BCE.

This piece of evidence is the only one which comes from the Phoenician territory itself. Only a couple of other references remain to be taken into consideration, both of which derive from those parts of North Africa inhabited by a Punic-speaking population. These sources may indicate that the Levantine origin of this Punic-speaking population had not been totally forgotten even as late as the 4th century CE. The first example is an inscription from Constantine in modern Algeria which dates from the 3rd-2nd century BCE. Here a certain ʿEbedʾešmun calls himself *bn mʾdr ʾš knʿn*, 'son of Madar, a Canaanite man'.[8] Some scholars are of the opinion that ʿEbedʾešmun in this way indicates that he is of Phoenician origin, in other words, a Canaanite by birth, but this explanation is unnecessarily complicated. In light of the following quotation from the letters of St Augustine, ʿEbedʾešmun could just as well have been born in North Africa proper. St. Augustine informs us that in the 4th century CE awareness

6 Eusebius, *Praep. ev.* I, 10, 39 (Ed. Karl Mras; vol. I [1954], p. 50, ll. 20-21). The translation cited here is the one by H.W. Attridge and R.A. Oden, *Philo of Byblus. The Phoenician History. Introduction, Critical Text, Translation Notes* (CBQMS 9; Washington, DC, 1981), pp. 58-61.

7 Cf. O. Eissfeldt, *Sanchunjathon von Berut und Ilumilku von Ugarit* (Beiträge zur Religionsgeschichte des Altertums 5; Halle, 1952). See also the introduction in Attridge and Oden, *Philo of Byblus*, esp. pp. 3ff. Pp. 11-14 include a full bibliography.

8 See KAI 116:3. The reading is not absolutely certain. Thus R. de Vaux expresses his doubts as to the correct transliteration, 'Le pays de Canaan', p. 23 n. 11. He prefers to read *ʾš kn ʿl*, 'préposé à'. Cf., however, also the commentary in H. Donner and W. Röllig, *KAI*, III, p. 120.

of the Canaanite origin of the local population of Tunis was very much alive:

> Interrogati rustici nostri quid sint, punice respondentes chanani.[9]
>
> If you ask our peasants who they are they will answer in Punic, 'Canaanites'.

It is a surprising fact—according to the surviving documents—that these peasants of the 4th century CE may have been the first persons who considered themselves to be Canaanites. We must, on the other hand, not forget that St Augustine's letter is only a second-hand source; after all, the possibility still exists that it was St Augustine who 'knew' that the peasants were 'Canaanites' because of their Punic origin. On the other hand, when viewed in light of the discussion of ethnicity to which I have already called attention, the testimony of these peasants as to their origin makes sense. Displaced persons, who may have lost their homeland and have settled in other parts of the world, as was the case with the Punic population of North Africa, could very well have kept an old ethnic identity alive although this very identity had never been equally evident to their forefathers in Western Asia.

It is interesting that the testimony of St Augustine's Punic peasants in North Africa can to some degree be compared to additional evidence which is, however, only found in the New Testament, in the Gospel of Matthew (15.21-22):

> Καὶ ἐξελθὼν ἐκεῖθεν ὁ Ἰησοῦς ἀνεχώρησεν εἰς τὰ μέρη Τύρου καὶ Σιδῶνος. καὶ ἰδοὺ γυνὴ Χαναναία ἀπὸ τῶν ὁρίων ἐκείνων ἐξελθοῦσα . . .
>
> Jesus then withdrew to the region of Tyre and Sidon. And a Canaanite woman from those parts came . . .[10]

It is evident that the women described as a 'Canaanite' came from Phoenicia ('Tyre and Sidon' is clearly an elliptic expression meaning Phoenicia in its totality, because Phoenicia is here marked out by the inclusion of its two most important cities). In addition, the person thus described as a Canaanite woman most probably belonged to the peasant population of ancient Phoenicia. It is more important to

---

9 Augustine, *Ep. ad Romanos inchoata expositio* 13 (Migne, *Patrologia Latina*, XXXV, p. 2096).

10 The New Testament quotations are from the REB.

58   The Canaanites and Their Land

realize that this New Testament passage may be considered independent testimony to the identification of Phoenicia with Canaan in the
Hellenistic period, because no Old Testament passage exists which
could have been the source of this narrative in the New Testament.
The parallel version in the Gospel of Mark (7.24, 26) cannot be used
as evidence against this interpretation of Matt. 15.21-22:

Ἐκεῖθεν δὲ ἀναστὰς ἀπῆλθεν εἰς τὰ ὅρια Τύρου . . . ἡ δὲ γυνὴ ἦν
Ἑλληνίς, Συροφοινίκισσα τῷ γένει . . .

He moved on from there into the territory of Tyre . . . (The woman
was a Gentile, a Phoenician of Syria by nationality. . .)

The term συροφοινίκισσα, literally 'the Syro-Phoenician woman', is,
as far as I know, a hapax legomenon. The meaning of the expression
is, however, absolutely clear: the woman coming from the territory of
Tyre was a Phoenician by birth, while Phoenicia itself in those days
formed a part of the political and administrative district of greater
Syria (or had traditionally been a part of greater Syria). She was, at
the same time, as Matthew acknowledges, a Canaanite, although Mark
adds Ἑλληνίς, 'a Greek woman', which in the language of the time
meant a 'gentile'.

The few other New Testament passages where Canaan is mentioned[11]—a situation which is comparable to the likewise limited use
of the term Phoenicia in the New Testament[12]—stands in contrast to
the relatively more frequent use of 'Sidon and Tyre' to indicate the
area in question.[13] However, this conforms well with the impression
gained from other Hellenistic evidence, that Canaan was in that
period generally understood to encompass the Lebanese coastal areas,
including its two flourishing centres of trade, Sidon and Tyre.

The few instances in the Septuagint where the Greek does not
translate Hebrew כנען and כנעני with Χανάαν and Χαναναῖος
(which is the usual rendering in the LXX) but with Φοινίκη and
Φοῖνιξ, cannot, of course, be looked upon as totally independent
evidence, these few instances may represent a specific interpretation
of the content of the geographical name 'Canaan' in the Hellenistic

11 Acts 7.11; 13.19.
12 Φοινίκη is only used three times in Acts: 11.19; 15.3; 21.2; cf. also Φοῖνιξ in
Acts 27.12.
13 Sidon: Matt. 11.21, 22; 15.21; Mark 3.8; 7.31; Luke 6.17; 10.13, 14; Acts 27.3.
Tyre: Matt. 11.21, 22; 15.21; Mark 3.8; 7.24, 31; Luke 6.17; 10.13, 14; Acts 21.3, 7.

period. These unusual transliterations of the LXX may, however, not always be so easily understood, as when, for example, in Exod. 6.15, in a genealogical list of the Simeonites, a certain Saul, who in the Hebrew version is called בֶּן־כְּנַעֲנִית, 'the son of a Canaanite woman', is described as ὁ ἐκ τῆς Φοινίσσης, 'the one who came from the Phoenician woman'.

The problematic character of this last example is stressed by the parallel passage in Gen. 46.10, where the Hebrew text is identical with Exod. 6.15. Here LXX transliterates the Hebrew as υἱὸς τῆς Χανανίτιδος, 'son of the Canaanite woman', which is absolutely identical with the Hebrew original. It could well be that the translator of Exod. 6.15, in order to demonstrate his learning, has here decided to 'modernize' the text. His 'improvement' is, however, meaningless, because the historical Simeonites never had any geographical affinity with the Phoenician territory. The Simeonites belonged to the southern part of Palestine, especially to the northern part of the Negeb, and were originally the allies of the tribe of Judah. Moreover—as many scholars have correctly observed—the independent tribe of Simeon had probably ceased to exist already before the emergence of the Hebrew monarchy c. 1000 BCE. The tribe of Simeon had already in those early days—together with a number of other tribes in Southern Palestine—been absorbed by the dominant tribe of Judah.[14] There was therefore no sociological entity called Simeon in the Hellenistic period which could explain the the Greek translation of Exod. 6.15.

The two passages where the LXX has rendered the Hebrew אֶרֶץ כְּנַעַן, 'the land of Canaan', as εἰς μέρος τῆς Φοινίκης (Exod. 16.35) and τὴν χώραν τῶν Φοινίκων, 'the land of the Phoenicians' (Josh. 5.12), cannot be considered to be mutually independent, although the two examples are placed in two different parts of the Old Testament, the first in the Torah, and the second in the Prophets. In Exodus 16 the provision of manna for the Israelites in the desert is described. At the end of the narrative a note is included, indicating

---

14 Martin Noth's summary of the source material on the tribe of Simeon, in his *Geschichte Israels* (Göttingen, 1950), pp. 58f., reflects the usual notion of the history of this tribe: in the historical period the tribe of Simeon played no independent role, because it had already at the beginning of this period been amalgamated into the much greater and more powerful tribe of Judah. See also E. Nielsen, *Shechem. A Traditio-Historical Investigation* (2nd edn; Copenhagen, 1959), pp. 259ff.

that the manna was to cease when the Israelites arrived אל־קצה ארץ
כנען, 'at the border of the land of Canaan'. In connection with the
narrative in Joshua 5 this note is referred to again: now the manna
could stop.[15]

It is unnecessary in this place to discuss the information contained
in Exod. 16.35. When Exod. 16.35 is compared to Joshua 5, we get the
impression that the river Jordan was considered the borderline
(according to Joshua 5 the manna ceased while the Israelites camped
in the environs of Jericho, just a couple of miles from the river). The
geographical implications of these texts will be reviewed later in
connection with other geographical information about Canaan in the
Old Testament. It is, however, more important here to realize that,
without discussion, the translators of the two interconnected passages,
Exod. 16.35 and Josh. 5.12, identified Canaan with Phoenicia, which, in
this case, they obviously understood to include more territory than
Lebanon: the latter was, perhaps the more usual interpretation of
Phoenicia in Hellenistic times. Here, in Exod. 16.35 and Josh. 5.12,
according to the evidence of the LXX translators, Phoenicia must also
have comprised Palestine. However, we are not in a position to
decide whether the translators were motivated by an understanding of
Canaan current in their own time, or whether their decision about
how to translate 'Canaan' in these two passages was based on their
knowledge of what Old Testament authors generally regarded as
constituting the land of Canaan.

In favour of the last mentioned explanation we may point to the
fact that this more comprehensive understanding of Canaan/Phoenicia
accords well with the description of the ideal borders of Canaan
elsewhere in the Old Testament. This is further supported by the fact
that the picture of Canaan/Phoenicia in Josh. 5.12 is absolutely at
variance with the one presented in Josh 5.1:

15 The two chapters, Exodus 16 and Joshua 5, form the textual basis for Martin
Rose's re-evaluation of the relations between the oldest part of the Tetrateuch,
the Yahwistic stratum, and the Deuteronomistic history, according to which the
Yahwist should be later than the oldest Deuteronomic version of the Deuteronomistic history. See M. Rose, *Deuteronomist und Jahwist. Untersuchungen zu
den Berührungspunkten beider Literaturwerke* (AThANT, 67; Zürich, 1981), pp.
25-54. There is no reason to comment on Rose's study in this place; however,
the strong emphasis placed upon the connection between the two chapters is
important in this connection.

ויהי כשמע כל־מלכי האמרי אשר בעבר הירדן ימה וכל־מלכי
הכנעני אשר על־הים

When all the Amorite kings to the west of the Jordan and all the
Canaanite kings by the sea-coast heard. . .

Καὶ ἐγένετο ὡς ἤκουσαν οἱ βασιλεῖς τῶν Αμορραίων, οἳ ἦσαν πέραν
τοῦ Ιορδάνου, καὶ οἱ βασιλεῖς τῆς Φοινίκης οἱ παρὰ τὴν θάλασσαν
. . .

And it happened when the kings of the Amorites, who dwelt on the
other side of the Jordan, and the kings of the Phoenicians who dwelt
along the sea, heard . . .

In this passage the Canaanite kings ruled over the Canaanites at the
sea. Although the wording of the passage is likely to be just conventional, the Canaanite territory might well have been understood also
to embrace Phoenicia, that is, the coastal area of Lebanon. The
translator of this verse in the LXX was, of course, of this opinion and
therefore—in contrast to the translator of Josh. 5.12—he rendered the
passage in accordance with the interpretation of Phoenicia current in
his own time.

The review of the evidence from the 1st millennium BCE and later
can be concluded at this point, and the last mentioned passages from
the Greek Old Testament, which belong to the Hellenistic period, can
thus form a bridge with the review of the evidence from the Hebrew
Bible in the next three chapters.

Thus the result of the investigation of this chapter is relatively
clear. The source material from the 1st millennium BCE—outside the
Hebrew Bible—points in the same direction, that 'the land of Canaan'
in the Hellenistic period was mainly to be identified with the central
areas of the Phoenicians in Lebanon, and perhaps also included the
neighbouring areas to the south on the coastal plain of Acre, and
perhaps even the Valley of Jezreel.[16]

It is, on the other hand, incorrect—or at least imprecise and even

16 This may be the most obvious interpretation of Josh. 5.1. The geographical
direction of Josh. 5.1 is perhaps not east-to-west—first the mountains in the
central part of Palestine, then the coastal areas (which were not densely
populated in antiquity, and where only very few city-states were situated
between Dor near Carmel and the Philistine cities in the south)—but rather
south-to-north—first the mountains of central Palestine, then the Galilaean
lowland, the valley of Jezreel and the coastal plain between Carmel and Rosh
Hanniqra, and finally the Lebanese coast. At least this much can be said, that
the translators of the LXX have interpreted the map of Israel this way.

impossible—to claim, as Roland de Vaux did, that the geographical concept of Canaan had by now returned to its original meaning after a digression which had lasted for centuries and which had been particularly popular among the Old Testament writers, who understood Canaan to embrace a territory far more extensive than Lebanon proper.[17] It was made clear by the discussion in the preceding chapter that the testimony of the sources belonging to the 2nd millennium BCE is less than certain as to the precise geographical demarcation of the Canaanite territory, and this evidence should hardly be called upon in support of the opinion of de Vaux and other scholars. The task which remains to us is to survey the evidence of the Old Testament itself, which quantitatively as well as qualitatively surpasses all other references to Canaan in the ancient world.

17 See R. de Vaux, 'Le pays de Canaan', p. 30.

Chapter 4

THE CANAANITES AND THEIR LAND ACCORDING TO
THE OLD TESTAMENT. I: INTRODUCTION

The terms 'Canaan' and 'Canaanite' appear quite frequently in the
Old Testament. Thus Hans-Jürgen Zobel, in his entry on כנען in the
Theologisches Wörterbuch zum Alten Testament, records ninety-four
examples of 'Canaan'; its derivative כנעני is found seventy-four
times.[1] In the same article, Zobel offers a careful survey of the Old
Testament evidence concerning Canaan and the Canaanites. Therefore,
to undertake another study of the Canaanites and their land may
seem superfluous, were it not for a number of factors which Zobel
did not take properly into consideration.

Zobel, who is a disciple of Otto Eissfeldt, must be considered as
belonging to the classical German tradition of Old Testament scholarship. His interpretation of the Canaanites and their land is therefore in
accordance with the view of the Canaanites generally held by the
members of the German school (or perhaps better, those with the
'German approach'). Some examples of this have already been
mentioned here, for example, the older contributions to the issue of
the Canaanites by Johannes Hempel and Albrecht Alt found in
various German encyclopaedias of this century. Another scholar to be
mentioned here is Martin Noth, with his balanced view on our
theme.[2] The approach to this problem which is followed by these
scholars is characterized by a remarkable scepticism about the
historical value of the Old Testament references to the Canaanites.
This sceptical attitude is very apparent when one considers how these

1 Zobel, *TWAT*, IV, col. 226.
2 On Canaan and the Canaanites see especially Martin Noth, *Die Welt des Alten
   Testaments* (4th edn; Berlin, 1962), pp. 45-49.

scholars evaluate the geographical boundaries of Canaan as presented in the biblical books of Numbers and Joshua: the geographical information contained in these books cannot, in their opinion, be thought to represent any ancient 'knowledge' about the land of the Canaanites. The biblical documents in question belong to a rather late literary context—the Priestly source, or sources, which must be considered to be in close agreement with the ideas of the Priestly writers; these passages were hardly drafted before the beginning of the Babylonian exile in the middle of the first millennium BCE at the earliest.[3]

If we continue our investigation according to the rules laid down by the classical German school of Old Testament study, we have initially to consider the literary layers in the Old Testament traditions and the evidence they each present relating to the development of the concept of Canaan in Old Testament times. As a result of such a procedure, it should prove possible to date the individual layers or source documents to different periods of Israelite history, thereby creating a kind of framework on the basis of which we could evaluate the various references to the Canaanites and their land contained in the various literary layers. This should enable the investigator to propose a stratigraphy of the material in the Old Testament historical literature of interest in this connection. It should be equally possible to trace the development of the Israelite concept of Canaan and its inhabitants, which covered a substantial span of years, perhaps more than half a millennium. The investigator is, then, supposed to begin with the references present in the 'Yahwistic' source (or 'J', after the German *Jahwist*), which was formerly attributed to the work of a scribe, or a circle of scribes, who lived in the days of King Solomon at the end of the 10th century BCE, or else a couple of decades after Solomon's death, at the beginning of the 9th century BCE. The latest references to Canaan would then be those contained in the Priestly source, which dates from the post-exilic period, as late as the 5th century BCE.[4] This 'stratigraphy' of the

4 Cf. Noth, *Die Welt*, p. 46. The important passages are those like Num. 35.10, 14 and Josh. 22.10, 11.
4 An almost classic example of this approach is Karl Jaroš's analysis of the attitude of the Israelites to the Canaanite religion, in his *Die Stellung des Elohisten zur kanaanäischen Religion* (Orbis Biblicus et Orientalis, 4; Freiburg, Schweiz, 1974). In his study Jaroš tries to describe a development from the rather neutral evaluation of Canaanite civilization in the Yahwistic stratum to

various opinions expressed by the Old Testament about Canaan could at a later phase of the investigation be compared to the evidence of the Deuteronomistic literature from the book of Deuteronomy to 2 Kings, which together form a literary composition which was compiled just before the Babylonian exile, during the exile, and in the years following the official end of the exile in 538 BCE. Likewise, it would be possible to broaden the comparison also to include the Chronistic literature and the books of Ezrah and Nehemiah. As a result of this investigation sholars should be able to describe how the concept of Canaan developed among the Israelites from c. 900 BCE until c. 400 BCE, and some scholars who would use such an approach as their starting point would even be prepared to trace this development back into the dark non-literary ages preceding the rise of the Hebrew monarchy.

In spite of the opposition which the formerly dominant position of the German school of Old Testament research provoked in other more conservative circles of biblical scholarship, where the German scholars were believed to be negative and nihilistic, scholars of Scandinavia and the Anglo-Saxon world generally followed the same approach to the study of the historical literature of the Old Testament. Thus scholars like Martin Noth and William F. Albright followed the same approach to the literary evaluation of the Old Testament sources, but they differed in their evaluation of the historical content of these sources. Whereas Martin Noth was very sceptical as to the historical value of the information contained in the Old Testament narratives about the early history of Israel, scholars belonging to the circle of Albright were far more willing to accept the testimony of the historical books at face value. Thus even the geographical descriptions of the land of Canaan, which have been transmitted in rather late literary contexts, and therefore relevant to, for example, the post-exilic period, would in such circles of Old Testament study be evaluated as containing very old information about the size and composition of the ancient Canaanite territory, the only reason being that the literary sources themselves relate events which were supposed to have happened during the course of Israelite prehistory.

the almost categorical dismissal of the entire Canaanite culture in the Elohist stratum. Jaroš considers this change of attitude to have developed in the period which separates the composition of the Yahwist stratum from the Elohist one.

We may easily find other examples of the more conservative attitude of research in the works of a number of Israeli scholars, who—following their old master, Benjamin Mazar—have been working with the most ancient history of Israel. Younger American scholars belonging to the circle surrounding Albright have also continued to produce rather biblicist reconstructions of the Israelite history. We are, however, entitled to ask whether these scholars have really advanced the interpretation of the biblical sources beyond the level attained by their old teachers. In some cases we may even argue that their approach is below the level of scholarly analysis which can be found in their masters' works. I shall try to illustrate this argument with an example taken from more recent Israeli scholarship.

The combination of an advanced analytical approach to the Old Testament historical literature with rather conservative viewpoints is already evident in a study published by Benjamin Maisler (later Mazar) in 1930.[5] In his study Maisler surveyed the demographic composition of Syria and Palestine in ancient times. Among the sources included in his work is the geographical information contained in the books of Numbers and Joshua.[6] It is Maisler's avowed aim to reconstruct the original text of the description of the land of Canaan in Josh. 13.2ff. by submitting the present text of Joshua to careful literary scrutiny. The reconstructed text of Joshua is then compared to other geographical evidence from ancient Near Eastern sources. As a result of this analytical approach Maisler is able to conclude that the original biblical understanding of Canaan allows this geographical entity to be identified with Phoenicia. This result, which compares favourably with the result of our survey of the sources concerning Canaan in the 1st millennium BCE, that Canaan was in the Hellenistic period another name for Phoenicia, does not, however, lead Maisler to the rather obvious conclusion that the biblical descriptions of Canaanite territory therefore derive from the Hellenistic age, or at least from the post-exilic era.[7] Instead Maisler

5   B. Maisler, *Untersuchungen zur alten Geschichte und Ethnographie Syriens und Palästinas* I (Arbeiten aus dem Orientalischen Seminar der Universität Gießen; Gießen, 1930), esp. pp. 59-67. Concerning methodology, see also his 'Lebohamath and the Northern Border of Canaan', in his *The Early Biblical Period. Historical Studies* (ed. S. Ahituv and B.A. Levine; Jerusalem, 1986), pp. 189-202.
6   Maisler, *Untersuchungen*, pp. 59-63.
7   Mazar comes as near to this conclusion as is possible without actually reaching it: 'Wenn auch die griechischen und phönizischen Quellen mit den

maintains that the biblical sources contain information about the land of Canaan at the end of the 2nd millennium BCE, the only reason being that these biblical sources are found in books which are supposed to tell the story of Israel before its formation as a nation around 1000 BCE.[8]

Maisler's basically critical and analytical approach is, on the other hand, not taken up by some of his younger Israeli successors, such as the late Yohanan Aharoni,[9] although the theories of these scholars follow the views of Maisler nearly to the end of the road. By maintaining this I want to stress that whereas Maisler based his analysis of the demographic composition of ancient Palestine and Syria on a reconstructed original text of Joshua, his younger fellow-countrymen only seldom follow him in the application of a truly critical method to their study of the biblical text. Scholars such as Aharoni have without reservation accepted the Old Testament text as it stands and have used this text as the principal basis of their evaluation of the extent of Canaanite territory in the 2nd millennium BCE. We may say that because the Old Testament evidence is left 'as it stands', the geographical landscape of Canaan has attained a size which surpasses by far the extent allotted to it by more critical scholars.[10]

It would, on the other hand, be unfair to Aharoni and other scholars following him to claim that they have no 'critical' ideas at all, that is, to maintain that they have based their idea of 'Greater Canaan' exclusively on the evidence of the Old Testament. It is rather that these scholars believe their high evaluation of the geographical information of the Old Testament text to be corroborated by external evidence, by other ancient Near Eastern documents. Thus they maintain that there exists a remarkable identity between the notion of the land of Canaan in the Old Testament and the known extent of the Egyptian empire in Western Asia in the second half of the 2nd

biblischen darin übereinstimmen, daß sie Şidonier = Phönizier bzw. Şidonier = Kanaanäer setzen . . .' (*Untersuchungen*, p. 67).

8 See Mazar, *ibid.*: 'Diese Phönizier, die bald Kanaanäer, bald Şidonier heißen, waren in der vorköniglichen Zeit zweifellos nicht auf das Küstengebiet allein beschränkt, sondern besaßen auch anderwärts im nördlichen Palästina Kolonien'. Hereafter the author continues with an investigation of the Phoenician-Canaanite historical expansion in the 2nd millennium BCE, and this on the basis of late biblical sources from the 1st millennium BCE.

9 Cf. Aharoni, *The Land of the Bible*, pp. 64-80, esp. pp. 67ff.

10 Cf. the map of the 'Greater Canaan' in Aharoni, *Land of Bible*, p. 71.

millennium BCE, and this comparison is particularly valid as far as the time of the 19th Egyptian dynasty is concerned. Aharoni believes that such an identity of concepts cannot be fortuitous.[11] According to the Old Testament the land of Canaan was the land of promise, or, simply, Israel's land.[12] However, never in its history did Israel embrace all of the territory which is included in the biblical boundaries of Canaan—which comprises at its maximum the territory between 'The Brook of Egypt' (*Wādi el-ʿArīš*) in the south and Lebo Hamath in the north, or even, in addition, the territory in the north between Sidon and the Euphrates.[13] Aharoni, accordingly, considered it likely that an old memory of the extent of the defunct Egyptian empire lay behind the description of Canaan in some Old Testament texts, and he explicitly indicated when such a concept of the territory arose, at the moment when the Egyptians and their political adversaries, the Hittites, divided Western Asia at the beginning of the 13th century BCE into two spheres of interest, the northern part, belonging to the Hittite empire, and the southern part, belonging to Egypt. In the treaty which was concluded between the two great powers of the day, Egypt and Hatti, the exact border between the two empires was drawn up and this border, according to Aharoni, coincides with the description of the northern boundary of Canaan as delimited in the Old Testament.[14]

It is a serious flaw in Aharoni's argument that neither of the two versions of this treaty between Egypt and Hatti contain any indication as to the precise location of the border between the empires. Thus when Aharoni and other scholars decided to build their notion of Canaan upon the Egyptian-Hittite treaty, the reason may have been not the actual wording of the treaty documents but a presupposition amongst these scholars that the northern part of the Egyptian empire, which once also encompassed the small Syrian kingdoms of Ugarit and Amurru on the Mediterranean coast, had already in the el-Amarna age lost these and other possessions in Syria to the recovering

---

11 *Land of the Bible*, p. 74.
12 Although the borders of 'the land of Canaan' and 'the land of Israel' are not always the same.
13 See Aharoni, *ibid.*
14 Aharoni, *Land of the Bible*, pp. 74f. The treaty (which dates from the beginning of the 13th century BCE) is preserved in two editions, a Hittite and an Egyptian. The Egyptian version has been translated by J.A. Wilson in *ANET*[3], pp. 199-201, the Hittite by A. Goetze, *ANET*[3], pp. 201-203.

Hittite power. Since the Egyptian-Hittite treaty confined itself mostly to confirming an already existing political and geographical situation in Syria, the modern scholars already *knew*—irrespective of the actual text of the treaty—where to look for the border between the two great powers.

Another important question which may limit the usefulness of Aharoni's argument is the fact that this treaty was destined to be valid for a only relatively short period, because of the demise, not only of the Hittite empire in Syria, but of the Hittite state itself, which followed only a couple of generations after the conclusion of the treaty, a treaty which was meant to end the state of war prevailing in Syria during the latter part of the Late Bronze Age. After all, we may question the likelihood that the ensuing short period of peace in the long and troublesome history of ancient Syria and Palestine could have had any lasting influence on the geographical ideas of 'Canaan'. Is it likely that these ideas survived during the several centuries after Hatti had passed into oblivion and before the emergence of the ancient Israelite state? It is, on the other hand, not to be totally ruled out that a remembrance of the treaty could have survived in the Egyptian administrative tradition after the dissolution of the Egyptian empire in Western Asia at the end of the 2nd millennium BCE, and, furthermore, that this remembrance could have been operative in the formulation of the ideological concepts of Egyptian foreign policy of the early 1st millennium BCE, when dealing with the former vassals of Egypt in Western Asia.

It must, however, at the same time be realized that it is normally assumed by the Israeli scholars who agree with Aharoni that the historical sources in the Old Testament are fairly old, and belong for the most part to the pre-exilic period. Even the Priestly source in the Pentateuch, which is normally believed by European scholars to be the work of a post-exilic writer, is considered pre-exilic by an important fraction of Israeli scholarship.[15]

15 Among the younger proponents of such a view which has been construed in outspoken opposition to the classical quotation from Julius Wellhausen, that the Israelite prophets historically predate the 'Law', we may include Avi Hurvitz, who in a series of studies tries to defend on the basis of linguistic arguments a pre-exilic date for P. See the recent effort by A. Hurvitz, 'Dating the Priestly Source in Light of the Historical Study of Biblical Hebrew. A Century after Wellhausen', *ZAW* 100, *Supplement* (1988), pp. 88-100 (where more bibliographical information is provided).

This defence of the antiquity of the Priestly source, however, presupposes that this part of the Pentateuch can be put into a closer connection with the other Pentateuchal sources, that is, the Yahwist and the Elohist sources, than was formerly assumed.[18] The argument, is, nevertheless, futile if we have to give up the traditional idea that the two oldest literary layers in the Pentateuch belong to the early part of the Hebrew monarchy and instead consider the works of the Yahwist and the Elohist to have been composed not before the end of the independent history of the two Israelite states, or even after the fall of the kingdom of Judah in the 6th century BCE. In this case a defence of the presumed early date of the Priestly source—and I shall not deny that some linguistic affinity exists among all three sources—will not prove the Priestly source to be pre-exilic. On the contrary, the affinity between J, E and P instead indicates that the historical and geographical information contained in all three documents must belong to roughly the same era, that is the middle of the 1st millennium BCE, or to the latter part of the same millennium.

Since I have already expressed my support elsewhere for the last-mentioned position, that none of the Pentateuchal sources or layers are earlier than the middle of the 1st millennium BCE, I see no reason to repeat the argument here, and the question of dating the Pentateuchal sources will not be dealt with on this occasion.[17] It might, nevertheless, be reasonable in this place to remind the reader of the consequences which follow such a reorientation of Pentateuchal studies. In my earlier volume, *Early Israel*, the argument for a late date of the Pentateuchal writings was challenged on the basis of an analysis of the historical remembrances present in the *possibly* pre-exilic sources in the prophetic literature and in the Psalms[18] with the result that it is not to be expected that the Old Testament contains traditions about the 2nd millennium BCE which can be valued as historical sources as far as Israel's formative period is concerned.

It was thus not very difficult to show that even the pre-exilic sources outside the Pentateuch have only a little to add about the early history of Israel. It was at the same time possible to demon-

---

16 I am here disregarding the obvious fact that the Elohist cannot be considered to represent an independent source but rather a redactional layer of the Yahwistic stratum. Although this is certainly true, it is of no consequence in this connection.

17 *Early Israel*, pp. 357-77.

18 *Early Israel*, pp. 306-57.

strate that in comparison to the historical 'knowledge' of the Prophets and the composers of the biblical Psalms the interpretation of early Israelite history had attained quite a different level in the historical books in the Old Testament, where we see preserved a continuous history until the Babylonian exile. The consequence is that this continuous history was hardly drafted before the end of Israelite independence in 587 BCE.

In the next chapter the information about the Canaanites and their land in the historical literature in the Old Testament will be surveyed. Then there will follow an analysis of the references to Canaan and the Canaanites in other Old Testament books. This should enable us not only to evaluate the character of this information in the Old Testament and to delineate a history of tradition of the Old Testament understanding of Canaan and its inhabitants, but also to put forward hypotheses concerning the intention lying behind the Old Testament writers' description of the Canaanites and their society.

Chapter 5

THE CANAANITES AND THEIR LAND ACCORDING TO
THE OLD TESTAMENT. II:
THE PENTATEUCH AND THE HISTORICAL BOOKS

A classic procedure when reviewing the Pentateuchal references to
Canaan and the Canaanites would be to start the investigation by
surveying the occurrences of these terms in the Yahwist stratum and
to continue with an investigation of the references contained in the
Elohist stratum (or maybe by combining these two 'sources' into one
and the same document, in the JE stratum), and to conclude with an
analysis of the material contained in the Priestly stratum. The next
step would be to trace the information included in the Deuteronomistic literature, while the final part of the investigation would consist
in a comparison of the evidence of all three or four strata.

As long as the scholar believes that a difference in time between
the oldest stratum (J) and the youngest (P) covers a period of five
hundred years or more, such a procedure makes sense, because it
seemingly enables the investigator to stratify the evidence of the
various sources, thereby providing the scholar with an opportunity to
describe the development of the idea of Canaan and the Canaanites
among the Israelites from the beginning of the 1st millennium BCE to
the post-exilic period in, say, the 5th or the 4th century BCE.

On the other hand, if the investigator is of the opinion that all of
the various traditions of the Old Testament historical books—except a
very few interpolations from older sources, like the Song of Deborah
(Judges 5)—belong roughly to the same age, about the middle of the
1st millennium BCE, the foundation of a diachronic survey of the
evidence concerning the Canaanites and their land will cease to exist.
Instead of this, a synchronic approach to this evidence will make

more sense. The differences supposed to exist between the use of the geographical and ethnic designations 'Canaan' and 'Canaanites' in J, E and P[1] may now be considered to represent differences of opinion which existed among Old Testament writers, who were mostly children of the same age, and the differences between the various strata in the Pentateuch can now be understood as indicative of differing evaluations of the Canaanites from one part of Israelite society to the next.

Such a synchronic approach will be mostly followed in this chapter. It is the aim of this writer first to isolate the various kinds of information about the Canaanites and their land in the historical literature in the Old Testament, in order to present a general picture of how the concepts were employed by the ancient Israelite historians, and, secondly to describe the purpose of the application of these two terms, 'Canaan' and 'Canaanites', in the historical books.

It is necessary, at the same time, to supplement this investigation with a specific review of the evidence which does not conform to the general picture. This 'extraordinary' evidence may be used to provide a contrast to the more normal occurrences of 'Canaan' and 'Canaanites' in the historical literature, thereby providing at least a kind of a diachronic perspective to our study, and thus creating a basis upon which tradition-historians may pursue their task. Nevertheless, a procedure such as the one described here should enable us to escape the historical simplifications which are all too common among students of the history of ancient Israel.[2]

---

1 The most important differences are these: according to the usual literary-critical source division, the expression כנען ארץ is characteristic of P; in J and E the only section where this expression can be found—except for a very few instances—is the Joseph novella. In contrast P never uses the gentilic form, כנעני. In place of P's ארץ כנען J sometimes uses ארץ הכנעני.

2 Therefore it should be unnecessary seriously to discuss such 'anti-historical' opinions as those presented, for example, by A. van Selms, 'The Canaanites in the Book of Genesis', *OTS* 12 (1958), pp. 182-213. Here the author tries to demonstrate that there was a specific moment in Israel's earliest history when the Canaanites presented no serious problems to the patriarchs (or 'the early Israelites'). By now it should be clear to most scholars that the patriarchal narratives in Genesis have no bearing on any historical period at all. Instead they are expressions of a non-historical and ideological interpretation of Israel's past. The two fundamental studies on this are still Thomas L. Thompson, *The Historicity of the Patriarchal Narratives. The Quest for the Historical Abraham* (BZAW, 133; Berlin, 1974), and John Van Seters, *Abraham in History and Tradition* (New Haven, 1975). It is now possible to supplement

Finally, the result of this survey should be compared to the evidence from other parts of the Old Testament, a comparison which, however, is left to the next chapter.

This procedure makes it unnecessary to produce a complete history of all the biblical passages where Canaan and the Canaanites are mentioned, because it will soon be obvious to the reader that most of the occurrences of Canaan and the Canaanites in the historical literature can be distributed among only a limited number of different categories of evidence. At the same time it is clear that, although sometimes belonging to different 'categories', most examples of the application of 'Canaan' and 'Cananaites' can be united into one and the same general picture.

In reality, nearly all references to the Canaanites and their land may be placed in one of only two thematic 'categories', which, although they are not totally to be kept apart, may be treated individually. We may describe these two categories of evidence as either embracing the theme of 'the land of Canaan and its inhabitants' or 'the land of promise'. It is also possible to subdivide each category into smaller sections. Thus the theme of 'the land of Canaan and its inhabitants' consists of subdivisions such as 'the borders of the land of Canaan' and 'the original inhabitants of the land of Canaan, the Canaanites, the Hittites, the Hivites, etc.', whereas the second category of 'the land of promise' may be split among such subthemes as 'covenant and promise' and 'the land of Canaan and foreign countries'. It is of course equally possible to divide the various subdivisions further. Thus the subdivision 'the land of Canaan and foreign countries' could be split among texts describing the fate of Israel 'in the land of Canaan' and others according to which Israel has not yet arrived in Canaan, or has left or is returning there.

The Land of Canaan and its Inhabitants

The basic description of the borders of the land of Canaan is already included very properly in the passage concerning the descendants of

these two important books with the minute analysis of the patriarchal narratives by Erhard Blum, *Die Komposition der Vätergeschichte* (WMANT, 57; Neukirchen, 1984), and with Thomas L. Thompson's recent 'narrative' analysis of Genesis and Exodus as far as the theophany on Mt Sinai, *The Origin Tradition of Ancient Israel. I. The Literary Formation of Genesis and Exodus 1-23* (JSOTSup, 55; Sheffield, 1987).

Canaan in Gen. 10.15-20, a part of the so-called 'table of nations' in Genesis 10. The passage of interest here is Gen. 10.19:

ויהי גבול הכנעני מצידן באכה גררה עד־עזה באכה סדמה ועמרה
ואדמה וצבים עד־לשע

. . . and then the Canaanite border ran from Sidon towards Gerar all the way to Gaza; then all the way to Sodom and Gomorrah, Admah and Zeboyim as far as Lasha.

The geographical horizon of this text encompasses the coastal areas along the Mediterranean from Sidon in the north to Gaza in the south. From there the border turns east to Sodom and Gomorrah on the Dead Sea. The text does not specify the eastern border, but five localities are mentioned which are either unknown, as is the case of Lasha, or included in order to pave the way for the narrative in Genesis 19. This applies to the two cities of Admah and Zeboyim, which always appear as twins together with Sodom and Gomorrah. In this way the writer here foreshadows the coming destruction of these four localities, which follows in Genesis 19, or at least we may say that the later destruction of these four cities was in the mind of the writer of Genesis 10 when he drafted his version of the descendants of Canaan.

In the text immediately preceding this passage, which is devoted to the Canaanites, the sons of Canaan are enumerated. The list may be divided into two sections, one of which includes Sidon and Heth, the other the Jebusites, the Amorites, the Girgashites, the Hivites, the Arkites, the Sinites, the Arvadites, the Zemarites, and the Hamathites. Thus Genesis 10 not only delimits the extent of the country but it also lists the original inhabitants of this country by name. In this way the description of Canaan and the 'Canaanite' nations form the background for all the following references to Canaan and its inhabitants in the Pentateuch. It is therefore not very interesting whether or not the passage in which Canaan is mentioned is an original part of 'the table of nations' in Genesis or is only a secondary supplement to it.[3] Thus Claus Westermann, in his comprehensive commentary on Genesis 10, follows the general scholarly opinion that this section of the table is the result of a Yahwist revision of the whole chapter, and that this revision is especially marked in the section dealing with

3   On this question see esp. C. Westermann, *Genesis* (BKAT, I; Neukirchen, 1974), pp. 665-73, and pp. 694-99.

Ham and his descendants. Westermann's view of the redaction of this section of Genesis 10 must be looked at together with his analysis of Gen. 9.18-27, where he had already expressed himself in favour of the removal of Canaan from this short narrative about the crime of Ham.[4]

There is no reason in this place to limit the discussion solely to the identity of the 'Canaanite' nations in Gen. 10.15-20. It is just as relevant to consider the territories which they are supposed to represent. It is evident that Sidon is the oldest son of Canaan (v. 15), but he evidently also indicates where the northern boundary of Canaan should be sought. In this text Sidon is obviously understood to be both the *heros eponymos* of the city called Sidon and the city itself. The eponymous quality of Sidon is here meant to designate the Phoenicians, or at least the Phoenicians who lived in southern Lebanon. Heth, the second son of Canaan, looks like a representative of the historical Hittites, who originally belonged in Asia Minor in the 2nd millennium BCE. However—irrespective of the evidence of one of the letters from the Tyrian king in the days of el-Amarna, Abi-Milku (EA 151), who considered Cilicia (Danuna) to be part of 'Canaan'—we shall not look for an explanation for the inclusion of Heth among the Canaanite peoples of Genesis 10 in the ethnic composition of Syria and Phoenicia at the end of the Late Bronze Age. The inclusion of Heth here obviously depends on other Old Testament passages where we find references to Heth and the Hittites. In this case, Heth in Genesis 10 is the *heros eponymos* of all the Hittites of the Old Testament who lived in Palestine. It was, accordingly, unnecessary to include the Hittites in the subsequent listing of Canaanite nations in Genesis 10.

In other passages where the Canaanite nations are listed, Heth—or rather החתי 'the Hittites'—is normally reckoned a part of the pre-Israelite population of Palestine. In Gen. 10.18, however, the name of Heth is used to bridge the gap between the Sidonians and the rest of the Canaanite nations.[5] This indicates that the author who drafted the

---

4   The inclusion resulted from a firmly established anti-Canaanite attitude among the Israelite population already in the days of J. This has at least often been maintained. See further on Gen. 9.18-27 below, pp. 114-15.

5   In most lists enumerating the original inhabitants of Canaan, the Hittites are only one among the various nations of pre-Israelite Canaan. It is, however, at least possible that Genesis 10 at an earlier stage of the tradition might only have contained the two names of Sidon and Heth, while the enumeration that

table of nations in Genesis 10 (or who revised an earlier document, if this was the case) never considered the eventuality that Heth in the past should have come from Asia Minor; the Hittites were, evidently, thought of by the Israelite writers as belonging to the ancient Palestinian population.

Such an evaluation of the appearance of Heth in Genesis 10 must also have consequences for the other peoples mentioned in this section of Genesis 10. Among the nations listed here, the Amorites, the Arvadites, the Zemarites and the Hamathites historically never belonged to the ancient population of Palestine. Two of these four names represent cities situated on the Mediterranean coast in Lebanon, the Arvadites, that is the citizens of Arvad in Phoenicia, and the Zemarites, who were most likely the citizens of ancient Simura. In contrast, the Hamathites must be the citizens of the Syrian city of Hamath, whereas the historical Amorites inhabited the state of Amurru to the north of present-day Lebanon.[6] The list in Genesis 10, accordingly comprises more than the Palestinian territory proper and is seemingly in conflict with the information in Gen. 10.19. Consequently we can say that the author in this case made use of a number of traditional ethnic names without connecting them with concrete political and geographical entities. Thus, in Genesis 10, the Amorites hardly represented the old Syrian state of Amurru, while the Arvadites, the Zemarites and the Hamathites were in this passage not looked upon as the populations of some Syrian and Phoenician cities, after which they were named; rather, all the nations mentioned in the list were believed to have lived in the territory, the border of which is described in the same passage, from Sidon in the north to Gaza in the south and Sodom in the east.[7] This indicates that the Canaanite

follows could be secondary. Arguing in favour of such an idea is the relationship between the list in Gen. 10.18 and a number of other enumerations of the original population of Palestine in the Pentateuch. Arguing against it, on the other hand, is the fact that the list in Gen. 10.18 is different from the other lists in that it mentions some names of peoples who are not elsewhere included among the Palestinian population: the Sinites, the Arvadites, the Zemarites and the Hamathites.

6   The Sinites are only mentioned in this text. The same applies to the Arkites, possibly to be connected with the city of Irqata, situated north of Tripolis in Lebanon; cf. Westermann, *Genesis*, p. 697.

7   The 'archaic' use of old ethnic names in this passage may remind us of the interesting and probably correct conclusion by John Van Seters that the likewise archaic reference to the Hittites and the Amorites in the Old Testament tradition was not due to any concrete historical knowledge about the two

territory as marked out in Gen. 10.15-20 was understood to be of rather limited extent—we could say that the geographical horizon of this text is definitely 'Palestinian'. The author had no intention of explaining how the descendants of Canaan populated all of Syria and Palestine, from Asia Minor in the north to the Egyptian border in the south; he wanted only to emphasize that the land of the Canaanites comprised no more than the area bounded by Sidon, Gaza and Sodom.

The description of the land of Canaan in Gen. 10.19 thus accords well with other delimitations of the Canaanite territory as presented by the Old Testament, the most complete being Num. 34.2-12:

> . . . the land of Canaan thus defined by its frontiers. Your southern border will start from the wilderness of Zin, where it marches with Edom, and run southwards from the end of the Dead Sea on its eastern side. It will then turn from the south up the ascent of Akrabbim and pass by Zin, and its southern limit will be Kadesh-barnea. It will proceed by Hazar-addar to Azmon and from Azmon turn towards the wadi of Egypt, and its limit will be the sea. Your western frontier will be the Great Sea and the seaboard; this will be your frontier to the west. This will be your northern frontier: you will draw a line from the Great Sea to Mount Hor and from Mount Hor to Lebo-hamath,[8] and the limit of the frontier will be Zedad. From there it will run to Ziphron, and its limit will be Hazar-enan; this will be your frontier to the north. To the east you will draw a line from Hazar-enan to Shepham; it will run down from Shepham to Riblah east of Ain, continuing until it strikes the ridge east of the sea of Kinnereth. The frontier will then run down to the Jordan and its limit will be the Dead Sea. The land defined by these frontiers will be your land.

The problems present in this passage seem to be confined to the fixing of the northern boundary. The other borders are easy to locate. The western border is of course the Mediterranean, the eastern border the line from the Sea of Kinnereth in the north to the southern end

ancient peoples. Rather, this usage reflects the Assyrian understanding of the two names Ḫatti and Amurru, which in the Assyrian tradition were intended to express Western Asia: Ḫatti was the Assyrian name for Northern Syria, while Amurru was used for Southern Syria and the Mediterranean coast. Cf. J. Van Seters, 'The Terms 'Amorite' and 'Hittite' in the Old Testament', *VT* 22 (1972), pp. 64-81.

8   On Lebo-hamath, לבא חמת, which was in older translations often understood as 'the region leading to Hamath' in agreement with the vocalization of the Massoretes, cf. B. Mazar, 'Lebo-hamath and the Northern Border of Canaan', in his *The Early Biblical Period*, pp. 189-202.

of the Dead Sea, a borderline which perhaps continues down through the Arabah depression to the area south of the Dead Sea. The southern border presents some small problems as to the precise line, but seems to run from *Wādi el-ᶜArīs̆*, 'the wadi of Egypt', via *ᶜĒn Qudēs*, 'Kadesh-Barnea', in Northern Sinai to the desert of Sin somewhere in the southern part of the Negeb desert. The fixing of the northern border, which is the problematic one in this description, depends on whether we opt for a 'maximum' solution, as most Israeli scholars have done, reckoning an extended part of Syria to belong to the Canaan of Numbers 34, or a 'minimal' solution, as advocated, for example, by Martin Noth who included among the non-Palestinian territory only the southern end of the Beqah valley.[9]

The correct solution to this dilemma is most likely the one chosen by Noth, but the decision cannot be based exclusively on the text of Num. 34.2ff. As this text stands, it might very well represent an ideal border of the ancient land of Israel, which in the north also encompassed a large part of present-day Syria, although this northern border did not necessarily coincide with the actual northern border of the Davidic empire. This empire, according to 1 Kgs 5.1, should have embraced the whole territory between the Euphrates in the north and Egypt in the south—certainly an ideological interpretation of the kingdom of David rather than a reflection of the actual size of the Israelite territory in the 10th century BCE—or, according to a more realistic evaluation, it should have encompassed the southern part of Syria, where Damascus was ruled by Israelite governors.[10] Noth, for

9 Among the 'maximalists' we may include B. Mazar, 'Lebo-hamath and the Northern Border of Canaan'. The maximal interpretation is prominent in Aharoni, *Land of the Bible*, p. 71; cf. his map of the territory of the Canaanites. Among the minimalists we must include M. Noth; cf. *Das vierte Buch Mose. Numeri* (ATD, 7; Göttingen, 1966), pp. 215-16.

10 It ought to be clear that the demarcation of the kingdom in 1 Kgs 5.1 must be ideological rather than historical. Included among the provinces of the Davidic-Solomonic empire are all countries west of the Euphrates, which according to the claim of the Assyrian and later the Babylonian kings formed part of the Assyrian and later the Babylonian empires until the middle of the 1st millennium BCE. In the Books of Samuel and Kings it is actually made clear that the Davidic kingdom must have been much less extensive. Thus the story of Solomon's financial troubles, when he had to pay the Tyrian king for contributing to his building projects, shows that Solomon did not even control the Phoenician states of Lebanon. The treatment which Solomon experienced from the king of Tyre (1 Kgs 9.10-14) would also have been unheard of should the king of Israel really have ruled over an empire as extensive as the

his part, bases his argument upon the identity between the northern border as laid down by Num. 34.7-9 and the northern border of the territory of the Danites according to Ezek. 48.1 (which may, again, be compared to the description of the northern border of all Israel in Ezek. 47.15-17). Noth is obviously right in maintaining that the Danite tribal territory hardly ever included the whole of southern Syria. If so, then we are forced to dismiss the opinion of the Israeli scholars who maintain that the Old Testament concept of the northern border of the Land of Israel relies on an age-old remembrance going back to the time of the Egyptian Empire at the end of the Bronze Age.

It is a remarkable fact that none of the descriptions of the land of Canaan in Gen. 10.19 or Num. 34.2-12 includes Transjordan, although this territory, or at least a major part of it, was certainly Israelite at some time. Without exception, all Old Testament passages where we find a delimitation of the geographical extent of Canaan consider the course of the Jordan to form the eastern borderline. This eastern border of the land of Canaan is also the one understood to be valid in the narrative parts of the historical literature of the Old Testament. Thus, according to Exod. 16.35, Israel was to live on the manna עד־באם אל־קצה ארץ כנען, 'until they came to the border of Canaan'. A biblical narrator later remembered this instruction, when he in Josh. 5.12 expressly mentions that the manna ceased to be once the Israelites had arrived in the country. In the future the Israelites had to live off the produce of their land. The place where the manna ceased was Jericho, close to the Jordan. A similar role is allotted to the Jordan—understood to form the border between the land of Canaan and the other side of the river—in the narrative in Numbers 32, containing the prelude to the conquest of the land of Canaan. In this narrative it is told that the tribes of Reuben and Gad and sections of the tribe of Manasseh settled in Transjordan, an act which in the eyes of the narrator must have been considered contrary to the instructions of Yahweh, because Transjordan was not the land of promise; if these tribes were to remain in their newly acquired territories, they had to assist their fellow-countrymen in subduing *the land*, that is, the area

one indicated by the Old Testament description of the borders of Solomon's kingdom. Another striking fact is the absolute silence about the territories north of Damascus in the biblical sources. In contrast, Damascus itself is mentioned in connection with the loss of control over this part of Syria (1 Kgs. 11.23-25).

west of the Jordan.[11] Finally—and this may be the most decisive evidence—Moses was allowed to stand on Mt Nebo to catch only a glimpse of the land of Canaan, since he was forbidden entry to the land of promise.[12]

In this connection a number of questions must be answered. First, we have to investigate the reasons for the confinement of the land of Canaan, 'the land of promise', to the areas west of the Jordan. Secondly, it must be noted that the concept of the land of Israel in the Old Testament is not always limited to the Palestinian territory west of the Jordan. Even in texts belonging to the same tradition we find different opinions as to the extent of the land of Israel. In order to answer the second question, it is obvious that in some Deuteronomistic circles different ideas were entertained about the extent of the land of Israel than in other circles of the same movement. In the opinion of some Deuteronomistic writers, the land of Israel embraced some territory lying east of the Jordan, while others considered Israel's land to be identical with the land of Canaan, that is, confined to the territory west of the Jordan.[13] It is possible that this second question must be answered by referring to a historical development of the concept of Israel's land in Israelite society, as maintained by Eduard Nielsen, who distinguishes between an old Deuteronomic concept and a younger Deuteronomistic one. The Deuteronomic concept is present in the older parts of the book of Deuteronomy, according to which we may speak of a Greater Israel, which includes Transjordan and parts of Syria. The Deuteronomistic notion, however, which may be found in other parts of the Deuteronomistic literature, places the eastern border of Israel at the Jordan. In the opinion of Nielsen, the older version may reflect an ancient North Israelite concept, whereas the younger understanding was influenced by the

---

11 In Num. 32.22 the juxtaposition of הארץ, 'the land' (in the determinate form), used about the territory west of the Jordan, and הארץ הזאת, 'this land', used about Transjordan, should be noted.

12 Deut. 32.48ff. Cf. also Deut. 34.1-3, where the borders of this country are indicated. Here, however, a reference to 'Gilead as far as Dan' is included, that is, the whole area east of the Jordan. On the other hand, we miss here the formula 'the land of Canaan', and thus the system is preserved, according to which the land of Canaan included only the territories west of the Jordan.

13 On this theme cf. esp. P. Diepold, *Israels Land* (BWANT, 95; Stuttgart, 1972).

geographical horizon of the Judaean kingdom, because Transjordan was never a part of the Judaean state.[14]

Irrespective of what can be said about this from a tradition-historical point of view, there should be no doubt that the supposed older concept of Canaan plays a very reduced role of the historical literature in the Old Testament. In this literature any idea of the land of Israel which does not coincide with the territory of the Canaanites—although present in some passages in the Old Testament where allusions are found to events which took place in Transjordan—has been substituted by the contrasting interpretation of the territory of Israel. We may say that the idea of a greater Israel was no longer actual, either historically or ideologically, when the Old Testament version of the history of Israel was conceived and put into writing.

The ancient Israelite 'historians' who composed the historical sections of the Old Testament also 'knew' that a number of nations had lived in the land of Israel before Israel conquered Canaan, namely the Amorites, the Canaanites, the Perizzites, the Jebusites, the Hivites, the Hittites, and the Girgashites. Israel was to exterminate all these nations before it could take possession of the land, although it is pointed out by the biblical tradition that every single nation was greater than Israel itself.[15] All of these nations are supposed by the biblical writers to have dwelt west of the Jordan and had—apart from the Amorites (cf. Num. 21.21-31)[16]—nothing to do with territories lying to the east of this border. The nations of Transjordan, the

14 See E. Nielsen, 'Historical Perspectives and Geographical Horizons. On the Question of North-Israelite Elements in Deuteronomy', *ASTI* 11 (1978), pp. 77-89, reprinted in *Law, History and Tradition. Selected Essays by Eduard Nielsen* (Copenhagen, 1983), pp. 82-93.

15 Cf. Deut. 7.1: 'When the Lord your God brings you into the land which you are entering to occupy and drives out many nations before you—Hittites, Girgashites, Amorites, Canaanites, Perizzites, Hivites, and Jebusites, seven nations more numerous and powerful than you . . .'

16 In Num. 21.21-31 the king of Heshbon is called 'the king of the Amorites', and the short narrative ends with the Israelite conquest of 'the territory of the Amorites'. The area in question is, however, identical with the Ammonite and at least the northern part of the Moabite territories in Transjordan. Cf. also the parallel version in Deut. 2.26-37, where the Amorites are not mentioned. On this narrative see John Van Seters, 'The Conquest of Sihon's Kingdom: A Literary Examination', *JBL* 91 (1972), pp. 181-97.

Ammonites, the Moabites and the Edomites, are not normally included in the enumeration of Canaan's pre-Israelite population.[17]

Hardly any of the stereotyped lists of the pre-Israelite population can be taken to contain real historical knowledge. The total number of nations in these lists is seven, but in most places only a fraction of them is included, from the first, in Gen. 13.7 (Gen. 10.16-18 is an exception, but here the list has been broken up by the inclusion of several other names) where only two, the Canaanites and the Perizzites, are mentioned to the final one in 2 Sam. 24.7, where we find only the Canaanites and the Hivites. Outside the Pentateuch and the Deuteronomistic History some exceptions may be found. In this connection the list of these peoples in Ezra 9.1 is interesting in that it includes, besides the usual Canaanites, Hittites, Perizzites, Jebusites and Amorites (if not the Edomites as read by some LXX manuscripts; cf. BHS), also the Ammonites, the Moabites and the Egyptians. In the case of Ezra 9.1 the traditional list of nations living in Palestine proper has been augmented by the inclusion of three other ethnic names denoting nations who never dwelt in the land of Canaan, and thus all the eight nations which are enumerated by the author of Ezra 9.1 are understood to represent the עמי הארצות, literally 'the nations of the world'. It is most likely that the author of this passage simply listed eight traditional names because of their symbolic value. Especially the inclusion of the Egyptians, which the LXX has evidently misunderstood (it transliterates ὁ Μοσερι) indicates that the motives of the author who drew up this list were ideological and certainly not historical.

I would therefore like to stress that these lists of the pre-Israelite nations of Palestine cannot be considered historical documents from which we may draw information as to the ethnic composition of the Palestinian population before the arrival of the Israelites. It is, accordingly, meaningless to invest much energy in studying the identity and history of the nations mentioned by the lists as if they had ever played a role in the history of Palestine. Although such discussions about the historical identity of these nations are quite common, the reason being that some of the names may be compared

---

17 Even in the apocryphal book of Judith (ch. 5), the nations who belonged to these lists of the Canaanites have not yet been forgotten. Newcomers to the list in Judith 5 are the people of Shechem (v. 16: τὸν Συχεμ), who probably are substituting for the Hivites (cf. Genesis 34: Shechem, the son of the Hivite Hamor).

to the names of nations of ancient Syria in the Bronze Age, they have hardly anything to contribute to the actual history of the Land of Israel in the 2nd millennium BCE, not to say the 1st millennium BCE. Irrespective of the fact that, apart from the Canaanites themselves, both the Hittites and the Amorites may be compared to ethnic entities of the Bronze Age, neither of these two peoples had ever had anything to do with Palestine. Both names were transmitted in later Near Eastern traditional circles without representing the nations which they once were.[18] Thus 'Amorites', or more correctly 'Amurrites', had since the 3rd millennium BCE been a commonly used Sumerian/Akkadian designation for 'the peoples of the West'. Later on this concept of the peoples of the West, i.e. the peoples belonging to Western Syria, was transferred to the Syrian state of Amurru, which arose duirng the course of the Late Bronze Age and was situated between Ugarit in the north and the Lebanese coastal states in the south. The kingdom of Amurru, whose kings for a short period only succeeded in maintaining its independence, was normally a tributary of either the Hittites or the Egyptians, but succumbed as a result of the general unrest at the end of the Late Bronze Age, never to emerge again. Only the name of Amurru survived as an Assyrian designation of Western Syria and its population, or maybe the Assyrians just returned to the traditional language of the ancient Sumerians and Babylonians, who understood Amurru to be the general name of the whole of Western Syria without speculating about the actual ethnic composition of this foreign country.[19]

18 Cf. the reference above to Van Seters's article in *VT* 22 (1972), where he tries to view the Old Testament application of these terms as loans from Assyrian tradition and usage in the 1st millennium BC. The inflexible formulation here does not mean that an 'Amorite' or a 'Hittite' might not occasionally have settled in Palestine. However, it is impossible to think of these two ethnic designations as representing two influential and comprehensive ethnic groups in 1st millennium Palestine.

19 In addition to the article by Van Seters mentioned in the preceding note—cf. M. Noth, *Die Welt des Alten Testaments* (4th edn; Berlin, 1962), p. 70. Noth (who for his part follows the older literary critics) is evidently of the opinion that whereas the older document J uses 'Canaanite' to refer to the pre-Israelite population of Palestine, J's definite Palestinian horizon has been replaced by a Mesopotamian horizon in the two younger documents E and P. In E the original inhabitants of Palestine are called 'Amorites' and in P 'Hittites'. On the modern understanding of the Amorites, cf. the two important articles by M. Liverani mentioned above, p. 24 n. 20. On the state of Amurru in the Late Bronze Age, cf. H. Klengel, *Geschichte Syriens im 2. Jahrtausend v.u.Z.*, II, pp. 178-325.

The Hittite state also disappeared in connection with the dissolution of the Bronze Age society of the ancient Near East at the end of the 2nd millennium BCE. The name of the Hittites, however, survived the demise of the empire, partly in the form of a number of North Syrian states ruled by dynasties who claimed to be descendants of the Hittite royal family, partly ideologically in the traditional language of the Assyrians and the Babylonians as a name for Northern Syria in the 1st millennium BCE. Thus the name of Ḥatti in the Neo-Assyrian documents may be a late reflection of the old competition between the Hittites and the Assyrians in the 2nd millennium BCE, both of whom wanted to control the North Syrian territory.[20] The Hittites never reached Palestine, at least not in any substantial numbers. This does not, of course, exclude the possibility that an Indo-Iranian population element was present in Palestine. It is well-known that such an element is attested in the el-Amarna letters where, among other things, a number of Indo-Iranian personal names are present. However, when Abraham in Genesis 23 is confronted by the 'Hittite' Ephron, this is not to be considered a piece of historical information about the origin of Ephron. That Ephron is here called a 'Hittite' may better be looked upon as a kind of pseudo-historical invention by the author of Genesis 23 (P according to the traditional interpretation), and the reason may be that the author of Genesis 23 chose the Hittites because they were already familiar to him as a consequence of their inclusion in the traditional enumerations of the Canaanite nations, and because he wanted to tell a story about these Hittites in order to present them in the flesh as members of the original Palestinian population.[21]

---

20 On the Hittites in general cf. O.R. Gurney, *The Hittites* (rev. edn; Harmondsworth, 1964), and the contributions by O.R. Gurney and A. Goetze in *CAH*[3], II, 1-2 (Cambridge, 1973-1975).

21 It is amusing to read the various explanations of the presence of these 'Hittites' at Hebron. We may refer to an explanation like the one presented by Gerhard von Rad, in his commentary on Genesis, *Das Erste Buch Mose. Genesis* (ATD, 2/4, 7th edn; Göttingen, 1964), p. 211, that 'schon im 2. Jahrtausend gab es in Syrien und Palästina eine z.T. weit nach Süden abgewanderte hethitische Herrenschicht'. This explanation, which has been proposed in lieu of a better one, can only draw support from the presence of a number of Indo-Iranian personal names in the el-Amarna letters from Palestine (although these letters were composed perhaps a thousand years before the time of the author of Genesis 23 [usually considered to be P]). We may also mention the explanation in Ephraim A. Speiser, *Genesis* (AB 1; New York, 1964), p. 172.

If the 'Hittite' Ephron is the invention of a late biblical narrator (P), we may ask whether this also applies to the inclusion of the 'Hittite' Uriah, the husband of Bathsheba, in 'David's Court Story' (2 Samuel 8-1 Kings 2). Two explanations of how Uriah could have been a Hittite exist, the first of them being the more traditional, and based on historical arguments, the second relying on literary considerations. According to the first explanation, Uriah was a Hittite by birth (that is, perhaps, coming from one of the new small Hittite kingdoms of Syria), but employed in the position of a mercenary by the king of Jerusalem, thus excluding the possibility that he was a representative of a major Hittite population element in Palestine. The second explanation considers the literary context of the narrative about Uriah. The evaluation of whether this episode about Uriah is historical or not will therefore largely depend on the decisions taken about when the Court Narrative was composed. If we opt for a date of composition in the 10th or 9th centuries BCE, then the historical Uriah might actually have been a Hittite, but if we follow the evaluation of this story by John Van Seters, who places this story in the post-exilic period, then the mention here of Uriah 'the Hittite' can be compared to the mention of Ephron 'the Hittite' in Genesis 23, and the historicity of this Uriah may thus be of the same kind as the historicity of Ephron.[22]

If we are entitled to call the the information about the two 'Hittite' persons, Ephron and Uriah, pseudo-historical inventions of the writers who composed the narratives in Genesis 23 and in 2 Samuel 8-1 Kings 2, the same verdict equally applies to the insignifi-

Speiser argues that these Hittites in Hebron were not Hittites proper but some other people who were the descendants of Heth (Genesis 10), who could thus not be the apical ancestor of the Hittites. Both explanations, as well as most of the discussions about the seven pre-Israelite nations of Palestine, are fine examples of what happens when the biblical narratives have seduced the critical mind of the modern scholar into writing paraphrases of the narratives in the Old Testament instead of critically analysing their content.

22 For the opinion of traditional modern scholarship on the Succession History we only have to mention the classic study by L. Rost, *Die Überlieferung von der Thronnachfolge Davids* (BWANT, III/6; Stuttgart, 1926), repr. in L. Rost, *Das kleine Credo und andere Studien zum Alten Testament* (Heidelberg, 1965), pp. 119-253. A radical reassessment of this story is presented by J. Van Seters, *In Search of History* (New Haven, 1983), pp. 277-91. According to Van Seters 'the Court History is a post-Dtr addition to the history of David from the post-exilic period'.

cant amount of information which exists about the other members of the pre-Israelite Palestinian population. Among these sources the most important information is, perhaps, that the Jebusites dwelt in Jerusalem, which is sometimes called Jebus (Josh. 18.28*; Judg. 19.10, 11; 1 Chron. 11.4), and that when David conquered Jerusalem, the Jebusites were still living there (2 Samuel 5). The evaluation of this information about the Jebusites of Jerusalem will, however, depend on the date of the Court Narrative, just as was the case with Uriah the Hittite. Should the Court History belong to the early part of the Hebrew monarchy, the information about the Jebusites may be trusted. If, on the other hand, the Court History is only a late, post-exilic literary product, then the historicity of Jebusite Jerusalem may be seriously questioned.[23] After all, the only existing references to the Jebusites are found in the Old Testament, and no Near Eastern document ever says that ancient Jerusalem was sometimes called Jebus. From the beginning of the 2nd millennium BCE to the 2nd century CE, when the Roman emperor Hadrian after the rebellion of Bar-Kochba changed the name of the city, Jerusalem was invariably called Jerusalem and nothing else.[24] It is therefore understandable that J. Maxwell Miller has proposed to distinguish between Jerusalem and Jebus as two different localities both situated in the same part of the country. Jebus was, however, according to Miller, later forgotten and therefore identified with the better-known Jerusalem. The proposal of Miller may, on the other hand, be regarded as a desperate attempt, based on the literary inventions of the biblical writers, to explain away existing historical sources, which may contradict the evidence of the Old Testament.[25]

23 Cf. J. Van Seters, *In Search of History*, pp. 264-71.
24 In the el-Amarna letters the city is invariably called URU-*salimu* , and in Egyptian tradition, since its first mention in the execration texts from the 19th-18th centuries BCE, the name is also without exception 'Jerusalem'; cf. on these texts Helck, *Beziehungen*, p. 52 n. 12 (12th dynasty) and p. 59 n. 45 (13th dynasty). Hadrian renamed the city Aelia Capitolina, after having forbidden the Jews to enter it, but still the name remained Jerusalem in the Jewish tradition. In the later Arabic tradition the city has been called *al-Quds*, 'the holy one', but this can hardly be considered a new name for the city; it is rather a reflection of its sacred status.
25 Cf. J. Maxwell Miller, 'Jebus and Jerusalem: A Case of Mistaken Identity', *ZDPV* 90 (1974), pp. 115-27. It is, however, interesting that Jerusalem is called Jebus only in passages the Deuteronomistic origin of which may be questioned, as Josh 18.28*; Judg. 19.10, 11, and (of course) 1 Chron. 11.4. The

Neither can the references to the Hivites, who according to Gen. 34.2 dwelt in Shechem (Shechem was the son of a Hivite called Hamor), be considered historical. Shechem is in this narrative obviously the *heros eponymos* (if we may say so) of the city of Shechem. Nevertheless, it would be presumptuous to maintain that this narrative about Shechem who raped Dinah the daughter of Jacob contains an old remembrance of the city of Shechem which once upon a time offended the early Israelites who dwelt in the environment of Shechem. It is far more reasonable to base our evaluation of the content of Genesis 34 on an analysis of the narrative plot and consider this story to cover conflicts which existed at the time when the narrative was drafted, and the content of the story is definitely anti-Shechemite. This evaluation of the narrative in Genesis 34 is valid irrespective of the date of the narrative, whether it originated in the dark ages of Israel before the emergence of the Israelite kingdom, thus representing on an ideological level the conflict between Shechem and other sanctuaries in those remote days,[26] or in the period of the monarchy, when its intention could have been to legitimate the reduction of Shechem's importance after Jeroboam moved his capital from Shechem and created new national sanctuaries at Bethel and Dan, or, finally, in the post-exilic period, when Shechem became the home of the Samaritans and was thus in open conflict with the official Jewish sanctuary in Jerusalem.[27] Instead of providing real historical information about the Hivites, the author of Genesis 34 decided, by introducing the Hivite person Hamor to his reader, to

name of Jebus may have been invented because the Deuteronomistic historians connected the Jebusites with Jerusalem, the point of convergence between the Deuteronomistic usage and the invention of the name of Jebus being Judg. 1.21: 'the Jebusites have lived on in Jerusalem alongside the Benjaminites to this day.' This note in Judg. 1.21 does not necessarily rely on old information; it could just as well have been included to prepare for the mentioning of Jebus in Judg. 19.10, 11. This may seem controversal in view of the traditional view of Judges 1 as containing old pre-Deuteronomistic information, which is more likely to be in accordance with the real facts of Israel's earliest history. This view of Judges 1 may, however, be questioned (Judges 1 hardly conveys a picture which is more 'historical' than the one presented by the Deuteronomistic writers).

26 Cf. E. Nielsen, *Shechem*, pp. 213-59 (a pro-Shechemite tradition of Manassite origin, now, however, endowed with an Ephraimite and anti-Shechemite layer, the whole narrative complex later receiving its present Judaean shape).

27 In favour of such an understanding cf. B.J. Diebner, 'Gen. 34 und Dinas Rolle bei der Definition 'Israels', *DBAT* 19 (1984), pp. 59-76.

create a historical narrative about the ancient Hivites, who were otherwise unknown. It must be remembered that, just like the Jebusites, the Hivites are totally unknown outside the Old Testament. Thus no Near Eastern source from the 2nd millennium BCE, neither the Egyptian execration texts of the early part of the millennium nor the el-Amarna letters of the latter part of the same millennium, has anything to tell us about these two 'nations' of Canaan, although Jerusalem and Shechem are mentioned in both groups of texts.[28]

The evidence provided by the other references to the Canaanites and the Amorites, *et al.*, in the historical literature in the Old Testament must be evaluated alongside the evidence about the Jebusites and the Hivites. Rather than representing real historical knowledge these references must be seen as indications of how the Israelite history writers more or less freely 'played' with ancient peoples and places. In order to present an example of this I would like to refer to the text of Num. 13.29, which has already been described as the birthplace of quite an amount of speculation about the ethnic composition of the Palestinian population before the emergence of Israel.[29] In this passage in Num. 13.29, the Amalekites are said to dwell in the Negeb, which accords well with all the narratives in the Old Testament where the Amalekites play an active part. All the events narrated by these texts are said to have taken place either on the Sinai Peninsula or in the southern part of Palestine.[30] Following the Amalekites, the Hittites, the Jebusites and

---

28 On Shechem in these sources, cf. in the execration texts, Helck, *Beziehungen*, p. 54, and in the el-Amarna letters, E.F. Campbell, 'Shechem in the Amarna Archive', Appendix 2 in G.E. Wright, *Shechem. The Biography of a Biblical City* (London, 1965), pp. 191-207. According to G.E. Mendenhall, who has dealt with the problem of the Hivites in his *The Tenth Generation* (Baltimore, 1973), pp. 154-63, the Hivites should historically be connected with the groups of 'Sea-peoples' in Palestine. Thus the Hivites were the descendants of such invaders from the last days of the Late Bronze Age. It is, however, difficult to escape the feeling that Mendenhall's hypothesis is actually based on a flowering fantasy.

29 See above p. 23.

30 This is the case from the first mention of the Amalekites in Gen. 14.7, according to which the great foreign kings defeat the Amalekites, who here live around Kadesh-Barnea, to Exodus 17, where Israel had to fight against the Amalekites during the wanderings in the desert, to the narratives about the Amalekite war of Saul in 1 Samuel 15 and David's defeat of Amalek while he was a Philistine vassal in Ziklag on the northern edge of the Negeb, in 1 Samuel 30.

the Hittites are described as the inhabitants of the mountains in Central Palestine. However, as already indicated above, the Hittites never populated Palestine in great numbers, and the same applies to the Amorites, but the names of Amurru and Ḥatti were two traditional Assyrian names for the peoples of Western Asia, and thus the use of these traditional names may represent a Mesopotamian 'imprint' on our narratives. We may therefore judge the inclusion of the Jebusites to be in line with the inclusion of the Hittites and the Amorites. They are mentioned not because of any trustworthy historical remembrance on the part of the biblical author, but because this author without regard for the historical realities of the past simply employed some names which he knew from tradition. Finally, according to Num. 13.29, the Canaanites lived by the Sea and along the Jordan, which is often considered to be reliable historical information which can be compared to other information about the original home of the Canaanites.

Another text, the content of which can be compared to Num. 13.29, is Deut. 1.7:

פנו וסעו לכם ובאו הר האמרי ואל־כל־שכניו בערבה בהר ובשפלה
ובנגב ובחוף הים ארץ הכנעני והלבנון עד־הנהר הגדול נהר־פרת

. . . up, break camp, and make for the hill-country of the Amorites, and pass on to all their neighbours in the Arabah, in the hill-country, in the Shephelah, in the Negeb, and on the coast, in short, all Canaan and the Lebanon as far as the great river, the Euphrates.

This is, of course, one of the passages in Deuteronomy which expresses the idea of a greater Israel surpassing the Jordan on its eastern frontier and reaching the Euphrates in the north-east. This is not the interesting point in this context, however. It is more interesting to discuss the possibility that an old idea of the original home of the Canaanites should appear in this text, that the Canaanites were originally the inhabitants of the coastal plains only. It is, on the other hand, more natural to understand the words 'all Canaan' as a kind of summary of the whole passage, thus encompassing all of the territories already mentioned in this text, while considering 'Lebanon as far as the great river, the Euphrates' a secondary gloss on the text.

There exists, however, another text according to which Canaan was actually identified with only a part of Palestine, in this case the

northern part of Palestine. The passage in question comes from the
Song of Deborah, Judg. 5.19:

באו מלכים נלחמו אז נלחמו מלכי־כנען

Kings came, they fought; then fought the kings of Canaan.

It is necessary to discuss this text and its literary context more
extensively, because it is considered to be part of what most scholars
regard as being unquestionably the oldest text contained in the Old
Testament. Most scholars date the Song of Deborah to the period of
the Judges, and a more exact dating of the composition of this poem
fixes it around 1125 BCE, although it is true to say that such a dating
is more conventional than founded on hard facts.[31] In the last decade
some scholars have expressed doubts about this dating of the composition of the Song of Deborah. Instead of a very early date for the
poem, later dates have been proposed, such as the latter part of the
pre-monarchical period and, especially the second half of the 11th
century BCE, because of the name of the main Canaanite champion,
Sisera, whose name cannot be Semitic.[32] Sisera is often considered to
have acted as the leader of a Philistine-Canaanite military alliance
which arose as an answer to the ever-increasing threat to the city
states of the plains by the growing Israelite tribal society in the
mountains of Central and Northern Palestine just before the emergence of the Israelite kingdom under Saul.[33] Very few scholars have

31 Among the host of studies of the text and its supposed literary and historical
   context in the period of the Judges we shall only mention a few examples,
   because the same general attitude is also represented in most commentaries (a
   classic example is the formulation of Karl Budde, *Das Buch der Richter*
   [KHCAT, 7; Freiburg i. B., 1897], p. 39: 'Sicher aber stammt das Lied aus
   der Zeit des Sieges selbst'). Important studies are A. Weiser, 'Das Deboralied.
   Eine Gattungs- und traditionsgeschichtliche Studie', *ZAW* 71 (1959), pp. 67-97;
   R. Smend, *Jahwekrieg und Stämmebund* (FRLANT, 84, 2nd edn; Göttingen,
   1966), pp. 10-19; and Noth, *Geschichte Israels*, pp. 139-40. On the endeavours
   of various scholars to create a relationship between the battle which is described in Judges 4-5 and the destruction of Hazor, cf. my *Early Israel*, p. 394.
32 Scholars cannot be blamed for not being inventive: the name of Sisera has
   been considered either Ḥurritic, Luwian (Neo-Hittite), or Illyrian (although the
   last language is almost unknown).
33 Thus originally A.D.H. Mayes, 'The Historical Context of the Battle against
   Sisera', *VT* 19 (1969), pp. 353-60; cf. also the same author, *Israel in the Period
   of the Judges* (Studies in Biblical Theology Second Series, 29; London, 1974),
   pp. 84-105, later followed by H. Donner, *Geschichte des Volkes Israel und*

dared to propose lower dates for the poem, although Gösta W. Ahlström considers the poem to have been composed a long time after the days of Deborah and Jael,[34] while Giovanni Garbini, on the basis of a series of linguistic arguments, maintains that the composition of the Song of Deborah does not precede the rise of the Israelite kingdom, but rather that the evidence speaks of a date in the 10th or 9th century BCE.[35]

Some other points must be considered in this connection. First of all, it is believed to be an important argument in favour of an early date of the poem that it has never been fully integrated into its context in the Book of Judges. Thus the Song of Deborah contains a substantial amount of historical information which either contradicts the evidence of the surrounding historical narratives, and especially Judges 4, or which may seem somewhat 'antiquated' in comparison with the historical information of the other sections of Judges. One of the more traditional arguments is that the understanding in the Song of Deborah of the Israel that fights against the Canaanite kings does not absolutely coincide with the picture of Israel held by the authors of the historical literature of the Old Testament in general, according to whom Israel in the period of the Judges formed some kind of a union of twelve tribes. Another point which is sometimes considered is that the Song of Deborah mentions a tribe which, according to the evidence elsewhere in the Old Testament, was not normally considered an independent tribe in Israel but a tribal section of another tribe. The tribal unit in question is Machir, a tribe which is elsewhere reckoned to be a section of the tribe of Manasseh. Recently, sociological arguments have also been adduced which are supposed to speak in favour of an early date of composition, in that some of the sociological information of the Song of Deborah is supposed to reflect very early social institutions in the pre-monarchical Israelite tribal society.[36]

---

seiner Nachbarn in Grundzügen (ATD Ergänzungsreihe, 4/1; Göttingen 1984), pp. 159-63, and J.A. Soggin, *A History of Israel* (London, 1984), pp. 175-78.

34 G.W. Ahlström, *Who Were the Israelites?* (Winona Lake, 1986), p. 54; cf. already his 'Judges 5:20f. and History', *JNES* 36 (1977), pp. 287ff.

35 G. Garbini, 'Il Cantico di Debora', *La Parola del Passato* 33 (1978), pp. 5-31; cf. also his *History and Ideology in Ancient Israel* (London, 1988), p. 32 and n. 5.

36 Cf. the opinion of N.K. Gottwald, *The Tribes of Yahweh*, pp. 503-07. Gottwald belongs to the circle of scholars who consider an early date of

It is an undeniable fact that the Song of Deborah contains some information which may be called 'abnormal'. This indicates that the song was composed without regard for the literary context in which it is now found and most likely also before the historical narratives were composed. However, this does not necessarily mean that the Song of Deborah has to be very early; we may say that because the date of the composition of the historical literature of the Old Testament in general has been lowered and may not precede the Babylonian exile in the 6th century BCE,[37] it is also reasonable to reconsider the dating of the Song of Deborah in light of this development. Irrespective of whether the historical literature of the Old Testament was drafted and written down just before the Exile, during the Exile or in the post-exilic period, there is reason to believe that the Song of Deborah must belong to an earlier phase of the history of ancient Israelite literature. Thus the song must be older than its literary context in Judges, composed without knowledge of the general content of the later historical traditions of Israel. However, this does not say that the song originated in the pre-monarchical period, or even in the earliest phase of the Hebrew monarchy. I would rather say that it is hardly possible to propose an incontestable date for the song. This view is also valid in light of the linguistic evidence, which certainly looks 'archaic' in comparison to the Hebrew of the historical literature in general, but there is actually nothing which proves this kind of Hebrew to be, say 500 years older than the standard Hebrew used by the authors of the historical books. We may argue that it is today only a postulate to refer the song back to the period of the Judges, because—irrespective of the scholarly tradition—this early date cannot actually be proved or disproved.

In view of such a re-evaluation of the date of the Song of Deborah, there is no reason to explain away the presence of the kings of Canaan in Judg. 5.19. On the contrary, it may be the most important single piece of information about the Canaanites contained in the Old Testament historical books. There is, at the same time, no reason to see the description of Canaan and the Canaanites elsewhere in the historical literature as dependent on the understanding of the Canaanites in Judg. 5.19. We may say that such evidence in other

composition to be likely; see *The Tribes of Yahweh*, pp. 117-19 and esp. pp. 153-54. In the same vein as Gottwald, see R.G. Boling, *Judges* (AB, 6A; New York, 1975), pp. 92-120.

37 On this cf. *Early Israel*, pp. 306-85.

parts of the historical literature has its own 'history' as part of a more comprehensive narrative scheme.

As to the time factor, nothing of course prevents Judg. 5.19, from a literary or tradition-historical point of view, to have exacted its influence on the interpretation of Canaan and the Canaanites in other sections of the historical books of the Old Testament. In order to decide whether such an influence is likely, we have to discuss some points of resemblance between the prose narrative in Judges 4 and the poem in Judges 5. As to the use of 'Canaan' in Judges 4, it is interesting that 'Canaan' only appears as a part of the title of King Jabin of Hazor, who is called מלך כנען (Judg. 4.2, 23, 24), whereas the gentilic form כנעני is not used. This indicates that Jabin was not called 'king of Canaan' because of the connection between Judges 4 and 5, nor because he was regarded as the leader of the coalition of Canaanite kings in Judg. 5.19. Instead, it is more likely that this title is a reminiscence of the other Old Testament text where Jabin is mentioned, Joshua 11, as the head of a coalition of Canaanite kings who fought against Joshua and the Israelites. Instead of viewing Judg. 5.19 as the origin of the title of Jabin in Judges 4, it is just as likely that the argument should be reversed, that the mention of the kings of Canaan in Judg. 5.19 owes its existence to a redactional note in Judges 5 which was added to the text of the poem as part of its incorporation into the greater Deuteronomistic narrative in the Book of Judges. Should this be the case, then 'the kings of Canaan' is used here in a more general way in line with the understanding of Canaan and its kings elsewhere in the Old Testament historical literature.

Isolated from their narrative context, Judges 4-5 tells the story of the battle between sections of Israelite tribal society, led by Barak, the son of Abinoam from Kedesh in Naphtali, and Deborah the prophetess and judge of Israel, the wife of Lappidoth (Judg. 4.4-6), and the combined forces of the city-states, led by the king of the Canaanites Jabin of Hazor and his general Sisera. The geographical outlook in Judges 5 is, as often noted, specifically North Israelite, and the centre of interest is Galilee and the Israelite tribes living in the northern and central parts of Palestine. The tribes living east of the Jordan are also mentioned by the composer of Judges 5, but only as tribal units who never showed up for the battle, and both Reuben and Gilead are reproached because of their defection. The same applies to the two northern tribes of Asher, who 'lingered by the sea-shore', and Dan, who 'did tarry by the ships'. The battle itself was located in the surroundings of Taanach and Megiddo, and the 'Canaanite' war-party evidently consisted of the local heads of the small city-states on the plain of Acre and Jezreel, although the poet never states the identity of the opponents of Israel in any precise way. Sisera, the champion of the enemy of Israel in Judges 4-5, is, of course, expressly mentioned in the poem in Judges 5, without, however, any information as to his place of origin. Only in Judg. 4.2 is this place mentioned: Harosheth-Haggoyim ('Harosheth-of-the-Gentiles'), the geographical location of which should perhaps be sought in the environs of the battlefield itself.[38]

This geographical information indicates that Judg. 5.19 can be taken to support an understanding of Canaan according to which it should be located in Galilee, or at least in northern Palestine. However, a more precise demarcation of the Canaanite territory cannot be found in the text of Judges 4-5. In Judges 4, no precise characterization of the enemy of Israel is included, except in v. 3, where it is remarked that the rule of Jabin the king of the Canaanites based its existence on the presence of 'chariots of iron'. This note should be placed in connection with Josh. 17.18, according to which the Israelites were supposed to be able to exterminate the Canaanites in spite of their chariots of iron. In this way the narrative in Judges 4 about the battle between the Israelite tribes and the kings of Canaan may be looked upon as a part of a more comprehensive historical narrative which covers Israel's history from the beginning of its settlement to the end of its conquest of the land of Canaan. In this way the enemy of Judges 4 becomes less concrete, and he actually functions in the narrative in a typological way, as the representative of the original inhabitants of the land of Canaan, who were to be extirpated by the Israelites.

As concerns the man named king of the Canaanites in Judges 4, Jabin of Hazor, it has a long time ago been noted that he is an 'odd man out'. It is commonly believed that Jabin originally belonged to the narrative context of Joshua 11, where Jabin the king of Hazor (who is not here expressly called 'the king of the Canaanites') becomes the leader of an anti-Israelite coalition of city-states of north Palestinian origin:[39]

> When King Jabin of Hazor heard of these events, he sent to King Jobab of Madon, to the kings of Shimron and Akshaph, to the northern kings in the hill-country, in the Arabah opposite Kinnereth, in the Shephelah, and in the district of Dor on the west, the Canaanites to the east and the west, the Amorites, Hittites, Perizzites, and Jebusites in the hill-country, and the Hivites below Hermon in the land of Mizpah (Josh. 11.1-3).

This passage introduces the narrative about the battle between the Israelites and the Canaanites 'at the waters of Merom' (vv. 6-9).[40] It is easy to recognize how the author in this text becomes less and less specific. The enumeration of the enemies of Israel begins with the kings of Hazor and Madon, and the personal names of both kings are mentioned. The following two kings are only characterized by their place of origin, while they themselves remain anonymous. Finally, the enumeration continues without mentioning further kings of the Canaanites. Instead of names, only general indications are presented, information which, however, derives from the traditional enumerations of the pre-Israelite nations of the land of Canaan found in different parts of the Pentateuch. The first to be mentioned are the Canaanites (who because of stylistic considerations are said to live 'to the east and the west'); thereafter there follow five other 'nations' of the land of Canaan.[41]

We may ask whether or not this passage actually limits the Canaanites to being the inhabitants of the northern part of Palestine. It is more likely that the expression 'the Canaanites to the east and

39 This has been the opinion since at least J. Wellhausen, *Die Composition des Hexateuchs und der historischen Bücher des Alten Testaments* (here cited after the fourth edition, Berlin, 1963), p. 216. See also the presentation of the problem in K. Budde, *Richter*, pp. 33f.

40 On the topography and the place names cf. Noth, *Josua*, pp. 67f., and J.A. Soggin, *Le livre de Josué* (Commentaire de l'Ancien Testament, Va; Neuchâtel, 1970), pp. 103f.

41 The Hivites in this text are located in the environment of Mt Hermon to the north. We should, however, note the commentary of Noth on this text (*Josua*, p. 68). According to Noth the information in this passage relies on 'einer theoretischen geographischen Anordnung', without historical value, and thus Noth's view of this text is in agreement with the general argument here that a number of 'geographical' references pertaining to the pre-Israelite population are nothing more than ornamental elaborations on the narratives, and certainly do not represent any historical knowledge.

the west' is used here in a more general sense, as encompassing the total pre-Israelite population of the land of Canaan. The general information in the second half of Josh. 11.1-3 may thus be compared to the lists of the Canaanite nations in the Pentateuch, and it cannot literally be separated from these lists. From a historian's point of view we may regret this outcome. After all, it would have helped enormously if this text could be understood to speak in support of a Galilaean Canaan only, and therefore was to be placed in the same context as the other information inside and outside the Old Testament which points in this direction.

The Canaanites are not mentioned in the enumeration in Josh. 11.1-3 in any specific way (as a matter of fact none of the Canaanite nations of the list is). Thus we cannot infer that the coalition headed by King Jabin of Hazor was 'Canaanite' in the historical sense of the word. This coalition must be regarded as representing the 'Canaanite' population in its totality in the act of fighting against the Israelite intruders under Joshua. In light of the modern historical discussion about Israel's settlement in Palestine, any claim that such a narrative could be historical must be considered invalid. It is therefore likely that the inclusion of the Canaanites and the other pre-Israelite nations in this place only represents a literary theory according to which the Canaanites played a role as Israel's archetypal enemy, a topic which is also present in some other passages. In Num. 21.1 and 33.40 the king of Arad is called הכנעני מלך־ערד, 'the Canaanite king of Arad', and it is also mentioned that he 'lived in the Negeb' (ישב הנגב, Num. 21.1), although Negeb is located at the opposite end of Palestine.

The full text in Num. 33.40 is:

וישמע הכנעני מלך ערד והוא־ישב בנגב בארץ כנען

The Canaanite king of Arad, who lived in the Canaanite Negeb, heard
. . .

This text is, however, only the first among a series of interrelated passages which are characteristic because of the inclusion of the expression כשמע/וישמע to report the reaction of the Canaanites to the arrival of the Israelites. The next passages in this series are Josh. 5.1:

ויהי כשמע כל־מלכי האמרי אשר בעבר הירדן ימה וכל־מלכי
הכנעני אשר על־הים

When all the Amorite kings to the west of the Jordan and all the Canaanite kings by the sea-coast heard . . .

and Josh. 9.1:

ויהי כשמע כל־המלכים אשר בעבר הירדן בהר ובשפלה ובכל חוף
הים הגדול אל־מול הלבנון החתי והאמרי הכנעני הפרזי החוי
והיבוסי

News of these happenings reached all the kings west of the Jordan, in
the hill-country, the Shephelah, and in all the coast of the Great Sea
running up to the Lebanon, and the kings of the Hittites, Amorites,
Canaanites, Perizzites, Hivites, and Jebusites . . .

The series ends with Josh. 10.1—which is the only example where the
Canaanites are not expressly mentioned; the kings of Jerusalem,
Hebron, Yarmuth, Lachish and Eglon are here called 'the kings of the
Amorites' (Josh. 10.5)—and Josh. 11.1, which was our point of
departure.[42]

Some of these texts have been called upon to prove that the
authors of the historical narratives in the Old Testament were in
possession of real historical knowledge about the original home of the
Canaanites. This applies to Josh. 5.1, according to which the Canaanites
should have lived along the Mediterranean coast while the Amorites
inhabited the mountains—just as was the case in Num. 13.29. The
historical value of these texts is, however, in no way certain. It would,
accordingly, be preferable to deal with these texts and their
geographical information in connection with the discussion which
concerns the fictitious and literary motives which may lie behind the
inclusion of the Amorites in other Old Testament texts. This
information about the Amorites in the books of Numbers and Joshua
can hardly represent any historical knowledge. Other, presumably
literary or ideological, motives must be the reason why they are
mentioned at all. If this is true, then the same can be said of the
other so-called geographical information in these passages. It would
hardly be appropriate to maintain that, although the information
about the Amorites is unhistorical in these contexts, the references to
the Canaanites in the same passages may be seen to reflect an ancient
historical remembrance of the original home of the Canaanites. I
would like to stress that there is no reason to believe that the biblical

---

42 Josh 7.9, וישמעו הכנעני וכל ישבי הארץ 'When the Canaanites and all the
other natives of the country hear of this. . .', is only an indirect part of this
series because it belongs to a speech made by Joshua in which he refers to the
reaction of the Canaanites to the arrival of the Israelites. But clearly the
wording of the other places is presupposed here.

writers were better informed about to the original home of the
Canaanites than they were about the origin of the Amorites. It is only
modern authors who claim that such knowledge was present among
the Old Testament 'historians'. We may say that the modern
argument here is more or less circular. Thus it has sometimes been
assumed that the geographical information in passages like these must
be reliable because of the historicity of the context. On the other
hand, so the argument runs, the historical information is reliable
exactly because of the presence of the geographical information which
is believed to be correct.

According to the Old Testament, Palestine in pre-Israelite times
was the home of a myriad peoples and nations. Some of these
original inhabitants of the land survived until a later date in the
history of Israel. However, the only place where references to all
these nations can be found is in the Old Testament. It can be
maintained that none of these national groups actually represents
historical, ethnic elements which were present in Palestine before the
emergence of the Israelite state in the 1st millennium BCE. This does
not mean that some of the names of these 'Canaanite' nations may
not, at some date, have referred to national entities (this of course
applies to the Hittites and the Amorites). The Old Testament context
is, however, so far removed from historical reality that it must be
stressed that the Old Testament writers never tried to write or to
publish historical information about these peoples; instead of this they
actually 'played' with strange and foreign ethnic names. The names
of the nations who are included in the various enumerations of the
inhabitants of Canaan in the Old Testament (as well as some names
which appear elsewhere) do not represent historical peoples; they are
mentioned in order to *populate the land of Canaan,* which is at the
same time the land of Israel. The lists of the various pre-Israelite
peoples of Canaan and the references to their whereabouts cannot be
separated from the major narrative 'project' of the Old Testament
historians; their appearance in the biblical sources should rather be
analysed in connection with the narrative parts of the historical books
in order to discern their true functions in the Old Testament context,
which is to stress Israel's claim to its land.

The Land of Promise

So far the result of this analysis of the references to the Canaanites and their land in the Old Testament indicates that the biblical historians operated not with historical facts but with ideological stereotypes when they expressed their opinion about the land of Canaan and its original inhabitants. The borders of Canaan as presented by the Old Testament did not coincide with the later borders of Israel and the inhabitants of Canaan were not historical nations who once upon a time lived in Palestine. 'The land of Canaan' was intended by the Old Testament writers to represent an ideal concept of the land of Israel irrespective of whether its various borders can historically be delimited. Accordingly it may be claimed that the concept of the land of Canaan/Israel in the historical books in the Old Testament is an intentional, programmatic expression of the authors of the historical narratives.

In this section it is my aim to present a survey of the connections between Israel and Canaan as presented by the ancient Israelite historians who wrote the historical books of the Old Testament. The argument here builds on the result established in the preceding part of this chapter, that in the historical narratives of the Old Testament the land of Canaan was not a concrete and historical place, but rather a place of ideological importance to the biblical writers and their readers. We may compare this result with the equally obvious fact that the picture in the Old Testament historical literature of Israel as a society of twelve tribes who towards the end of the 2nd millennium BCE conquered Palestine does not reflect historical events in Palestine during that period. Instead, the notion of the early Israelite tribal society in the Old Testament expresses an idea of Israel which was alive in a much later Israelite, or even Jewish, society of the 1st millennium BCE, according to which Israel was already, from its first appearance on the historical stage, a national unity.[43]

In light of the ideological importance of the concept of Canaan in the Old Testament historical narratives, these narratives can—at least from the book of Exodus to the book of Joshua—be understood as

43 An immediate consequence of the disappearance of the amphictyonic hypothesis is the breakdown of the historical basis of the assumption that Israel was united before the monarchy. On the various endeavours to revive the amphictyony (or a tribal league very much like the amphictyony), and the one made by N.K. Gottwald, cf. *Early Israel*, pp. 291-305.

presenting more or less one coherent narrative devoted to the relationship between these two ideological concepts, Israel on the one hand and the land of Canaan on the other. This is not to say that the narrative is uniform. On the contrary, it consists of a whole series of smaller literary units. However, this is not the place to discuss the redactional history of the Pentateuchal and Deuteronomistic literature; I only claim that, as it stands, the historical literature may be understood as united by this motif of Israel *en route* to conquering its land. Neither do I want to argue that this motif is the only one in the historical books—far from it. Nevertheless, the theme of Israel and its land may be seen as a kind of framework for all the individual episodes.

As a consequence, this story of Israel and its land ends only when Israel has attained its goal of having Canaan subdued by the Israelites and divided among the Israelite tribes. Other elements in the narratives also have a part to play and therefore become important from an ideological point of view. Thus Egypt becomes the place which Israel has to leave in order to reach the land of promise, and the desert becomes the place of tribulation through which Israel has to travel before it comes to the border of the land of Canaan.

When the biblical narratives about the history of Israel from the Exodus to the conquest are viewed in this fashion, it becomes obvious that the sections preceding and following them are also in accord with the general narrative theme of Israel and its land. Thus the patriarchal narratives of Genesis represent a prelude to the narratives of Israel on the way to its land. In this way the real conquest of Canaan, when Joshua and his tribesmen swept over the Canaanite countryside, is prepared for by the repeated arrivals of the patriarchs in the land of Canaan. And if we continue along this line, it would be equally possible to maintain that the later history of Israel, from the death of Joshua to the Babylonian exile, represents a kind of epilogue to the conquest narrative, but this epilogue is also prepared for by the patriarchal narratives: just as the patriarchs had to leave their country, so the Israelites were forced, at the end of their history, to settle in a foreign country, and thus the epilogue turns the whole narrative into a tragedy, with Israel being reduced to a small group of deportees in Mesopotamia.

We might say that the narratives in the historical literature take place on a stage where a number of localities are confronted by a single actor who represents Israel or the Israelite nation. The plot of the play concerns the relationship between the actor and the various localities visited by the actor during the course of the performance. The following terminology has been borrowed from a Danish New Testament scholar, Geert Hallbäck, according to whom the acting player may be styled an anti-place, as he is actually never resting in one place but, until the end of the plot, is always on the move to the next place. Together the various places visited by the hero form the stage of the play. To Hallbäck it is important that the places which make up the stage cannot be considered irrelevant or even neutral. Actually, both the stage and the various places are themselves of the utmost importance to the plot of the play.[44]

The point of departure in the New Testament studies of Hallbäck is the acknowledgement that this dialectical interplay between the anti-place, the hero of the play, and the various localities or places, decided the very composition of the Gospel of Mark. It is in the same way possible to argue that the equally dialectical interplay between Israel and the land of Canaan established the compositional basis of the historical narratives, from the election of Abraham until the death of Joshua at the end of the Israelite conquest of Canaan.

---

44 Geert Hallbäck's use of the notions of 'the place' and 'the anti-place' can be found in his article 'Sted og Anti-sted. Om forholdet mellem person og lokalitet i Markus-evangeliet' ('Place and Anti-Place. On the Relation between Person and Locality in the Gospel of Mark'), *Religionsvidenskabeligt Tidsskrift* 11 (1987), pp. 55-73. In Hallbäck's article we find an elaboration on the theme that in its structure the Gospel of Mark follows the changing relations between two places, on one hand Galilee and on the other Jerusalem, and the anti-place, that is Jesus, who is travelling from one place to another. Jesus, who is always on the move between the two places, at the same time defines the role of the two places, but in a fashion which is absolutely contrary to the usual Jewish interpretation of the two places (Galilee being understood as the negative place, and Jerusalem the positive). In the Gospel of Mark their respective roles have been exchanged, in that the connotations usually connected with Jerusalem are attributed to Galilee, and *vice versa*. The anti-place, Jesus, is at the same time on the move between the two places, and his very movement can be looked upon as expressing the dynamism of his work, a dynamism which only comes to an end when Jesus is identified with a place, in Jerusalem at the crucifixion. At this moment the circle of his disciples dissolves and the progress of the gospel is checked. However, the triumphal testimony of the Gospel of Mark is that the empty grave can be understood as Jesus' refusal to be identified with a place. Now the dynamic movement of the gospel can begin again.

The interaction between the place and the anti-place in the Old Testament historical narratives is, obviously, very different from the dialectical interplay between Jesus and Galilee on one hand and Jesus and Jerusalem on the other. We may say that the Old Testament narratives are governed by exactly the opposite intentions of the ones which lie behind the New Testament narratives. Instead of promoting the dynamism of Israel's movements, the Old Testament historical narratives always try to halt them and to confine Israel to one place, the land of Canaan. From the first moment, when Yahweh promises Abraham that his descendants shall inherit a certain country and until Joshua realizes that this promise has become true, the anti-place, Israel, struggles in order to become rooted in one place, that is, in the land of Canaan. The goal of these historical narratives in the Old Testament means that at the same time the dynamism of Israel's history comes to a halt. The narratives only end when this goal is achieved, although we may also say that from now on a new series of narratives follows concerning the struggle of Israel to remain in its land. Thus the metamorphosis of Israel into a place cannot last forever. From the moment when Israel finally settles in Canaan its possession of the country becomes a problem, and the narratives covering the period from Joshua to the destruction of Jerusalem tell the story of how Israel, in spite of its efforts to remain in Canaan, at the end has to leave its country again. Israel re-emerged as an anti-place, so to speak, when it left Canaan in order to travel to Babylonia in exile.[45]

Although such a narrative analysis of the historical narratives of the Old Testament may be feasible, this does not mean that we at the same time have to deny that different layers of traditions or new editions of older narratives, sources or documents can be present in the narratives. In the story of Israel and Canaan several different

---

45 One may be tempted, because of the basic difference between the Jewish foundation narrative and the Christian one, to find here an explanation of the fundamental difference between the Jewish and the Christian religions. We may argue that the adherents of a religion which tries to be rooted in one place must at the same time want to constitute a closed society and stop their missionary activity, while a religion always on the move will try to keep its momentum. It is a fact that the Jewish religion, in spite of the missionary activity of the early Jews, was destined later to become the religion of a closed society whereas the Christian religion always reacted against becoming identified with a place and therefore acknowledged no limit to its growth.

strata are also obviously present, irrespective of whether we speak about the presence of a Yahwist, an Elohist, a Priestly document or Deuteronomistic writings, or supplements to the Deuteronomistic literature. Scholars have a long time ago demonstrated that a number of differences exist among the various literary strata when it comes to designating Canaan or the land of Canaan, and it has at the same been noted that in some layers we may speak of a certain preference for the stereotypical lists of the pre-Israelite inhabitants of Canaan. Furthermore, such differences of terminology have been used to mark the presence of different literary sources as well. It is at the same time also acknowledged that none of the various expressions and devices applied to characterize Canaan and its inhabitants is exclusively found in one literary stratum alone (as is the case with the use of the various names of Israel's God). Although we may speak of a certain preference in the so-called Elohist parts of the Tetrateuch for listing the pre-Israelite population of Canaan, such lists may also be found in the Deuteronomistic literature and—at least in a fragmentary state—in the Yahwist stratum. There is accordingly no reason to invest much energy in categorizing the varying terminology in the literary strata of the historical narratives, neither is there reason to deny that such literary strata do exist. My point here is, however, that there is no need to base the analysis of the evidence of the historical narratives on these rather unimportant literary differences, especially if the general impression is that most if not all the literary strata express the same general idea about the function of Canaan and the Canaanites in the complex of narratives.[46]

Neither is it reasonable to maintain that this story of the interplay between the place and the anti-place, about Canaan and Israel,

---

46 By applying so-called narrative techniques when analysing the Pentateuchal narratives as well as the narratives in the Deuteronomistic History, it is, of course, possible to deny the existence of different sources, documents or layers. It is at the same time equally possible that the text may be interpreted 'as it stands'—and to be honest, the ambitions of the scholars who invest their energy in such studies seldom go further than this. It cannot, however, be denied that a dividing line has appeared during the last decade between Old Testament scholars who consider themselves to be historians or historical-critical scholars and their colleagues who maintain that they are studying literature, however ancient this literature may be. This dividing line may at some point become a gap that cannot any longer be bridged. It is therefore important to try to stop the different approaches from drifting apart, One way

exhausts the content of the Old Testament historical narratives. A series of other partly related themes concerning the fate of Israel are also present in the historical narratives of the Old Testament, some of which are related to the narrative of Israel and its land while others are independent stories with their own aims and points to make. Furthermore, it would be wrong to argue that the people who either themselves invented the narratives or transmitted traditional stories from the past were always in a categorical way concerned with the theme of Israel and its land to such a degree that other literary motifs and themes were left out of consideration. Thus it is very relevant to argue that in the whole complex of the Sinai narratives the theme of possession of the land plays a very reduced role, irrespective of the fact that the themes of Israel and its land seem to be presupposed even in these narratives, in Exodus 19ff. However, it would hardly produce relevant results to base an analysis of the Sinai pericope exclusively on this narrative theme.[47]

We may begin the discussion of this narrative scheme concerning the conflict between the place and the anti-place by introducing an example of how it works and how it has so to speak structured the

to do this is to demonstrate on a historical-critical basis that the so-called 'historical' narratives of the Old Testament cannot be considered dry historical reports written by real historians of the ancient world. Instead, they represent a genuine narrative tradition and ought to be appreciated as narratives. Such preparatory historical-critical work has to be done if the narrative analyses are not to end up as non-critical and—in some places—almost fundamentalistic essays. It is possible to understand my monograph *Early Israel* as such a preparatory study, but a better example of the relation between a historical analysis and a narrative study of a text are the two monographs by Thomas Thompson, *The Historicity of the Patriarchal Narratives*, and *The Origin Tradition of Ancient Israel*.

47 The Sinai pericope may be the best example of this, because it seems to be intrusive in its literary context. Therefore the basic assumption of G. von Rad, in his *Das formgeschichtliche Problem des Hexateuch* (1938, repr. in his *Gesammelte Studien zum Alten Testament* [Theologische Bücherei, 8; München, 1958], pp. 9-86), will survive in spite of narrative analyses intended to demonstrate coherence rather than difference. On the other hand, an analysis which divides the Pentateuch into a number of originally independent narrative cycles which were only at a later date combined into one great narrative (cf. R. Rendtorff, *Das überlieferungsgeschichtliche Problem des Pentateuch* [BZAW, 147; Berlin, 1977]) may very well be in conflict with modern narrative analyses, especially because a scholar like Rendtorff holds a degrading view of the Old Testament writers, who are reduced to collectors rather than considered true authors.

content of the narratives. We shall start at the beginning of the
narratives, in Genesis 11-12. At the start of the story, the narrator has
taken us to Ur in Chaldaea, where Abraham (or Abram, as his name
still was) lived in the house of his father, Terah, together with his
family. Abraham, that is the ancestor of Israel, is not yet a 'place'
and has not yet initiated his journey to the land of Canaan. No
conflict has arisen, and no narrative has started, not before Terah
leaves for Harran with his family in order to travel to the 'land of
Canaan' (Gen. 11.38). Terah, however, settles in Harran in Northern
Mesopotamia, and the narrative has seemingly ended before it started.
Harran is, on the other hand, not the land of Canaan, and thus cannot
be the place where Israel is to settle. Obviously Harran cannot be the
place where the narrative of Israel's journey to its land comes to an
end.[48] At this point the story needs a 'deus ex machina' in order to
make progress again, and already in the next chapter the God of
Israel is introduced, who can impel the journey of Abraham to
Canaan (Gen. 12.1-3). Here Yahweh simply orders Abraham to leave
his father and go to the land which will be his and his descendants'.
Abraham of course obeys immediately and travels to the land of
Canaan, which he reaches.[49]

Still, neither Abraham nor the reader of this narrative can yet be
assured that this land is actually the right place. Abraham continues
his journey through the country until he reaches Shechem, or rather,
he arrives at 'the place of Shechem' (in Hebrew מקום שכם), to 'the
oak (or 'terebinth') of the soothsayer', in the days when 'the
Canaanites lived in this land' (Gen. 12.6)—a note which actually points
towards the later conquest and extirpation of the Canaanites as
described in the book of Joshua. Only in Shechem can Abraham
receive the confirmation that he has arrived at the right spot: 'I give
this land to your descendants' (Gen. 12.7). Now the land has a name

48 It might be the case that the author plays with the etymology of the name of
Harran, 'caravansary', but this is unimportant for the interpretation of the text.
49 That it was mandatory for the narrator immediately to disclose the importance
of the land of Canaan in the narrative context is obvious because of the
wording of v. 5: ויצא ללכת ארצה כנען ויבאו ארצה כנען 'and they departed
to go to the land of Canaan and they entered the land of Canaan'. A translation like the one proposed by REB '. . . and they departed for Canaan.
When they arrived there . . .', although certainly better than the older one in
the NEB ('and they started on their journey to Canaan. When they arrived
. . .'), hardly pays justice to the Hebrew original.

and Abraham can start taking it into his possession, an act which is symbolized first by his building two altars, one at Shechem and another at Bethel, and secondly by Abraham's journey through the country 'by stages' (Gen. 12.9) until he arrives in the Negeb in the south.

The wanderings of Abraham indicate at the same time that he has not yet become a place. He is still travelling, and soon is forced to leave the country again and continue his journey to Egypt in order to survive when a severe famine strikes the land of Canaan (Gen. 12.10-20). Although it is a place, Egypt cannot be the land of Israel. It is a foreign and therefore dangerous country. Thus it can never become the home of Abraham and his descendants, so Abraham travels back to the land of Canaan, to the Negeb and then to Bethel, to the same place where he had already built an altar for Yahweh before he left for the south. His travelling ends with an invocation of Yahweh (Gen. 13.4). We are now back in the right place.

But Abraham has not yet become a place in the narrative. Immediately after his return from Egypt his family splits into two sections when Lot leaves with his part of the household and settles in Sodom, which, according to Gen. 10.19, was situated on the border of the land of Canaan.[50] We are at the same time informed that in those days the Canaanites and the Perizzites lived in the land (Gen. 13.7). Abraham himself settles in the land of Canaan, and here Yahweh once more confirms that this place is the right one, which his descendants are going to inherit. Furthermore Yahweh instructs Abraham to mark out his land by travelling through the whole country: 'Now go through the length and breadth of the land, for I give it to you' (Gen. 13.17). Finally, Abraham settles with his family in Mamre near Hebron, and this story ends with another altar being built by Abraham.[51]

It would now be possible to continue with the remaining parts of

50 It is obvious that the text follows the demarcation of the land of Canaan which was already presented in Gen. 10.19. The description of the borders of Canaan in Genesis 10 was presumably drafted with an eye on the following narratives. Therefore Genesis 10 does not represent an independent tradition about the geographical dimensions of Canaan.

51 It is possible that in an independent cycle of narratives about Abraham we have now arrived nearly at the end of the story. Abraham settles in Mamre and becomes a 'place'. Now even the messengers of God have to travel in order to visit Abraham. Perhaps the original arrangement of events has been

the patriarchal narratives about Abraham, Isaac and Jacob. There is, however, hardly any reason to do so. These narratives continue in the same manner as Genesis 11-13, and hardly contribute any new aspects to the main theme, except for one important matter. As long as the patriarchs are alive, they can never become a place, but have to continue their journey and remain an anti-place. After all, Canaan is never to become theirs; only their descendants are going to take Canaan into their possession. However, even patriarchs die, and in connection with the immobility and inactivity of a deceased person, a patriarch also becomes a place. This point is expressed in the narratives more than once. Thus Abraham buys a burial cave for Sarah and himself at Hebron (Gen. 23.19), to be buried there later on (Gen. 25.9-10). After his son Isaac's death, Isaac is also buried in the same cave as his parents (Gen. 35.29).

It is more reasonable to continue with a discussion of the concept of Canaan expressed by the Joseph novella in Genesis 37-50, because of the fact that this text should most likely be considered from a literary and tradition-historical point of view an independent narrative unit among the narratives of the Pentateuch. We follow the authors who have indicated that the Joseph story should be regarded as an independent novel, the composition of which must be considered separate from the origin of the other parts of the Pentateuch.[52] By submitting this comprehensive and independently conceived narrative unit to analysis here, it should be possible to decide whether the theme of Israel and the land of Canaan really played such a decisive role for the layout and composition of the Pentateuchal narratives as we have proposed.

The Joseph novella is extremely stereotypical in its application of the term 'the land of Canaan'. The narrator evidently knew only one name for this country, ארץ כנען. The only occasion when this name is substituted by another one is in Gen. 50.11, where in connection with

broken up because of the incorporation of the narratives about Abraham in the greater complex of patriarchal narratives. As it stands, Abraham once more has to leave for a foreign country, although this time he only has to go to Gerar. At the end of the story he is back again in Mamre, and his final resting-place will be in nearby Hebron.

52 Only a couple of the more important recent studies can be mentioned here: D.B. Redford, *A Study of the Biblical Story of Joseph (Genesis 37-50)* (SVT, 20; Leiden, 1970), and H.C. Schmitt, *Die nichtpriesterliche Josephgeschichte* (BZAW, 154; Berlin, 1980).

the description of the burial of Jacob we read וירא יושב הארץ הכנעני,
'when the Canaanites who lived there saw' (thus rather freely
translated in REB). In the novel the application of the expression 'the
land of Canaan' is, on the other hand, never casual. When Joseph is
sold by his brothers to be dragged to Egypt we are not informed that
he had to leave the land of Canaan. When the question of his land of
origin is put directly to him, Joseph answers: 'By force I was carried
off from the land of the Hebrews' (Gen. 40.15).[53] Only when the
high-ranking Egyptian official, Joseph, is confronted by his brothers
in Egypt, does the land of Canaan appear in the novel (Genesis 42ff.).

The initiative is still in Jacob's hands. By now Jacob has lived in
the land for many years. His lack of activity has so to speak turned
him into a 'place' and there is seemingly no reason why this situation
should not continue forever. The land was obviously firmly in Jacob's
and Israel's possession. If the story is to continue, Jacob has to leave
his country and become an anti-place again. And, as was the case in
Genesis 12, when Abraham was forced by a severe famine to seek
refuge in Egypt, although his country had already been legitimized
through the building of a number of altars to Yahweh, a famine
which harries 'the land of Canaan' (Gen. 42.5) forces Jacob to react
and end his period of inactivity. At first Jacob reacts rather hesitantly,
by sending all his sons—except Benjamin—to Egypt.[54]

Five more times 'the land of Canaan' is used in Genesis 42 (vv. 7,
13, 29, 32), and always with the intention to stress that—from an
Egyptian point of view—the home of Joseph and his brothers is 'the
land of Canaan', irrespective of whether the brothers indicate to
Joseph (whom they have not yet recognized) that they have arrived

53 On this not very clear expression, cf. my article, "Hebrew' as a National
Name for Israel', *Studia Theologica* 33 (1979), pp. 1-23 (p. 11).
54 Gen. 42.5: כי־היה רעב בארץ כנען. Cf. Gen. 12.10, ויהי רעב בארץ, and in
connection with Isaac, Gen. 26.1, ויהי רעב בארץ. The difference in expression
may be explained by maintaining that Gen. 12.10 and 26.1, represent a
'Canaanite' outlook: the principal character of the narrative is staying in the
land, and nobody needs to tell us that this is the land of Canaan. In the story
of Joseph the hero is, however, living in Egypt, and it is therefore necessary
to indicate the precise location of the famine. The identity of the plot between
the two narratives discloses first that the author works with his general
literary pattern in a very conscious way, and secondly that the narrative of
Genesis 42ff. must be considered a new and more elaborate variant of the
more basic narrative in Genesis 12, (20) and 26. Not only do Abraham and
Isaac have to leave the land; Jacob is also forced to depart, and their departure is always prompted by a severe famine.

from the land of Canaan, or whether they say that they are all sons of one man who lives in the land of Canaan, or whether they return home from Egypt to the land of Canaan.

In the following chapters the expression 'the land of Canaan' is used less often, perhaps because the narrator no longer considered it necessary to point out that one must distinguish between the land of Egypt and the land of Canaan, that is, the land of Israel. However, whenever the expression 'the land of Canaaan' is used, it is always to mark out this fundamental difference—in the Joseph novella—between the two places, Egypt and Canaan.[55] In Gen. 44.18 Joseph's brothers defend themselves, when they are accused of theft, by referring to the fact that they have brought back the money they found in their packs (even) from the land of Canaan, and in Gen. 45.17 Pharaoh instructs the brothers to return home and bring their families to Egypt. In Gen. 45.25 they leave Egypt to travel to the land of Canaan and in Gen. 46.6 Jacob finally gets up and travels with his family down to Egypt, etc.[56]

55 The complete list of examples in the Joseph novella is Gen. 42.5, 7, 13, 29, 32; 44.8; 45.17, 25; 46.6, 12, 31; 47.4, 13, 14, 15; 48.3, 7; 49.30; 50.5, 13. The wording of Gen. 50.11 is a little different.

56 In Gen. 46.6 a technical term appears which belongs to the more or less stereotypic expressions used by the Old Testament writers to describe the conditions of the patriarchs when travelling to or leaving the land of Canaan: Joseph's brothers and their father Jacob collect the belongings אשר רכשו בארץ כנען, 'they had acquired in Canaan'. Cf. also Gen. 12.5 (אשר רכשו רכושם), when Abram leaves Harran to go to the land of Canaan, Gen. 31.18 (אשר רכש and רכשו אשר רכש בפדן ארם), where Jacob collects his belongings in order to return to the land of Canaan, Gen. 36.6 (אשר רכש בארץ כנען), where Esau is said to leave the land of Canaan, and finally Gen. 46.6. These are the only passages in the Old Testament where this verb is used and its connection with the act of travelling to 'the place' or leaving 'the place' is obvious; the verb was seemingly used with such a distinctive meaning by the authors of the patriarchal narratives. In support of this we may draw attention to the fact that the noun רכוש is often used in comparable passages: Gen. 12.5; Gen. 13.6 (where too much רכוש forces Abram and Lot to split, and Lot nearly to leave the land again; cf. also Gen. 36.7, where too many belongings make it necessary in just the same way for Jacob and Esau to separate); Gen. 14.12 (about 'the great kings of the east' who drag Lot into exile); Gen. 14.16 (in 14.11, 21 the application of the noun seems to be less distinctive); and Gen. 15.14 (the promise of Yahweh to the Israelites that they shall leave Egypt again with many belongings). According to the usual literary-critical explanation all these places belong to the P-stratum of the Tetrateuch, or they are redactional additions. The reason is that all examples of רכוש outside the Pentateuch are found in very late books (in the book of

The expression 'the land of Canaan' is thus used in the Joseph novella to indicate to the reader that Israel has not yet settled in the right place, as long as Israel remains in Egypt. In Egypt Israel can only be a guest. The land of Israel, the land of promise, is situated in another place. The last four passages in the Joseph novella where the expression 'the land of Canaan' is mentioned (Gen. 48.7; 49.30; 50.5, 13) is the trump-card of the narrator, who uses this card to impress on his readers that Israel really has to settle in the land of Canaan and in no other country. In these four places it is stressed that just as the apical mothers of Israel, Sarah, Rebekah and Leah (Gen. 49.31), but also Rachel (Gen. 48.7) were buried in the land of Canaan, the body of the deceased Jacob also had to be carried back to the land of Canaan to be buried there. We may also note that the last piece of information in the Joseph novella is in accord with this theme of the narrative when it says that Joseph was not buried in Egypt, but was embalmed there and placed in a coffin, so that his remains would later be transferred and buried properly in Canaan (Gen. 50.25-26). This command of Joseph's is not forgotten by the narrators of the following sections of the Pentateuch. Exod. 13.19 explicitly mentions that Moses takes care of removing the remains of Joseph from Egypt in order to transport them back to Canaan, and even after it has been reported that Joshua died and was buried, the narrative of Israel's conquest only ends when the reader is informed that Joseph was finally entombed near Shechem. Only now does the narrative circle come to an end (Josh. 24.32).[57]

From the book of Exodus onwards the story aims directly at one goal: the land of promise which was given by Yahweh to Israel and its fathers as their inheritance. This is now the focus of attention. The introduction to this theme is remarkable, because the first time the theme of promise is expressed in the book of Exodus is in the revelation to Moses in the burning bush. Whereas the patriachs of Israel had to leave the country because of ravaging famines, new notes are now struck. Now the land of Israel will be the land flowing with milk and honey.[58] The promise of the possession of the land is,

Daniel, 1 and 2 Chronicles, and the book of Ezra), and in these books רכוש is normally used quite neutrally for 'possession'.

57 Cf. above, with respect to Abraham.

58 Thus Exod. 3.8, 17; 13.5; 33.2-3 (cf., without a direct mention of the land of Canaan, Lev. 20.24; Num. 13.27; etc.).

however, not unconditional: a negative condition is attached to it, the prohibition against any contact with the inhabitants of Canaan. The Canaanites have to be exterminated if Israel is to remain in its land.[59] The general tone is thus sharpened, as becomes obvious in a passage like Exod. 34.11-16. The warnings against the religious practices of the Canaanites should especially be noted:

> Observe all I command you this day; and I for my part shall drive out before you the Amorites, Canaanites, Hittites, Perizzites, Hivites, and Jebusites. Beware of making an alliance with the inhabitants of the land against which you are going, or they will prove a snare in your midst. You must demolish their altars, smash their sacred pillars and cut down their sacred poles. You are not to bow in worship to any other god. For the LORD's name is the Jealous God, and a jealous God he is. Avoid any alliance with the inhabitants of the land, or, when they go wantonly after their gods and sacrifice to them, you, anyone of you, may be invited to partake of their sacrifices, and marry your sons to their daughters, and when their daughters go wantonly after their gods, they may lead your sons astray too.

In this text we see the fully developed anti-Canaanite programme which is connected with Yahweh's promise to destroy the Canaanite inhabitants of Israel's future country. The redactional and tradition-historical problems of this passage—for example the connection between the prohibition against making covenants with the Canaanites and Yahweh's identification as the אל קנא 'jealous God'—is not the issue under discussion here. The passage quoted above is a part of the so-called 'cultic decalogue', but this redactional context is unimport-

---

59 The two themes appear either alone or as a pair; cf. Exod. 23.23, 28; 33.2; 34.11 (as a pair); etc. The theme connected with the extermination of the original inhabitants of the country has, however, already been touched upon more than once in Genesis: Gen. 24.1-9 (37); 26.34-35; 27.46-28.5; 28.6-9. In these passages the prohibition against marriage with Canaanite women is connected with the theme of departure from the land of Canaan, irrespective of whether the man to depart is a servant who has to leave the land of Canaan to fetch a wife for the son of his master the patriarch from some other place (Genesis 24), or whether the patriarch himself has to leave his country to find a wife, provoked by his brother's marriages with Canaanite girls (Gen. 27.46-28.9). Genesis 34 may also be counted among these anti-Canaanite passages, although the content of this chapter is different or rather contrary to the other examples: in Genesis 34 the question is whether or not it is allowable to an Israelite woman to marry a Canaanite (Hivite). The woman cannot, however, depart and therefore the Israelites are forced to destroy the Canaanites.

ant in this connection.[60] We only have to maintain that no part of this text needs to be old—except perhaps for the notion of 'the jealous God' (although the usual argument in favour of an early date for such a notion is, perhaps, problematic and based on notions of Israel's religious history that it is no longer possible to maintain[61]). The presence of a number of programmatic elements—in this connection most notably the stereotypical list of the pre-Israelite inhabitants of Palestine (only the Girgashites are lacking here)—shows that this passage actually expresses a religious and socio-cultural programme. To continue in this vein: this text so to speak blueprints the notion of the stereotypical inhabitant of Canaan in the historical literature of the Old Testament. Our task in the following will be to investigate how the blueprint influences the historical literature. We must especially look for information which does not accord with the general programmatic framework and which may indicate some independent 'knowledge' of the inhabitants of Canaan before the arrival of the Israelites.

The first time the Old Testament confronts us with a Canaanite is in Gen. 9.18-27, and, very appropriately, the first Canaanite is the eponymous ancestor of the Canaanites, Canaan himself, the son of Ham.[62] A number of questions may be raised on account of how the

---

60 On these questions I have only to refer to the standard commentaries by M. Noth, *Das zweite Buch Mose. Exodus* (ATD, 5; 3rd edn; Göttingen, 1966), pp. 215-16, and B.S. Childs, *Exodus* (OTL; 5th edn; London, 1984]), pp. 604-19.

61 It has often been assumed that this notion of 'the jealous God' is an idiosyncratic element of Israelite religion and therefore one of its original and genuine elements. Now the word 'original' may at least in some languages (in Danish and German for example) have two different senses: (1) 'original', 'earliest' and (2) 'strange', 'peculiar'. In the context of ancient Israelite religion the idea of a jealous God may sound strange, but this does not mean that this notion was also 'original'. I have tried elsewhere to delineate a history of pre-exilic Israelite religion according to which this religion was not a peculiar religious manifestation but just another version of 'West-Semitic religion' and therefore without the 'idiosyncratic' features which form part of the Old Testament version of Israelite religion. Cf. my *Ancient Israel*, pp. 223-37, which will be supplemented by my article, 'The Development of the Israelite Religion in Light of Recent Studies on the Early History of Israel', to be published in the *Congress Volume Leuven 1989* (SVT). On the notion of 'the original cultural elements' of Israelite society, cf. N.K. Gottwald, 'Domain Assumptions and Societal Models in the Study of Pre-Monarchic Israel' (SVT, 28; Leiden, 1975), pp. 89-100.

62 On the interpretation of this passage cf. Westermann, *Genesis*, pp. 644-61.

father of Canaan is presented in vv. 18, 22: וחם הוא אבי כנען (thus v. 18; v. 22: חם אבי כנען), and on account of the role of Canaan, son of Ham, in this short story about Noah and his sons. The problem is that Canaan is cursed in vv. 25-27, but has no part in the anecdotal narrative about Shem, Ham and Japhet in vv. 20-24. Here the sinner is Ham, Canaan's father. A number of scholars have therefore considered Canaan in vv. 18, 22 to be intrusive in the narrative context, and they have considered the curses in vv. 26-27 to represent the oldest—or at least an independent—section of the anecdote. However, it is just as feasible that the curses were dependent on the anecdote itself, and accordingly only to be understood in light of the present literary context. The reason could be that the linking of Ham and Canaan is a reflection of the genealogical speculations in Gen. 10.6, according to which Canaan, together with Cush, Mizraim and Put, is the son of Ham. It is of course not totally to be excluded that a historical remembrance lies behind this genealogy; however, that it should go back to the days of the Egyptian empire during the 2nd millennium BCE, when Canaan was a part of the Egyptian realm, is highly doubtful. The linking with Japhet, who is often considered to be the ancestor of the 'Indo-European' peoples (Gen. 10.2-5), including among other nations the Greeks (Javan = the Ionians), hardly seems to indicate an early date for this section. On the contrary, it must be rather late.[63] We therefore have to conclude that in the case of the appearance of Canaan in Gen. 9.18-27 only rather weak arguments can be adduced in favour of the author's possessing real historical knowledge about the ancient Canaanites. In actuality, the anecdote in Gen. 9.18-27 represents a notion of the Canaanites which is the same as the one found in the rest of the Pentateuch and in the Deuteronomistic literature. It is thus possible to consider Gen. 9.18-27 as expressing a fundamental rejection of the Canaanite culture and nation. The short anecdote in Gen. 9.18-27 thus cannot function as a starting point for an investigation of the Old Testament Canaanites. Rather, it should be interpreted in the light of the notion of the

---

63 Against the idea that Genesis 10 represents some kind of precise 'ethnographic' knowledge is the fact that Heth, the ancestor of the Hittites, who were of Indo-European origin, is here considered to be a son of Canaan. From a historical point of view this is wrong, but the reason may be either the late Assyrian application of the term Ḫatti or the literary fiction of the Old Testament according to which the Hittites belonged to the pre-Israelite population of the land of Canaan.

Canaanites expressed in other parts of the Old Testament historical literature.

In all the narratives that follow, only one mentions a Canaanite by name, although the person plays only an insignificant role in the story. This Canaanite is introduced in Gen. 38.2 as Shua, the father of Judah's Canaanite wife, who became the mother of Er, Onan and Shela. However, not even this name is certain, since in 38.12 the name of the wife of Judah is Batshua.[64]

Now the story in Genesis 38 about Judah and Tamar (beginning in v. 2) is a fine example of how the more comprehensive narrative discourse of the Pentateuch is interwoven with smaller anecdotes and narratives. It may be true, of course, that information which derives from such subordinate narratives cannot be decisive for the general evaluation of the role of the Canaanites in the historical books.[65] On the other hand, although this may be correct, it does not mean that it is impossible that such more or less independent narrative entities as Genesis 38 cannot contain historical information. After all, it may be that exactly in such short stories such historical information might appear.

It is remarkable that the present arrangement of the Old Testament books as well as the traditional literary critical division of the Pentateuch into a number of originally independent sources, according to which Genesis 38 is part of the J-source (ultimately 'early-J'; Eissfeldt says 'L'), has prevented the interpreter from understanding Genesis 38 as a parallel narrative to the Book of Ruth. The plot of the narrative is in both cases almost identical: a young childless widow procures a son for her deceased husband. At the same time the narrator(s) include in both stories civil laws connected with family arrangements, in Genesis 38 the Levirate marriage and in Ruth the institution of the redeemer. Both institutions are of fundamental importance for the happy ending of both narratives, but in both cases the conflict is solved only because of an 'incorrect' application of the laws. The connection between the two stories is further indicated by the inclusion in both narratives of genealogical information (Gen. 38.27-30 and Ruth 4.18-22). These genealogies are not necessarily

---

64 Cf., however, Gen. 38.12 where Bathshua seems to be the name of the wife of Judah.

65 On the usual exegesis of Genesis 38, cf. C. Westermann, *Genesis* (BKAT, I/3; Neukirchen, 1982), pp. 39-52.

secondary inserts in the narratives and, moreover, they link Tamar with Ruth (or Perez with Boaz). The interrelationship between the respective fates of Tamar and Ruth is also clear because of the cross-reference in Ruth 4.12.

John Emerton has proposed understanding Genesis 38 as a narrative originally to be located in a Canaanite milieu.[66] The opinion of Emerton is undoubtedly incorrect; the narrative comes without question from an Israelite environment. It is on the other hand quite true that the story of Genesis 38 did not originally belong to the greater narrative discourse of the Book of Genesis—although at the same time we should not forget that this original independence of the narrative is of course only hypothetical. Therefore, since a number of parallels between the two women, the Moabite Ruth and the Canaanite Tamar, are obvious, it cannot be excluded that Tamar also is to be understood as a 'foreign' woman. In the introduction to his narrative the author indicates such an understanding of Tamar's background, in that Judah is said to have married the daughter of a Canaanite. Foreign women are of course dangerous, because they manage to do things which to an ordinary Israelite woman are out of the question, being contrary to appropriate Israelite tradition. However, these foreign women at the same time can help Israelites who are in some sort of trouble (and childlessness is indeed a very real problem). Thus the two narratives do not deny that their heroines are foreign women, and thus both dangerous and unpredictable, but at the same time they contain an understanding of foreigners which stands

---

66 See J.A. Emerton, 'Judah and Tamar', *VT* 29 (1979), pp. 403-15. In the same article Emerton dates the story to the period of the Judges. Westermann may be critical towards this proposal, but with his own explanation, that the story of Genesis 38 goes back to a period characterized by a peaceful symbiosis between Israelites and Canaanites (cf. his *Genesis 37-50*, p. 44), he only substitutes one unlikely explanation for another. Closest to the mark is the explanation of E. Würthwein, in his commentary on Ruth, that such a narrative may be pre-exilic, exilic or even post-exilic, because it is actually without any concrete details which might help us propose a definite date for this story (cf. E. Würthwein *et al.*, *Die fünf Megilloth* [HAT, I, 18; Tübingen, 1969], p. 6). The reason why Genesis 38 has usually been considered early, even going back to the age of the patriarchs, or at least to the days of the Judges, is that this narrative is generally considered to be part of the Yahwist stratum of the Pentateuch, and of course scholars of this opinion have generally advocated a very early date of J.

in contrast to the usual Israelite hatred of all foreigners, of which the larger Pentateuchal narratives present ample evidence.[67]

When the story of Judah and Tamar was incorporated into the larger historical framework of Genesis, a narrative which attempts an over-arching thematic coherency, it was presumably extensively rewritten. One of the methods used by the redactor was to eliminate the family of Tamar, keeping the note about Judah's marriage alliance with a Canaanite family. In this way Tamar becomes an Israelite woman and her kindness to Judah's house may be understood as testimony of her true Israelite identity. The tragedy of the story—the childless state of Tamar, and the unnatural relations between a man and a woman, which are the issues dealt with in this text—is thus a result of Judah's mingling with the Canaanite world. In this manner Genesis 38 becomes an exemplary narrative used to support the prohibition against mixed marriages between Israelites and Canaanites, and a warning to every Israelite to avoid intercourse with Canaanite women. And thus it becomes obvious how the content of the story of Judah and Tamar changed when this narrative was included in the complex of patriarchal narratives in Genesis. Whereas the message of the story before its incorporation was mainly positive—the contribution of a foreign woman—it has now become a warning against mingling with foreign women.

The narrative about Judah and Tamar in Genesis 38 may in some early edition have contained some information about the original pre-Israelite population of the land of Canaan. As it stands, however, it is possible to compare the present thrust of the narrative, that is, the warning against foreign marriages, to similar warnings against such marriages in the Jacob-Esau cycle.[68] In contrast, when it is said in the Books of Joshua and Judges that the Israelites were unable entirely to exterminate the pre-Israelite population of Canaan, this has nothing to do with a historical recollection of the earliest Israelite presence in Palestine. The total extermination of the Canaanites had already been

---

67 As indicated to me by Charles Blair, Rahab of Jericho—another prostitute—provides us with a third example of extraordinary behaviour ascribed to non-Israelite women (Joshua 2 and 6).

68 Cf. Gen. 26.34-35; 27.46; 28.1; 36.1ff. These women are sometimes Hittites, sometimes Canaanites, but this is actually equivalent and the result is clear: Esau is not only forced to leave his country because of his intercourse with foreign women but Jacob also has to go, although he never married a Canaanite woman.

prepared for the narrative by the inclusion of the passage in Exod. 34.11-16 commanding Israel to avoid any intermingling with the Canaanites. However, it is apparent that two logically contrasting themes are included in the admonitions of Exod. 34.11-16: first, that all inhabitants of Canaan must be exterminated, and second that Israel is not allowed to make covenants with the inhabitants of the land. If the first point had in fact been realized, then the second point would be superfluous and contrary to normal logic. This problem has usually been addressed by pointing at the (supposed) historical fact that Israel was unable to destroy the whole population of Canaan when it captured its future land.[69]

It would be preferable to speak of an issue in the conquest narratives, the background of which must be the ideological struggle between the Israelite and the non-Israelite populations of Palestine at a time quite different from the one presupposed by the Book of Joshua. It goes without saying that should the analysis of modern historians prove that Israel emerged in Canaan, then it is no longer correct to consider the information about the surviving Canaanite population in Joshua and Judges as being historical.[70] In this case the stories in Joshua and Judges must contain some kind of ideological message intended for the contemporaries of the authors of these

69 The acceptance of the fact from the original inhabitants of the land of Canaan were never extirpated by the Israelites was crucial for the emergence of a modern scholarly understanding of the Israelite process of settlement. This process may be seen in the sophisticated studies by Alt devoted to the settlement of the ancient Israelites in Palestine. According to Alt this settlement was at first peaceful and only later did the first incidents of trouble between the Israelites and the Canaanites occur. Cf. A. Alt, 'Die Landnahme der Israeliten in Palästina' (1925) and 'Erwägungen über die Landnahme der Israeliten in Palästina' (1930) (both works are reprinted in A. Alt, *Kleine Schriften zur Geschichte Israels*, I [München, 1953], pp. 89-125 and pp. 126-75). But even Alt's reconstruction of the Israelite settlement contains some elements of the usual 'rationalistic paraphrase' of the biblical narrative, which is so often found even in modern historical studies of the history of Israel. Indeed, one might even say that from a logical point of view the settlement hypothesis of Alt is on the same level as the more primitive ones of W.F. Albright or Y. Kaufmann.

70 Although this is actually what the so-called 'revolution hypothesis' tries to do by maintaining that historical Israel was the outcome of a peasants' revolt against the supremacy of the cities. In this connection the Canaanites are considered to be the city-dwellers. On this point, as well as for a treatment of the 'meta-historical' reconstructions of the 'revolutionary' school, cf. my *Early Israel*.

stories. The narratives about Israel's relations to the Canaanites should thus—just like other pieces of information about the Canaanites and the other pre-Israelite nations of Palestine—be considered as exemplary narratives intended to inform the contemporaries of the authors about how they were to deal with persons of non-Israelite origin. I shall return to this theme at the end of the book. Here I shall only draw attention to the stereotypical form of the notes about the surviving Canaanite population in the Deuteronomistic literature, and especially to the repeated information that this Canaanite population was at some point reduced to villeinage. We may find that such notes are present not only in the so-called alternative conquest story in Judges 1 (vv. 28, 30, 33, 35; a number of different expressions are used, but the stereotypical formula is למס '[put them] to forced labour'), but that they are anticipated already in the Book of Joshua in the short notes about the Canaanites who were not driven out by Ephraim from Gezer (Josh. 16.10), or about Canaanites who survived in the territory of Manasseh (Josh. 17.13), as well as in the story of the covenant between Joshua and the Gibeonites in Joshua 9. It is the point of the narrative in Joshua 9 that these Gibeonites were to 'chop wood and draw water' in the temple of Jerusalem, when Yahweh chooses his place (9.27). The narrator does not, however, forget this information later. Therefore, at the time when he has described the inauguration of the temple in Jerusalem, he leaves it to Solomon to reduce the surviving 'Amorites, Hittites, Perizzites, Hivites and Jebusites' to corvée workers (1 Kgs 9.20-21). In the next sentence we are informed that the Israelites were not themselves included in this labour force, which directly contradicts the evidence concerning Israelite forced labour, which became the avowed reason for the breakdown of the Solomonic state in the days of Jeroboam ben Nebat (1 Kgs 11-12).

With this we shall conclude the analysis of the use of 'Canaan' and 'the land of Canaan' in the historical literature of the Old Testament. To include further examples and passages would only be repetitive. The land of Canaan is the land of promise, and thus the place where the anti-place, Israel, has to go in order to become unified with its place. The land and its inhabitants play no independent role in these Old Testament historical narratives; their role is always the same. The Canaanites and their land are not allowed by the biblical history writers to depart from their fixed roles in the narrative. The few examples where one might say that they at least try to play an independent role all belong to passages which may be considered secondary interpolations in the larger narrative framework of the historical books. However, if such an 'importation' of narratives or anecdotes which do not fully tally with the main narratives has taken place, the interpolations have been concealed by bending the original content of these additions to the intent of the biblical historiographers. In this manner they do not detract from the general theme of the biblical historians.

The remaining task is to discuss the original milieu or *Sitz im Leben* of the historical narratives and to decide in which historical framework their picture of the Canaanites and their land fits. Although this discussion will be included only in the final chapter of this book, it presupposes the results of the investigation in this chapter, that the Old Testament does not provide any description of the land of the Canaanites, or of their world, culture or religion, which we can call historical.

Chapter 6

THE CANAANITES AND THEIR LAND ACCORDING TO
THE OLD TESTAMENT. III:
THE PROPHETIC AND POETIC BOOKS

One task remains: to examine the use of 'Canaan' and 'the Canaanites' in the non-historical parts of the Old Testament. This summary
need not be long because the two expressions 'Canaan' and 'the
Canaanites' appear only in a limited number of passages, mostly
confined to the prophetic literature. We shall accordingly devote the
main part of this chapter to the prophetic books. Only at the end will
we turn to the other parts of the Old Testament, notably the Psalms.
We shall also review some occurrences in the wisdom literature, and
conclude with a couple of important occurrences in the Chronistic
literature. However, the small amount of material in these parts of the
Old Testament makes it difficult to continue with a systematic
description of the use of the two terms outside the Pentateuch and
the Deuteronomistic History. In this case the best approach will also
be a simple one, to discuss the relevant passages one by one, although
their evidence may, perhaps, seem casual and unsystematic.

Isaiah 19.18:

ביום ההוא יהיו חמש ערים בארץ מצרים מדברות שפת כנען
ונשבעות ליהוה צבאות עיר ההרס יאמר לאחת

When that day comes there will be five cities in Egypt speaking the language of Canaan and swearing allegiance to the LORD of Hosts, and one of them will be called the City of the Sun.[1]

The interpretation of this passage has—except in the most conservative commentaries—been almost unanimous and may be summarized by a quotation from Bernhard Duhm: 'In der Tat ist kaum ein Stück im ganzen Buch so 'unecht' wie v. 16ff.'[2] Not only is this passage placed next to the equally late oracle against Egypt, Isa. 19.1-15, but it must also be regarded as a secondary supplement to this oracle. The date is clearly post-exilic, and the only question worth discussing is the following: How late, in fact, is this text? According to Hans Wildberger we should look to the Persian period to find a context for this verse. Other commentators prefer to date the verse to the Hellenistic period. Duhm even considers the verse to be post-Maccabaean.[3]

The only controversal questions in connection with this text are (1) whether 'the language of Canaan' is intended to mean 'Hebrew' or else another West Semitic language, (2) whether the text speaks of Jews living in Egypt as members of the diaspora or else about the Egyptians, (3) finally, whether the text may be considered an apocalyptic prophecy of some sort or else a *vaticinium ex eventu.*

At first 'the language of Canaan' sounds like an extraordinary by-name for 'Hebrew'. In this connection Wildberger summarizes a discussion concerning the possibility that 'the language of Canaan' was actually Aramaic, but he rejects this conclusion.[4] The answers to the following two questions are interconnected: If the text must be considered a *vaticinium ex eventu*, the persons for whom it was meant were likely to be Jews of Egypt. However, should the text be a real prophecy, it is perhaps more reasonable to think of Egyptians as being the receivers of the message. Regardless of which solution we accept, the text was probably composed in Egypt.

However, to try solve these problems in this place would surpass

1 On the ample text-critical problems of this passage (although without relevance to the discussion in this section) cf. H. Wildberger, *Jesaja 13-27* (BKAT, X/2; Neukirchen, 1978), pp. 728f.

2 B. Duhm, *Das Buch Jesaia* (GHKAT, III/1, 4th edn; Göttingen, 1922 [repr. Göttingen, 1968]), p. 140.

3 Wildberger is rather vague here. That the Persian Period is preferred by him becomes, however, clear from his commentary on v. 18 in *Jesaja 13-27*, pp. 733-36. Among the several commentators who prefer to date this text to a very late period I shall only mention O. Kaiser, *Der Prophet Jesaja. Kapitel 13-39* (ATD, 18, 3rd edn; Göttingen, 1983), pp. 87f.

4 *Jesaja 13-27*, pp. 734f.

the scope of this monograph. Here it is enough to acknowledge that irrespective of whether the receivers for whom this 'prophecy' was intended were Jews or Egyptians, the expression 'the language of Canaan' in this text is quite neutral. No negative connotations seem to be attached to the use here of the expression 'Canaan'. It would even be possible to maintain that from a Jewish-Egyptian point of view the text indicates that the language which was spoken in the part of Western Asia bordering Egypt might one day become more widely known. Thus it cannot be excluded that Canaan in this text merely indicates Phoenicia. And the text might be thought to inply that the Jews who belonged to the Egyptian diaspora in the late Persian or Hellenistic periods had only a vague and imprecise knowledge of the linguistic and geographical conditions of Western Asia. In the sense in which the expression 'the language of Canaan' is used in this context, 'Canaan' may here be understood to be a more general name for Western Asia in its totality, the reason being, perhaps, that the author had borrowed a traditional *Egyptian* name for the language which was spoken in the foreign Asiatic world, going back to the heyday of the Egyptian empire—although this can certainly not be proved.

Isaiah 23.8:

מי יעץ זאת על־צר המעטירה
אשר סחריה שרים כנעניה נכברי־ארץ

Whose was this plan against Tyre,
a city with crowns in its gift,
whose merchants were princes,
whose traders the most honoured men on earth?

This text, which is directed against Phoenicia, belongs, like the one which shall be quoted below, to the oracles against the foreign nations in the Book of Isaiah (Isaiah 13-23). Two of the problems in this text might be of interest in this connection. The problem of the translation of the Hebrew word כִּנְעָנֶיהָ as 'merchants' may only be the least intricate one. More problematic is the dating of Isa. 23.1-14 (finally we have also to ask whether Isa. 23.1-14 constitutes one coherent text, or whether it must be considered a conglomeration of at least three independent fragments).

In this short space it is impossible to deal extensively with the dating of Isa. 23.1-14. In any case the decision will depend on redactional-historical considerations which are not directly relevant to the discussion in this chapter.

Today two different, although not mutually exclusive, approaches are relevant in the study of prophetic literature, (1) the prophet is considered the point of departure for the analysis of the book named after him, (2) the prophetic book is the starting point.

In the first case the scholar recognizes the prophetic book to rely on what may originally be utterances by the prophet himself, although later redactional contributions, glosses and elaborations on the message of the prophet, are also accepted. The aim of the scholar is, however, to isolate the *ipsissima verba* of the prophet and to study his message.

The second approach is characterized by a critical attitude towards 'textual archaeology' of this kind. Instead the general idea is that a prophetic book is first and foremost the work of a collector or editor. However, this editor was hardly interested in conveying the message of a certain ancient prophet. Instead he wanted to present to the peoples of his own time an actual message which might or might not have included material going back to a certain prophet. The important point is, however, that the editor included whatever material he found suitable for conveying his *own* message, and he was not very interested in whether this material really relied on a certain prophetic utterance or came from another source.[5]

The two methods are different in that in the first case it is the conviction of the scholar, for example, the Book of Isaiah (at least chs. 1-39) was mostly written by this prophet or building on utterances made by the prophet Isaiah at the end of the 8th century BCE, while a scholar belonging to the second school of thought might argue that Isaiah may not be the author of a single part of his book. The important point is not that one scholar maintains that it must be proved that a certain prophecy in the Book of Isaiah was not written or composed by this prophet, while his colleague argues that Isaiah has not contributed to his own book, except from lending it his name. The important issue is the procedures which are the consequences of

---

5 Knud Jeppesen presents the following well-chosen 'example': After being repeated several times, the original question, 'Did Isaiah not say . . . ?' was apt to change into 'It was Isaiah who said . . . !' He stresses that in their selection of material ancient editors and collectors were not hamstrung by proper methodological considerations (in our sense of the word). See K. Jeppesen, *Græder ikke saa saare. Studier i Mikabogens sigte*, I-II (Aarhus, 1987), p. 99.

the different scholarly attitudes to prophetic studies. The first scholar would argue that it must be proved that a certain part of the Book of Isaiah was not composed by this prophet, while the second scholar simply says that it must be proved that this passage was not written by the collector or editor of the book bearing Isaiah's name.[6]

If we opt for the first solution and reckon the Book of Isaiah to be based on the message of this prophet, then it simple to maintain that Isaiah was the author of Isa. 23.1-14, as Jesper Høgenhaven has recently done, and to connect this utterance in its original form with events that took place between 705 and 701 BCE, when the danger of an Assyrian invasion haunted the Western Asiatic states.[7]

If, on the other hand, we apply the insights of the second school of thought and consider the Book of Isaiah to be mainly the work of a late editor or compiler, then the Isaianic authorship of the passage in Isa. 23.1-14 may not be as obvious as it seemed at first. Under such circumstances it is entirely relevant to reconsider the long-standing arguments which speak against the assumption that Isaiah was the author of this text.[8] Actually, the case was already most simply and completely stated by Frants Buhl, who claimed that any destruction of Phoenician territory, from the days of Isaiah himself until Hellenistic

---

6 Among recent commentaries and studies written by scholars belonging to the second group, we may mention the second edition of Otto Kaiser's *Isaiah 1-12* (OTL; London, 1983 [German original, 1981]), and the aforementioned study by Knud Jeppesen, *Græder ikke saa saare*, pp. 51-84. Jeppesen's main interest is Isaiah's contempory Micah, whose book according to Jeppesen is the patchwork of a late collector. The differences of attitude are, however, more obvious when we compare a number of recent studies and commentaries on the Book of Jeremiah, notably R.P. Carroll, *From Chaos to Covenant* (London, 1981), *Jeremiah. A Commentary* (OTL; London, 1986), W. McKane, *A Critical and Exegetical Commentary on Jeremiah*, I (Edinburgh, 1986), and W.L. Holladay, *Jeremiah*, I-II (Hermeneia; Philadelphia, 1986-1989).

7 Cf. J. Høgenhaven, *Gott und Volk bei Jesaja* (Acta Theologica Danica, 24; Leiden, 1988), pp. 157-61, who has chosen, rather obstinately, to follow the opinion of W. Rudolph, 'Jesaja 23,1-14' (*Festschrift F. Baumgärtel*, ed. L. Rost; Erlangen, 1959), pp. 166-74.

8 Today the arguments for or against the Isaianic authorship are mainly the same as they were three generations ago. Cf., for example, F. Buhl's careful discussion of Isa. 23.1-14, *Jesaja oversat og fortolket* (2nd edn; Copenhagen 1912), pp. 298-304, with O. Kaiser, *Der Prophet Jesaja. Kapitel 13-39* (ATD 18; 3rd edn; Göttingen, 1983), pp. 131-33).

times, could be adduced as the historical background of a prophecy like Isa. 23.1-14.[9]

There may thus be reason to doubt the Isaianic authorship of Isa. 23.8. There is no compelling reason to date this passage to the end of the 8th century BCE. On the contrary, a date later than the time of Isaiah would for certain reasons be preferable. It is, however, impossible to decide exactly which political catastrophe occurring in Phoenicia formed the background of this specific prophecy. Should we prefer a date just before Israel's Babylonian exile, it is imperative that we be able to prove that the incorporation of Isa. 23.1-14 among the oracles against the foreign nations was the work of a redactor who lived and worked during the Exile, and who, perhaps, was active in connection with the so-called Deutero-Isaianic redaction of the Book of Isaiah.[10] Should such a redaction, however, be unlikely, or should we prefer another date because this passage may seem to be incongruous with the message of Deutero-Isaiah, it would make more sense to date this passage to the post-exilic period. In this case a date even as late as the 4th century BCE might not be absolutely unlikely.[11]

The question of when Isa. 23.8 was written down has, however, no direct bearing on the interpretation of the word כְּנַעֲנֶיהָ used here. The determining of the date of Isa. 23.8 will on the other hand help us to decide when כנעניה could be translated as 'traders'. This translation is certain because of the parallellism with the preceding סחריה, 'merchants'. There is no reason to emend the wording—not even *metris causa* as has sometimes been proposed.[12] As transmitted, the present Hebrew text evidently represents the *lectio difficilior*. It is, however, absolutely translatable. Neither is the translation of כנעניה as 'traders' problematic because it is supported by a number of other occurrences of the word which will be reviewed below.[13] A number of well-founded arguments in favour of this translation of an originally ethnic term as 'traders' or 'merchants' may be presented, and I shall return to this question later in connection with the

---

9   The complete list is in Buhl, *Jesaja*, pp. 300ff.

10 Cf. on this Jeppesen, *Græder ikke saa saare*, pp. 63-84.

11 In favour of such a date cf., for example, O. Kaiser, *Der Prophet Jesaja. Kapitel 13-39*, pp. 131-33. Cf. also H. Barth, *Die Jesaja-Worte in der Josiazeit* (WMANT, 48; Neukirchen, 1977), pp. 7f.

12 Thus incorrectly Buhl, *Jesaja*, p. 307.

13 On the form (and especially on the unusual vocalization), see Buhl, *Jesaja*, p. 307. See also Wildberger, *Jesaja 13-27*, p. 857 (note d on v. 8).

discussion of Hos. 12.8. We can only conclude here that in the context
of Isa. 23.8 the decision of the author to use the word כנעניה is
evidently connected with the use of כנען as a geographical or political
designation in v. 11. The wording of v. 11 has evidently induced the
author to make use of this particular word for 'traders' in v. 8, and
thus it is plausible that כנעניה was deliberately chosen, not because
these particular traders were Phoenicians, but because of the wording
of v. 11.

Isa. 23.11:

ידו נטה על־הים הרגיז ממלכות
יהוה צוה אל־כנען לשמר מעזניה

The LORD has stretched out his hand
over the sea
and made kingdoms quake;
he has decreed the destruction of
Canaan's marts

Most of the problems concerning the dating and authorship of this
passage will be of the same kind as the ones which have already been
discussed in connection with Isa. 23.8. What is left is to decide what
territory 'Canaan' was meant to designate. The question is fairly easy
to answer. The passage in question is part of the oracle against Tyre,
so 'Canaan' here may designate Phoenicia and nothing else. Irrespective of whether or not modern commentators prefers an early or a
late date for this passage, they will most probably refer to the fact
that the geographical or political term 'Canaan' here follows the interpretation of this term current in Phoenicia proper, which is to say
that Canaan is here understood to be the name of the Lebanese
coastal area. The only problematic thing is that some commentators
have not at the same time realized both how sparse and how late the
comparative material from Phoenicia actually is.[14]

14 Cf., for example, E.J. Kissane, *The Book of Isaiah*, I (Dublin, 1960), p. 254:
'The name is used here for Phoenicia. It was so used by the Phoenicians themselves' (with a reference to Abel and Cooke); cf. also Wildberger, *Jesaja
13-27*, p. 877, who, in spite of his own relatively moderate position as to the
dating of the passage about Tyre in Isaiah 23, finds room to present the
Phoenician sources (however, in a rather unsystematic way), without noticing
that in precisely this period, in which he considers this passage to have been
drafted, no Phoenician evidence of such a 'Phoenician' self-designation is
extant.

Ezek. 16.3

וְאָמַרְתָּ כֹּה־אָמַר אֲדֹנָי יְהוִה לִירוּשָׁלַ͏ִם מְכֹרֹתַיִךְ וּמֹלְדֹתַיִךְ מֵאֶרֶץ
הַכְּנַעֲנִי אָבִיךְ הָאֱמֹרִי וְאִמֵּךְ חִתִּית

Tell her that these are the words of the Lord God to her: Canaan is
the land of your ancestry and your birthplace; your father was an
Amorite, your mother a Hittite.

The use of 'the land of Canaan'—or rather of the 'land of the
Canaanites'—as well as the references to the pre-Israelite population
of Palestine in this passage[15] may at first glance seem to follow the
understanding of these geographical and ethnic terms in the historical
books of the Old Testament. Most exegetes are likely to agree on this
issue.[16] It is obvious that some sort of relationship exists between the
references to the original inhabitants of the land of Canaan in this
text and their appearance in the historical narratives. It is also likely
that the author of Ezek. 16.3 was acquainted with the enumerations of
the pre-Israelite nations which appear in the Pentateuch, although it
may be difficult to decide whether he derived his knowledge from
the Pentateuch itself (or one of its strata) or from some independent
source. It may, at the same time, be argued that the author of Ezek.
16.3 has used this information in his own way.

At the same time we have to ask whether this passage may not,
after all, contain some sort of criticism against an all too pronounced
complacency of the Jewish community in the days of the author of

---

15 W. Zimmerli remarks that the form אֶרֶץ הַכְּנַעֲנִי has been deliberately chosen
by the author to show the distance from the following two occasions (16.29;
17.4) where the usual אֶרֶץ כְּנַעַן is found; however, in this first instance in the
Book of Ezekiel the meaning is actually different. See W. Zimmerli, *Ezechiel.
1. Teilband. Ezechiel 1-24* (BKAT, XIII/1, 2nd edn; Neukirchen, 1970), p. 334.

16 Cf. Zimmerli, *Ezechiel 1-24*, p. 347, who among other things refers to the
determinate form הָאֱמֹרִי, literally 'the Amorite', which shows that the passage
here is not intended to be taken as a historical explanation of Israel's origin:
the determinate form of the word indicates that the usage is in this place
general (or even ideological). Zimmerli's argument is weakened because of the
following חִתִּית, without the definite article, and because both 'parents' of
Israel appear in 16.45 without the definite article. The interpretation of this
passage in the more recent commentary on Ezekiel by M. Greenberg, *Ezekiel
1-20* (AB, 22; New York, 1983), p. 274, who on the basis of this text considers
the possible historical relations between Canaanites, Hittites and Jebusites
(who are actually not referred to in this passage) and pre-Israelite Jerusalem,
has no historical foundation.

Ezekiel 16: 'We are all the children of Abraham'. The author here points out that according to their behaviour this assumption simply cannot be true because people are actually behaving like 'Canaanites'.[17] Ezek. 16.3, on the other hand, is not the only place in the Book of Ezekiel where the land of Canaan is mentioned:

Ezek. 16.29

ותרבי את־תזנותך אל־ארץ כנען כשדימה

You did spread out your fornications to the land of Canaan, to Chaldaea.[18]

Ezek. 17.4

את ראש יניקותיו קטף
ויביאהו אל־ארץ כנען בעיר רכלים שמו

. . . plucked its highest twig;
he carried it off to a land of traders,
and planted it in a city of merchants.

The first of these two passages must surely be reckoned among the most enigmatic references to the land of Canaan in the whole of the Old Testament. After all, regardless of how we try to translate the present wording of Ezek. 16.29, it locates the land of Canaan in Chaldaea, that is in Mesopotamia, in the country from which Abraham once—at the beginning of Israel's history—departed (from Ur in *Chaldaea*). This problem has usually been solved in two different ways. First of all it has been quite popular since the days of the translators of the LXX to emend the text and leave out the Hebrew word כנען. These translators have preferred to read simply ארץ כשדימה, 'the land of Chaldaea'.[19] Although being very old, this solution must be considered an obvious transgression of the critical principle of the *lectio difficilior*, and can never be considered to be absolutely satis-

---

17 This is the essence of A. Bertholet's concise commentary on this text, *Hezekiel* (HAT, I, 13; Tübingen, 1936), pp. 58f.

18 To make my argument clearer I have decided to present my own translation of this passage. Cf. below on the modern translations.

19 On the textual problems of this passage—not least in the LXX—cf. Zimmerli, *Ezechiel 1-24*, pp. 337f. Modern commentators have also made use of this escape route, among others G. Fohrer, *Ezekiel* (HAT, I, 13; Tübingen, 1955). p. 89. The philological problems which such an alternative explanation may raise (the unusual use of ה-*locale*), have also been remarked upon by Zimmerli, *ibid.*, who actually considers the reading ארץ כשדימה to be grammatically impossible.

factory. The second solution to our problem is the one usually chosen by modern translators, including the translators of the REB:[20] ארץ כנען here is not used of the geographical land of Canaan; it should rather be translated 'the land of the traders'. It may be of some interest to note that this tradition of translating Ezek. 16.29 cannot be traced back to Luther.[21] On the other hand, it is rather easy to explain the translation as being influenced by the wording of the following parable in Ezek. 17.4, where ארץ כנען can be translated as 'the land of the traders' because of the following line: 'and planted it in a city of merchants'.

The translation of Luther, however, contains a point which has been missed by more modern translators. Luther maintains that according to the text the adultery of Jerusalem not only encompassed the whole city of Jerusalem as well as the land of Israel, but in the end it caused the city, Jerusalem, to be dragged into exile to Chaldaea. The Hebrew wording of the passage, however, does not support such an understanding, because the two expressions 'to the land of Canaan' and 'to Chaldaea' are clearly used in apposition as two words for one and the same country.

The question is, nevertheless, whether the modern translators of Ezek. 16.29 have not paid too much attention to the understanding of the land of Canaan in the historical books of the Old Testament. According to the Old Testament historians the land of Canaan was of course to be sought in Palestine and was identical with the land of Israel. Furthermore, this understanding of the land of Canaan is evidently corroborated by other ancient Near Eastern sources. It therefore seems difficult to understand how it can be that we find in the book of Ezekiel not one but two references to the land of Canaan, both of which place this country in Mesopotamia and not in Palestine or at least on the Mediterranean coast. The evidence of Ezek. 16.29 and 17.4 accordingly seems to be so unlikely that it will have to be explained away.

The textual problems in Ezek. 16.29 are complicated, and the various readings of the different manuscripts of the LXX make it clear that the ancient translators were less than willing to accept the localization of the land of Canaan in these two passages. There is

20 'You committed countless acts of fornication in Chaldaea, the land of commerce.'
21 Cf. Luther: 'machtestu der Hurerey noch mehr im land Canaan / bis in Chaldea' (*Die gantze heilige Schrifft Deudsch* [Wittenberg, 1545]).

actually no reason to think that the translators of the LXX did not know that in some parts of the Old Testament the Canaanites were believed to be traders or merchants.[22] However, this knowledge has not prevented them from misinterpreting the use of 'land of Canaan' in these two passages—or perhaps it is better to maintain that they deliberately chose not to accept this translation of the expression in Ezek. 16.29.

Ezek. 17.4 poses no comparable problems for the translator, although the context clearly indicates that the eagle who removes the twig must be Nebuchadnezar, and that the saying refers to the Babylonian exile of Israel. It is, on the other hand, never said that the twig is transported to Chaldaea. Therefore the translator of the LXX decided to render the Hebrew text of Ezek. 17.4 as it stands: καὶ ἤνεγκεν αὐτὰ εἰς γῆν Χανααν.[23]

It has sometimes been maintained that the expression 'the land of Canaan', here as elsewhere where the translation of 'Canaan' as 'trader' suggests itself, is used in a markedly negative sense because Israel had not yet—after 700 years!—accepted the business of the trading.[24] It was therefore possible, when the book of Ezekiel was composed, to use the expression 'the land of Canaan' about any country which was considered to be a trading centre, and Babylonia was obviously a very prominent centre of international commerce.

This opinion, which may be seen even in a commentary by a respected scholar like Alfred Bertholet, owes its existence to the rather primitive sociological understanding of the sentiments and ideologies in ancient Israelite society, which was current in Old Testament scholarship before the Second World War. First and foremost it is in no way certain that such a negative view of trading by merchants played a important role in the mind of the Israelites in biblical times. We have little or no indication in the Old Testament of a fundamental antagonism between the trading class and other sectors of Israelite society. Furthermore, such a view can only be defended by referring to Israel's supposed nomadic origin—which of course was generally held to be true in Bertholet's day. Only if Israel

---

22 Cf. the translation in the LXX of Isa. 23.8: οἱ ἔμποροι αὐτῆς ἔνδοξοι, ἄρχοντες τῆς γῆς.

23 However, the tradition of the text is not without problems of its own, because some manuscripts evidently have 'to Chaldaea' in 17.4, apparently inspired by 16.29.

24 Thus, for example, Bertholet, *Hezekiel*, p. 59.

originated 'in the desert' is it feasible to imagine that the Israelites generally were negative towards the expressly urban world of trade. However, as is well known, the historical presuppositions which form the basis of a sociological argument of this kind are false and the assumption of an antagonism between the Israelites and the merchant class of the cities of Palestine have no historical or sociological foundation at all.[25]

The tendency to explain away the 'geographical' location of Canaan in these passages of the book of Ezekiel is understandable. Evidently the Hebrew wording of passages like Ezek. 16.29 and perhaps also 17.4 indicates that this land was located in Chaldaea. One possible explanation for this, which is indicated by Bertholet in his commentary on Ezek. 16.3, namely that the author of Ezekiel 16 did not have to base his description of Israel's fate on any normative edition of the Pentateuch or the Deuteronomistic History, can after all not be excluded.[26] The interpretation of the expression 'the land of Canaan' in these passages may thus represent an independent understanding of the concept of Canaan which was *not yet* influenced by the interpretation of Canaan in the historical literature; the concept of Canaan may represent an independent view of Canaan which will not necessarily coincide with the usual interpretation of this concept in other parts of the Old Testament. Maybe the author of Ezekiel 16 had not been 'brainwashed' by the ruling historical tradition of the Pentateuch and its view of the Canaanites. His ideas can be seen as running parallel to the interpretation of the land of Canaan in the Pentateuch and the Deuteronomistic History, although a number of common connotations are evidently attached to the concept of Canaan both in Ezekiel 16 and in the historical books.

25 On the study of nomadism in the Near East and the bearing of this study on the question of the early history of Israel, cf. my *Early Israel*, pp. 84-163. Neither can the anti-Canaanite attitude be explained as a feature of the antagonism between the rural and the urban populations of the country (which has been a fundamental issue among the adherents of the so-called 'revolution hypothesis'), since such a stage of antipathy between city and countryside cannot be taken for granted in the Near East. Cf. further on this *Early Israel*, pp. 164-201, and cf. *ibid.*, pp. 199-201, on the sociological stereotypes 'nomad—peasant—city-dweller'.
26 However, Bertholet only uses this to explain 'the idea of the origin' of Israel in Ezek. 16.3, which seems to depart from the concept of Israel's origins in the historical books of the Old Testament. Cf. also above pp. 130-31 on Ezek. 16.3.

It is at the same time not necessary to conclude that the author of Ezekiel 16 should have written his account of Israelite 'history' without knowing the description of this history in the Pentateuch and the Deuteronomistic History. A general knowledge of the content of these historical works is most conspicuous in Ezekiel. However, this does not imply that the author of Ezekiel 16 was forced to follow the guidelines set out by the historians who wrote the historical books of the Old Testament. He was evidently in a position where he could freely interpret this history in his own way. Thus we may argue that in Ezek. 16.29 he used the concept of Canaan, not in a geographical or historical sense, but in an ideological one, because of the specific negative and ideological attitudes which had already been attached to the concept of Canaan in the historical literature.[27]

Hosea 12.8-9 (*REB*: vv. 7-8):

[28]כנען בידו מאזני מרמה לעשק אהב

ויאמר אפרים אך עשרתי מצאתי און לי

כל־יגיעי לא ימצאו־לי עון אשר־חטא

> False scales are in merchants' hands,
> and they love to cheat.
> Ephraim says,
> 'Surely I have become rich,
> I have made my fortune';
> but despite all my gains
> the guilt of sin will not be found in me.

27 This might then be another reason to regard the Old Testament traditions about Canaan in the historical literature not as expressions of the historical or geographical preoccupations of the authors but as indications of the basically ideological character of the Old Testament historical tradition itself.

28 For the textual criticism of this passage, which is only relevant in the case of לעשק, which has often been corrected into לעקש, 'to practise usury', cf. T.H. Robinson, in T.H. Robinson and F. Horst, *Die zwölf kleinen Propheten* (HAT, I, 14; 3rd edn; Tübingen, 1964), p. 46. Cf. also K. Marti, *Das Dodekapropheton* (KHCAT, 13; Tübingen, 1904), p. 96. According to Marti the correction was proposed by F. Buhl. Another common correction in this place is to emend לעשק to לעקב, 'to swindle', with a word-play on the name of Jacob, 'the main character' of Hosea 12. This emendation goes back to J. Wellhausen and has been supported by, for example, W. Nowack, *Die kleinen Propheten* (GHKAT, III/4; 3rd edn; Göttingen, 1922), p. 72, who explains the exegetical consequences in a very thorough way. Modern commentators are generally more reluctant to change the consonantal text here; thus W. Rudolph, *Hosea* (KAT, XIII, 1; Gütersloh, 1966), p. 222, and H.W. Wolff, *Dodekapropheton I. Hosea* (BKAT, XIV/1; 2nd edn; Neukirchen, 1965), p. 268.

In a footnote to the new Danish translation of the Old Testament, the translators remark: '*Canaan* is the designation of the non-Israelite population of Palestine. We have, at the same time, a play of words on the basic meaning of the word, "trader" '.[29] More information can be found in the commentary of Svend Holm-Nielsen, who is the mainly responsible for this translation: '. . . and the name of Canaan is used here in a contemptuous sense about the Northern Kingdom. Here is a double feint. On one hand the meaning is of course that Israel is no better than the idolatrous Canaanites, while on the other the Hebrew word *Canaan* also means 'trader', and in this connection it concerns humbug in the world of business.'[30]

Surely the commentary of Holm-Nielsen cannot totally be ignored, but the note which was attached to the translation itself is meaningless and hard to explain in light of the tradition of translating this verse, which goes back to Jerome, according to which Canaan and Ephraim must here be one and the same person (or better, people).[31] If we disregard some of the more unnecessary implications, Holm-Nielsen's commentary makes sense. Among the unnecessary elements of this commentary belongs—apart from the irrelevant hint at the world of business—the reference to the idolatrous Canaanites, since Hosea never mentions these idolatrous Canaanites but only the *idolatrous Israelites*. It is only the modern scholar, and not Hosea's contemporaries, who knows about the idolatrous Canaanites. The modern interpretation of this verse is as usual dependent on the religious and ethnic interpretation of the Canaanites present in the historical books of the Old Testament.

It seems fairly easy to date this passage, because commentators generally agree in maintaining that—irrespective of whether vv. 8ff. are an original part of Hosea 12 (thus the majority of scholars) or an independent prophecy as maintained by W. Rudolph[32]—it is nevertheless a genuine prophecy by Hosea. As long as the point of departure for the analysis was considered to be the prophet himself, an evaluation like this was not to be doubted. However, should we prefer the alternative approach to the prophetic literature indicated above, some questions may be raised concerning the genuineness of

29 *Tolvprofetbogen. Det gamle Testamente i ny oversættelse* (Danish test translation; Copenhagen, 1985), p. 33 n.
30 S. Holm-Nielsen, *Tolvprofetbogen fortolket* (Copenhagen, 1985), p. 93.
31 On Jerome, see W. Rudolph, *Hosea*, pp. 233f.
32 *Hosea*, p. 224.

these verses; there may also be reason to qualify the usual interpretation of the passage.

If we consider it plausible that this passage was composed in the days of Hosea in the 8th century BCE, the importance of this text for our discussion cannot be overestimated. It must first of all be noted that Ephraim is here the same 'person' as Canaan. We may only guess whether this Canaan should be understood as a sociological term meaning 'trader'[33] or as an ethnic name. If 'Canaan' is here an ethnic name, the passage evidently plays on the hatred which already existed among the Israelites in the period of the kings against non-Israelite ethnic groups, and here especially against the Canaanites. But who were these Canaanites? Were they the Canaanites of the Pentateuch, that is, the original population of the country, or were they Phoenicians, the foreign traders who according to the stereotype and ideological understanding of the Israelites must be swindlers, not because they were traders but because they were *foreign* traders?[34] And is it possible in this prophecy of Hosea to find an indication that these Canaanites/Phoenicians had formerly (perhaps in the days of the Omride dynasty) played their own game to the detriment of the native Israelite population?[35]

If something can be said in favour of such an understanding of Hos. 12.8-9, it will be possible to extract other information from this passage as well. It would be possible to maintain that in Hosea's days it was common to identify the Canaanites with the Phoenicians. If so, this would be testimony to the fact that the identification of Canaan and Phoenicia here preceded the oldest known identification of the two ethnic terms from the Phoenician world itself by almost half a millennium.

It would, however, on the basis of this passage also be possible at least to indicate the direction in which the origin of the Old

---

33 H.W. Wolff is the only commentator I know of who does not translates כנען as 'Canaan' (*Dodekapropheton I*, p. 266). The REB translation cited here has little basis in modern scholarly commentaries.

34 In this connection K. Marti refers to the amusing fact that in the Greek tradition the Phoenicians were also considered to be 'swindlers'. He refers to *Odyssey* 14, 288f.: '. . . then there came a man of Phoenicia, well versed in guile, a greedy knave, who had already wrought much evil among men' (A.T. Murray's translation, *Homer. The Odyssey*, II [Loeb Classical Library, 105; Cambridge, MA, 1919]).

35 Cf. Rudolph, *Hosea*, p. 224, who actually refers to the prolonged period of peace under Jeroboam II.

Testament notion of Canaan and the Canaanites should be sought. If the Phoenicians were originally, that is, in the days of the Omrides, called 'Canaanites' and at the same time considered treacherous foreign traders, we here have an explanation both of the hatred against the Canaanites, that is very much in evidence in the Old Testament historical literature, and of the independent tradition that identifies the Canaanites with traders or merchants. Thus, in Hos. 12.8-9, Ephraim could be considered a Canaanite, not because he was foreign, but because he is here likened to a swindling tradesman. And when other prophetic books ascribed to prophets who lived later than Hosea himself use Canaan to mean 'trader', the reason may be not that Canaan originally meant 'trader' (which it certainly did not, being an ethnic designation of some sort), but that authors of these writings borrowed the expression Canaan and the interpretation of it from Hosea (or from a tradition which may go back even further into the history of Israel). Finally, it is also possible to argue that Hosea here as elsewhere was not influenced in his choice of concepts by any knowledge of the interpretation of Canaan in the Pentateuchal tradition. It is as a matter of fact far more likely that he based his understanding of Canaan on the existing political and ethnic differences of his own time.

Only one serious argument may be adduced to disprove this commentary on Hos. 12.8-9. If the passage was never composed by the prophet Hosea (or by one of his contemporaries) but was written by a later redactor who collected material which may not necessarily go back to Hosea or his contemporaries, it would be very difficult to date this passage. In that case the context of Hos. 12.8-9 could be the political and economic conditions of a much later period.

Which solution to choose must be discussed in connection with a more comprehensive study of the redaction(s) of the book of Hosea. Here it is only possible to say this, that it has often been noted that the book of Hosea displays a certain degree of independence when dealing with traditions and concepts which are well known from other parts of the Old Testament, especially from the historical literature. Therefore there may be reason to imagine that the independent usage of such concepts and traditions may, after all, go

---

36 It is possible to find traces of a parallel interpretation in the commentary of F.I. Andersen and D.N. Freedman, *Hosea* (AB, 24; New York, 1980), pp. 615f., although they do not pursue this.

back to an original mind, whether to Hosea himself or to some unknown redactor or author of the pre-exilic period.

Obadiah 20:

וגלת החל־הזה לבני ישראל אשר־כנענים עד־צרפת וגלת ירושלם
אשר בספרד ירשו את ערי הנגב

Exiles from Israel will possess Canaan as far as Zarephath, while exiles from Jerusalem will possess the towns of the Negeb.[37]

The date of this verse will depend on where we look for the 'exiles from Jerusalem'. The connection between the date of the passage and the dwelling place of the exiled Jerusalemites becomes obvious from the commentary of Theodore Robinson, especially when his commentary is compared with older ones going back to the school of Wellhausen, for example the commentaries by Karl Marti and Walther Nowack. Robinson is of the opinion that although vv. 19-21 may be a secondary supplement to Obadiah 1-18 belonging to the post-exilic period, it is impossible to propose a precise date for the passage, the reason being that Robinson has nothing to say about Sepharad except that the place is unknown. However, in his opinion the verses are not as late as assumed by the adherents of the Wellhausen school.[38] Marti and Nowack both indicate a date for this passage in the post-exilic period. Marti places it in the 2nd century BCE while Nowack considers it to derive from the end of the 4th century BCE. Both authors refer to Assyrian sources where indications of the location of Sepharad may be found, that is, in Asia Minor.

37 Thus REB. This translation must, however, be considered the result of a rather heavy-handed emendation of the Hebrew text. Should we propose another translation which follows the wording of the Hebrew Bible more closely it would read like this: 'Exiles of the army of the Israelites shall take possession of Canaan as far as Zarephath, exiles of Jerusalem, who are in Sepharad, shall possess the cities of Negeb'. This translation also presupposes a number of corrections and emendations to the Hebrew text, although in no way as comprehensive as the ones made by the translators of the REB. Thus the translation of 'Exiles from Israel will possess' presupposes an emendation of אשר to ירשו, as indicated by the BHS. The precise rendering of this enigmatic passage, however, presents some additional possibilities: 'Exiles of this army which belongs to the sons of Israel, who are Canaanites until Zarephath, and the exiles of Jerusalem, shall possess the cities of the Negeb'. The Israelites may in this way be identified with the Canaanites.
38 Robinson and Horst, *Die zwölf kleinen Propheten*, p. 116.

According to Marti and Nowack the passage presupposes that a Jewish diaspora was already in existence in Asia Minor, and in their opinion this indicates a very late date, perhaps even in the Hellenistic period.[39]

The information contained in Obadiah 20 may therefore be unimportant as far as the location of the land of Canaan in ancient times is concerned, since it is only relevant to the late post-exilic period. The two areas which are in the main focus of this text are the most northern part of the territory, especially the Phoenician coast as far as Zarephath, which was situated between Sidon and Tyre, and the Negeb, which in the post-exilic period was a possession of the Edomites. As part of his expectation of a future messianic kingdom, the author believes that Israel will reconquer the northern part of the country while Jerusalem (Judah?) will retake the southern part, and that at the end of history Israelites as well as Jerusalemites shall meet in Jerusalem to condem the Edomites.

Zeph. 1.11:

הילילו ישבי המכתש

כי נדמה כל־עם כנען   נכרתו כל־נטילי כסף

Those who live in the Lower Town will wail.
For all the merchants are destroyed,
and the dealers in silver are all wiped out.

Commentators generally agree that the prophecies of Zephaniah belong to the late pre-exilic period. Moreover, because of the general 'atmosphere' in Jerusalem described in this prophetic book, which is often thought to square well with the description of the period of King Manasseh in the second book of Kings, scholars often consider the era of this king to form the historical background of the prophecies of Zephaniah, and this also applies to Zeph. 1.11. Some scholars lay stress on the description of the religious circumstances found in the early part of the book of Zephaniah and therefore argue that this prophet was active in the early days of King Josiah, when this king was still an infant and the prospects of a religious reform

---

39 Marti, *Dodekapropheton,* pp. 229f., 239; Nowack, *Kleine Propheten,* pp. 172f.

including a dramatic reversal of cultic practices and general beliefs were never thought of.[40]

We are, however, entitled to question this evaluation of the work of Zephaniah. We may ask whether the present stage of research on the prophets has not brought scholarship beyond such positions, and whether this evaluation of Zeph. 1.11 is perhaps more conventional than fact-based. A remark included in the commentary of Holm-Nielsen may indicate that the redactional implications of Zephaniah are not as simple as generally believed: 'When one has finished reading the three chapters of this book it must be confessed that nothing new is said in them which cannot also be found in the prophecies of Amos, Hosea or Micah—and especially Isaiah—a hundred years earlier'.[41] If we should, therefore, depart from the idea that this prophetic book goes back to the work and sayings of a specific prophet, Zephaniah, and instead consider the book to be an agglomeration of sayings and prophecies of various origins which were put together in a book by a redactor, then the Book of Zephaniah will not be the expression of the sentiments of a single prophet, but rather of the evaluations and sentiments of its redactor. We may say that the attribution of the three chapters to one prophet is actually to the credit of the redactor who combined the material into these three chapters and who was able to disguise the non-homogeneous origins of the material collected by him. In the Book of Zephaniah no original points of view are found to indicate that an original prophetic mind stands behind the sentences of the book. Instead the material may come from different prophetic traditions, some of it from the tradition going back to Hosea, other parts from the tradition going back to Isaiah, etc. All of this was put together by a redactor who wanted to preach impending doom over Jerusalem, Niniveh and Israel's neighbours. Furthermore, this preaching of doom was drafted in such a way—at least the passages concerning Jerusalem—as to agree with the historical interpretation of the Deuteronomistic literature.[42]

40 There are actually only insignificant differences between so-called 'moderate' exegetes like F. Horst, in Robinson and Horst, *Die zwölf Kleinen Propheten*, p. 187, and the more radical exegetes belonging to the school of Wellhausen, for example Marti, *Dodekapropheton*, pp. 358f., or Nowack, *Kleine Propheten*, pp. 287f.
41 *Tolvprofetbogen*, p. 129.
42 Cf. also what the Deuteronomistic editors have done for 'Zephaniah's' contemporary, Jeremiah, in that the book which bears the name of this prophet is more or less their work. It may thus be reasonable to ask what we would

Thus there may be reason to question the usual dating of Zeph.
1.11. On the other hand, it is clear that—irrespective of the date of this
verse—it closely follows the Hoseanic tradition according to which the
Canaanites were tradesmen, and it is certainly not dependent on the
view of the Canaanites in the historical books. The Canaanites
of Zeph. 1.11 are definitely not to be considered an ethnic group;
כל־עם כנען is used here with a definite sociological meaning. The
persons called Canaanites were Judaeans by birth and their surname is
understandable: it is the rich Judaeans who were so called, the persons
who profited from the general prosperity and the social injustice of
the period.[43]

Zeph. 2.5

הוי ישבי חבל הים גוי כרתים דבר־יהוה עליכם
כנען ארץ פלשתים והאבדתיך מאין יושב

Woe betide you Kerethites who live by the coast!
This word of the LORD is spoken against you;
I will destroy Canaan, land of the Philistines.[44]
I shall lay you in ruins, bereft of inhabitants.

In this case the question of dating may be important. Scholars have
also displayed more ingenuity when discussing this passage than was
the case with the preceding text, because they have generally doubted
that this verse could go back to a late pre-exilic prophet.[45] The

have known about Jeremiah were it not for the editorial work of these
Deuteronomists. Cf. further on this R.P. Carroll, *Jeremiah* (London, 1986). It
should in this connection be remarked that our sources for the 'Deuteronomistic reform' in Josiah's days are contained in the *Deuteronomistic* 2 Kings
only, and in the sections of the Book of Jeremiah which are equally Deuteronomistic; the reform was evidently considered to be Deuteronomistic by the
Deuteronomists themselves. What the historical prophet Jeremiah thought
about the Deuteronomistic reform we do not know, nor that a reform with a
programme like the one described in 2 Kings ever did take place. If Josiah
actually did carry through such a religious reform, we have no sure indication
of the programme. The only things we know are what the Deuteronomist
historians want to tell us. If the Deuteronomistic reform under Josiah may be
questioned, then of course the proposal to date Zephaniah to the early part of
Josiah's reign is ill founded.
43 All these themes have a long prehistory in the prophetic tradition, and the
book of Zephaniah has nothing original to say in this connection.
44 Thus my translation of the Hebrew text. However most modern translations
emend the text, like the REB: 'Land of the Philistines, I shall crush you'.
45 Thus Nowack, *Kleine Propheten*, p. 287.

passage is obviously dependent on other prophetic texts and it is possible to trace the traditions behind the present formulation of Zeph. 2.5—as indicated by John Strange—back to seemingly older texts like Jer. 47.4 and Ezek. 25.16.[46] The dependency on prophetic writings which can hardly be older than the period of the Babylonian Exile makes it unlikely that Zeph. 2.5 originated before the last days of the Exile or in the post-exilic period. The specific problem which is connected with the כרתים 'the Kerethites' (or 'the Cretans') in this text is no concern of ours. It is, however, necessary to discuss the meaning of 'Canaan' in this passage. In the preceding verse four cities along the coast are mentioned by name, Gaza, Ashkelon, Ashdod and Ekron, all four of them belonging to the Philistines. The geographical horizon of this text is obviously confined to the coastal plain, especially the southern part. Therefore Canaan—if it is not just a very late gloss (which is the opinion of the editors of BHS)—must here designate the Philistine part of the coastal plain. Any other explanation, for example, that we should here distinguish between two parts of the coastal plain, one Canaanite and the other Philistine, cannot be supported by the wording of the verse.

Zech. 14.21:

והיה כל־סיר בירושלם וביהודה קרש ליהוה צבאות ובאו כל־
הזבחים ולקחו מהם ובשלו בהם ולא־יהיה כנעני עוד בבית־יהוה
צבאות ביום ההוא

> Every pot in Jerusalem and Judah will be holy to the LORD of Hosts, and all who come to sacrifice will use them for boiling the flesh of the sacrifice. When that time comes, no longer will any trader be seen in the house of the LORD of Hosts.

This verse, which concludes the book of Zechariah, also brings our review of the occurrences of 'Canaan' and 'the Canaanites' in the prophetic literature to an end. It is at the same time legitimate to maintain that this passage belongs among the most impenetrable of the citations from the Prophets. Thus we may ask whether 'the Canaanites' are here meant to be 'merchants' or 'tradesmen', which

46 Cf. J. Strange, *Caphtor/Keftiu. A New Investigation* (Acta Theologica Danica, 14; Leiden, 1980), pp. 119-20. It should be remarked that Strange—like the REB—chooses to follow the BHS and corrects כנען to אבנער, 'I shall crush you'. This emendation is, however, without support either in the Hebrew textual tradition or in the ancient translations of the Old Testament.

is the usual interpretation of the translators and commentators of the modern world, or whether the word here carries an ethnic meaning. And, if the content of the word is ethnic, then who were these 'Canaanites'?

The dating of the verse may be easy to ascertain because even scholars who maintain that at least some sections of Deutero-Zechariah (Zech. 9-14) belong to the pre-exilic period generally agree in seeing Zech. 14.21 as a clearly post-exilic and apocalyptic text. That Zech. 14.21 must belong to the post-exilic era was unproblematic to older commentators like Marti and Nowack because they were at the same time ready to date the whole of Deutero-Zechariah to the late post-exilic period, perhaps even as late as the Hasmonaean period at the end of the 2nd century BCE.[47] We may disregard the minor differences that exist among the various commentators and say that this text is evidently very late and hardly predates the Hellenistic period.

Such a late date for Zech. 14.21 does not preclude the translation 'No traders shall again be seen in the house of the LORD of Hosts', because this translation can draw support from other prophetic passages as well where the Canaanites were understood to be traders. On the other hand, the late date makes it preferable to use the 'ethnic' translation of Canaan here, as has been the case in a number of more recent translations—including the new Danish one.[48] First, and most important, it is reasonable to consider the corpus of the Old Testament historical literature to have been in existence when Zech. 14.21 was drafted. This means that, irrespective of whether or not the author of Zech. 14.21 understood 'the Canaanites' to be Canaanites or merchants, his readers would probably have considered them to be Canaanites because of the Old Testament historical tradition which was well known to them, or so we may suppose. Furthermore, the translation of the LXX makes it obvious that the Canaanites of Zech. 14.21 were believed to be ethnically speaking Canaanites because the

---

47 Cf. on this K. Marti, *Dodekapropheton* , pp. 396f., and Nowack, *Kleine Propheten*, pp. 367f., who both date Deutero-Zechariah in its entirety to the Maccabaean or the Hasmonaean era. A more moderate position is the one supported by F. Horst, in Robinson and Horst, *Die zwölf kleinen Profeten*, p. 214, and B. Otzen, *Studien über Deuterosacharja* (Acta Theologica Danica, 6; Copenhagen, 1964), pp. 200ff. Horst dates Zech. 14.21 to the transitional period between the 4th and the 3rd century BCE, whereas Otzen maintains that it must be 'aus später nachexilischer Zeit' (*Deuterosacharja*, p. 212).

48 The tradition goes through Luther back to the LXX.

word is here transcribed as Χαναναῖος. It may also be argued that
the context of Zech. 14.21 points in the same direction. Thus the
preceding passage (Zech. 14.16-20) speaks about the temple in Jerusalem as the centre of all nations of the world, and in this connection
we find a special admonition directed at the Egyptians if they will
not come and visit the temple. It would, accordingly, be reasonable to
consider the Canaanites of v. 21 (although it cannot be excluded that
this verse is a secondary gloss) an exception to the rule: The
Canaanites cannot be allowed entry to the temple. It may also be
likely, as maintained by Friedrich Horst, that the 'Canaanites' of this
passage were not real Canaanites but that the word was used here as
a synonym for Samaritans.[49]

We have now arrived at the conclusion of our review of the
prophetic passages which mention the Canaanites and their land. It is,
however, difficult to summarize the results of this review under a
single heading, although it may be possible to present a couple of
results. First it should be noted that the authors of the prophetic
literature generally show little or no dependence on the historical
literature of the Old Testament in their use of the two terms כנען and
כנעני. Even in very late texts such as Zech. 14.21—a text which must
have been drafted in a period when the historical literature had
already been collected and its interpretation of Canaan and the land
of Canaan was well known to most Jews—it is unlikely that the
author borrowed his formulation from the historical books. It is far
more likely that the authors of the prophetic literature made use of
the historical tradition in their own free way. It is on the other hand
very noticeable that the translators of the LXX version of the
prophetic literature were influenced in their choices by the interpretation of the Canaanites and their land in the historical literature.

This result may be seen as partly elaborating on and supporting a
theme which was already in evidence in my earlier volume *Early
Israel*.[50] There, the outcome of the section dealing with the historical
tradition in the prophetic literature was that the only prophet from
pre-exilic times who apparently reveals any acquaintance with Israel's
historical traditions was Hosea. As far as the other prophetic books
are concerned, they hardly ever mention traditions going back to the
early history of Israel—except in a limited number of passages which

49 *Die zwölf kleinen Propheten*, p. 260.
50 *Early Israel*, pp. 306-28.

clearly show Deuteronomistic influence.[51] Furthermore, it may be concluded that, apart from these few 'Deuteronomistic' passages in the prophetic books, the late redactors of the prophetic books did not usually consider the ideas of the historical writers to be normative and not to be departed from.

Another result of this survey of the prophetic literature is that Hos. 12.8 may provide a clue as to the problem of Canaan in the Old Testament. It may explain how the ethnic term 'Canaanite' was transferred to the sociological sphere with the meaning of 'traders' or 'merchants'. This sociological understanding of the Canaanites may go back to Hosea himself and may have survived in the Old Testament tradition following Hosea, or it may predate Hosea. There is, however, no longer any reason to consider the understanding of Canaan as 'trader', 'tradesman', 'merchant' or the like an integral part of the original sense of the word. The interpretation of the Canaanites as 'traders' may very well represent a specific 'Israelite' understanding of the ethnic term 'Canaan'.[52] Therefore, when this understanding of the Canaanites survives in some other passages, as for example in the book of Job (40.30) and in Proverbs (31.24), these few examples may be taken as indications of how the Hoseanic tradition in later times was also felt in other parts of the Old Testament. Neither Job 40.30 nor Prov. 31.24 should be considered independent testimonies of the Canaanites as being 'traders', as both texts are surely post-exilic.

Job 40.30 (*REB* 41.6):

יכרו עליו חברים יחצוהו בין כנענים

Do partners in the fishing haggle over it
or merchants share it out?

---

51 This does not mean that the redactors of these prophetic books were not acquainted with the historical traditions of ancient Israel. They most likely knew the historical traditions very well, and the best evidence of this can of course be found in the Deuteronomistic parts of the book of Jeremiah. It becomes especially obvious if these sections are compared to the non-Deuteronomistic passages in that book. Cf. also *Early Israel*, pp. 316-22.

52 In his commentary on Isa. 23.8 Buhl states that it is certainly not unknown for ethnic designations to acquire additional sociological connotations (*Jesaja*, p. 307). Buhl expressly mentions the 'Swiss' and the 'Savoyards'. However, both examples are meaningless today and this may be taken as evidence of how short-lived such additional meanings may be.

Prov. 31.24:

סרין עשתה ותמכר וחגור נתנה לכנעני

She weaves linen and sells it,
and supplies merchants with sashes.

There is hardly any reason to waste time on these two passages of Job 40.30 and Prov. 31.24. The Hebrew wording of both texts is in itself unproblematic. It is, on the other hand, more interesting to examine how they were translated in the LXX. In both cases the translators have chosen to understand the word as having an ethnic meaning and not a sociological one (which was also the case with Zech. 14.21). In Job 40.30 כנעני is translated as 'Phoenicians', and in Prov. 31.24 as 'Canaanites'. The first example may be taken as another proof of the identification of the Canaanites with the Phoenicians current in late post-exilic times, in the Hellenistic period.[53]

Neither is there much reason to waste much time when dealing with the three psalms where allusions to the Canaanites and their land can be found:

Psalm 105.11:

לך אתן את־ארץ־כנען חבל נחלתכם

'I shall give you the land of Canaan', he said,
'as your allotted holding'.

Psalm 106.38:

וישפכו דם נקי דם־בניהם ובנותיהם אשר זבחו לעצבי
כנען ותחנף הארץ בדמים

they shed innocent blood,
the blood of sons and daughters
offered to the gods of Canaan
and the land was polluted with blood.

Psalm 135.11:

לסיחון מלך האמרי ולעוג מלך הבשן ולכל ממלכות כנען

53 Job 40.30b: μεριτεύονται δὲ αὐτὸν Φοινίκων γένη; Prov. 31.24b: περιζώματα δὲ τοῖς Χαναναίοι. Cf. above pp. 55, 58ff. on the use of these ethnic terms, which are actually synonymous in the LXX.

Sihon king of the Amorites, King Og of Bashan,
and all the kingdoms of Canaan.

All three psalms are late post-exilic paraphrases of the historical
narratives of the Pentateuch. Psalm 135 even looks like a rather
anaemic reproduction of Psalms 104-106.[54] These three citations
cannot, accordingly, be considered independent examples of the use of
the terms 'Canaan' and 'the land of Canaan' in the Old Testament,
but all three passages are clearly dependent on the Pentateuchal texts
which they actually paraphrase. Now, the only examples of 'Canaan'
and 'the land of Canaan' which remain to be discussed are the
examples in the Chronistic literature, in the books of Ezra and
Nehemiah and Chronicles. However, we can safely leave out of
consideration the relevant passages in Chronicles. These are either
verbally identical with passages in the Pentateuch,[55] or—as in the case
of 1 Chr. 16.18—taken verbally from Psalm 105.11.

The references to Canaan in Ezra 9.1 and Neh. 9.8, 24 are more
promising. The interesting point here is, however, not that all three
places are dependent on the view of the Canaanites in the Pentateuch
and the Deuteronomistic History but that the Canaanites are used here
in a very peculiar sense in order to promote a specific goal of the
authors. In Ezra 9.1 the Canaanites are mentioned among the other
pre-Israelite nations of Palestine together with the Ammonites, the
Moabites, the Egyptians and the Amorites. This verse introduces the
account of Ezra's settlement of the problem of the mixed marriages
(Ezra 9-10) and the point is that the Israelites did not, as Yahweh
once had demanded, segregate themselves from the עמי הארצות,
literally 'the nations of the lands'. In Nehemiah 9 the references to the
Canaanites belong to the general summary of Israel's history which
closely follows the guidelines laid out in the Pentateuch and the
Deuteronomistic History, the conclusion being that 'the people' must
keep the Law. The concrete expression of the Jews' obedience to the
Law is their separation from the 'Gentiles', whether they have to
separate from their Canaanite wives or avoid mingling with the
Gentiles on the sabbath.

---

54 Cf. *Early Israel*, pp. 351-52.
55 Thus 1 Chr. 1.8-16, which is almost identical with the passage about Canaan in
   Gen. 10, and 1 Chr. 2.3, where the sons of Judah are enumerated (cf. Genesis
   38).

The problems which are at stake in these chapters of Ezra and Nehemiah will not occupy our attention here. I shall return to the testimony of these passages in the conclusions below, because they may present at least some clues to the understanding of the strongly anti-Canaanite tradition of the Old Testament.

Chapter 7

THE CANAANITES.
RESULTS, CONCLUSIONS, CONSEQUENCES

In this final chapter some of the historical consequences of a study of this type will be discussed. Should somebody in the future want to pursue the results and conclusions of this book, it will be evident that some changes have to be made in the scholarly understanding of Israel's ancient history, especially Israel's relations to the Canaanites. However, it must at the same time be said that it is mandatory, if a study like this is to make any sense, that the reader be prepared to change some of his or her basic ideas about the content, the presentation and the aims of the historical literature of the Old Testament. If the reader is convinced of the basically historical nature of the biblical historical writings, and believes that the ancient writers actually tried to write *history*, not *stories*,[1] then I suppose that not much of what follows will make sense. On the other hand, it should be equally clear that the biblical historians did not want to write stories simply in order to entertain their readers; instead they had a programme which directed their way of narrating the past history of their nation. This might serve as a reminder to those who all too willingly disregard the historical consequences of the new orientation in biblical studies.

1 In spite of Baruch Halpern's good intentions and well-written defence of the Old Testament historians as being actually *historians* who tried to write history and not novels (cf. B. Halpern, *The First Historians. The Hebrew Bible and History* [San Francisco, 1988]), it must be maintained that these historians—irrespective of their intentions—did not possess the necessary methodological tools to write a history which can be compared to the work of the historians of our age, except remotely.

It sometimes looks as if modern scholars have chosen to emphasize the literary character of the Old Testament historical narratives without discussing the historical consequences of these studies. The aim of this study is, however, not just to 'kill' another people, as someone might argue, but to show that a modern literary analysis of the Old Testament narratives can contribute to a reorientation of our understanding of Israelite history as well.

The Results

The Canaanites of the ancient Near East did not know that they were themselves Canaanites. Only when they had so to speak 'left' their original home, only when they lived in some other part of the Mediterranean area, did they acknowledge that they had been Canaanites.[2] The explanation for this is not to be sought in the mind of these ancient people; it should first be sought in our own presuppositions and ideas. When today it may seem absurd that the Canaanites should not have realized that they were Canaanites, this problem only arises because of our own interpretation of the source material, because of the obvious tendency to explain the behaviour of ancient people in modern 'Eurocentric' terms and categories. In this connection it is important to notice that our way of looking at peoples and nations may lead us astray especially when analysing the concepts of nations current among ancient peoples. Our concepts act like a kind of filter through which the sources from the ancient world have to be sifted and this filter is likely to distort our impression of these sources. It has always been difficult for Old Testament scholars—and they are not exceptional in this respect among Orientalists in general—to understand the nature of the differences between modern European scholars and the peoples of the ancient Near East. This problem is so fundamental that it may totally block the way to a correct understanding of—in this case—the concepts of 'ethnicity' and 'social communities' in non-European societies.

It is necessary to understand that the ideas of nationality and ethnicity which appear in ancient writings and which we easily

2 Cf. above, Chapter 3, dealing with the evidence of the 1st millennium BCE and later. Only in Northern Africa are some late descendants of the Canaanites known to have described themselves as 'Canaanites'—irrespective of whether they were physically descendants or had only inherited the notion of being Canaanites from some other people. Cf. above, pp. 56-57.

misunderstand as genuine expressions of a national self-consciousness had no roots in the awareness of the ordinary population of the ancient world. Such concepts were nourished by the members of the higher circles of ancient oriental society; they were so to speak the prerogative of an intellectual elite, irrespective of whether we speak of a political elite connected with the palace administration (usually considered to be 'the court', but in those days of far greater importance than a royal court in a European state) or of a religious elite which centred around the major shrines of the ancient states. If we really want to understand the issues at stake here, it is of paramount importance that we first acknowledge this state of affairs.[3]

Although the evidence of the ancient documents pertaining to the Canaanites and their land may seem utterly confusing and incongruous, our argument here is that the testimony of these sources is in no way contradictory or unintelligible. The seemingly conflicting evidence of these sources may be explained as the result of a lack of appropriate criteria among the ancients by which to distinguish among the different states and peoples of their own age. Because the concept of a 'nation' was first and foremost an idea nourished by the intellectual elite located at the centre of society and not a popular notion which was the common heritage of all people, the lack of clarity as to the precise understanding of Canaan and its inhabitants makes

3 It is important to realize that the modern notions of ethnicity, nations and peoples also emerged in comparable intellectual environments, and exactly at the moment when European society experienced some profound changes during the revolutions of the late 18th century CE and in the Romantic period of the 19th century CE. The new elite which appeared in this period actually considered itself to be the representatives of the *people* and the *nation*, and thus it is understandable that they at the same time misunderstood their own sentiments and ideas as being the sentiments and ideas of the common people as well, disregarding the fact that ordinary people do not necessarily harbour the same ideas of what a nation is. Only during the course of the 19th century CE may we speak of a widespread and common idea of what a nation actually is as having become the possession of ordinary people, although the really nationalistic ideologies of the late 19th century CE could not have appeared without the preparatory work done in the first half of that century. (Here especially the introduction of common schools and the diffusion of literacy among ordinary people were important factors.) Only a system of massive communication enabled the elite to convey its ideas and beliefs to the whole of the population in their states. We cannot go further with this theme here, but it is imperative to study the emergence and preconditions of our own concepts before we apply them to the study of societies which are quite different to ours.

sense. After all, it is more than likely that each centre had its own ideas as to the extent and composition of a certain nation or people. Only if Canaan was once a well-defined *political* and *ethnic* entity in ancient Western Asia, as was the case, for example, ancient Egypt, especially in contrast to the populations of Western Asia, should we expect the various references to Canaan and the Canaanite population to be precise and in mutual agreement. Furthermore, should Canaan have in those days been acknowledged as being a state or a nation, it would have been mandatory for it to be a state ruled by a king, because it seems evident that the notion of a state in the ancient Near East was almost invariably related to the notion of a kingdom. However, Canaan was never united under the rule of one king— except when it was governed by the king of Egypt, Assyria, Babylonia, etc.

Now the references to Canaan in the ancient sources from the 2nd millennium BCE mostly indicate that Canaan was a geographical entity of some sort, situated in Western Asia and often (if not always) a part of the Egyptian Empire. The general direction in which we should look for this Canaan is also easy to ascertain, because most sources indicate a location somewhere along the Mediterranean coast. However, the northern and eastern borders of the territory of the Canaanites have never been defined in any precise way; the southern border of Canaan was obviously Egypt itself. It is characteristic that the most precise information about Canaan which has survived to modern times is contained not in documents which come from the Western Asiatic territory itself but which originate in Mesopotamia. This information therefore comes from documents which were drafted in administrative centres far removed from Canaanite territory, by scribes who had never visited Canaan themselves. We are accordingly entitled to maintain that the information in such documents does not disclose any actual, precise knowledge about Canaan and the Canaanites, but mainly perpetuates the stereotypical ideas especially of the Babylonian scribes about where to look for this Canaan. Only in the Hellenistic period at the end of the 1st millennium BCE may we speak of a certain and fixed idea among the peoples of the ancient Near East as to the location of Canaan, because of the identification of Canaan with Phoenicia.

The Old Testament references to the Canaanites and their land may be divided into two main groups. The information in the first group is consistent and discloses a fixed idea as to the identity of the Canaanites and their importance for Israelite history (they were identified as being the principal enemy); the other displays a disturbing lack of inner coherence, painting instead a confusing and sometimes even contradictory picture. In the Pentateuch and the Deuteronomistic History there is no doubt as to the identity and character of the Canaanites, neither do the authors hesitate to tell us where we should look for the land of Canaan. This land is always understood to encompass the territory between the Jordan in the east and the Mediterranean Sea in the west, while the Canaanites are always identified with the people who lived in this area before the Israelites settled in the land. The understanding of Canaan and the Canaanites in these biblical books is, on the other hand, stereotypical and inflexible and makes it clear that the Canaanites and their land had no independent history of their own; they were only included in the historical narratives in order to further the intentions of the narrators. The biblical Canaanites thus had no historical role to play, and the Old Testament historical literature cannot be used as information about the *historical* Canaanites, simply because the Canaanites of the Old Testament are not historical persons but actors in a 'play' in which the Israelites have got the better, or the hero's part.

The second group of references to the Canaanites is found outside the historical books, especially in the Prophets, but a very limited number of examples can also be found in other parts of the Old Testament. As soon as we are confronted with this second group, the unreal character of the evidence of the first group becomes obvious, not because the references to the Canaanites in the prophetic literature create a picture of the Canaanites which does not conform with the one in the Pentateuch and the Deuteronomistic History, but because no comparably coherent picture emerges in the prophetic books. Of course it is possible to find references outside the historical books which conform well with the understanding of the Canaanites in the historical literature but in all such cases it is easy to show that the author has been influenced by the ideas of the Pentateuch and the Deuteronomistic History. In other cases such a dependence cannot be demonstrated, and in these places we find an almost unsystematic and rather vague interpretation of the identity and role of the Canaanites.

Conclusions

It is possible to summarize the results of this investigation in this way. Here it is our aim on the basis of these results to put forward a hypothesis which may be able to create a kind of coherence between the various and seemingly conflicting applications of the terms 'Canaanites' and 'the land of the Canaanites' in the Old Testament, and it is the opinion of this author that such a consistent hypothesis should be proposed, although we do not mean it to be exclusive, barring alternative hypotheses from contention. However, should the unhistorical nature of the references to the Canaanites and their land in the Old Testament historical literature be acknowledged by the reader, then the following reconstruction of the history of the notion of Canaan may seem feasible.

Although it cannot be proved with absolute certainty, it is reasonable to think that the oldest reference to the Canaanites in the Old Testament is the one found in Hos. 12.8. The reservation which has to be made concerns the eventuality that Hosea was not the author of this saying. Although it cannot be proved with absolute certainty that he was the author, neither can it be disproved, and I think that most scholars are ready to accept that this passage may go back to a prophet of the pre-exilic time. If Hosea was the author, the concept of Canaan in this place seems to contains more than one meaning.

In Hos. 12.8 Canaan is on one hand an Ephraimite and on the other a tradesman. Now this is the only evidence in the Old Testament of the identity between Ephraimites and Canaanites. It was therefore proposed above that Hosea in this place makes use of a foreign ethnic designation to disclose the true character of Ephraim, while at the same time imparting a sociological connotation to this ethnic term. In this way the Canaanite Ephraim also becomes a trader. Still, the Canaanite traders of Hos. 12.8 are at the same time Ephraimites, but there must have existed specific reasons why Hosea could change an ethnic expression into a sociological one. It was proposed that we look for a period in the history of the Northern Kingdom when a foreign element which could be compared to the Canaanites, or which was perhaps even called Canaanite, played a significant role in the history and economic life of the Northern Kingdom. Such a period was most likely the time of the Omride dynasty, that is, the first half of the 9th century BCE, when the Tyrian marriage alliance of the Israelite dynasty created an extraordinary opportunity for the Tyrians and the Phoenicians to make their influence felt in the state of Israel. Maybe already then, but evidently also later—under the more open-minded reign of the later kings of the dynasty of Jehu in the 8th century BCE—the ethnic term 'Canaanite', which was formerly used about this foreign element in Israel, changed into a sociological one. Now it became possible to describe not only the Phoenicians themselves but also the representatives of the main occupation of these Phoenicians, that is the merchants or tradesmen, as Canaanites. The expression 'Canaan', however, is never neutral, not even when it is used in this sense, but is always endowed with some negative connotations. It is therefore likely that it was originally used to describe merchants of foreign extraction who would invariably—in the mind of the Israelites—be potential swindlers. Later on this expression was also used of merchants of Israelite origin and often, if not always, endowed with the same negative connotations.[4]

In other prophetic utterances which belong to the time after Hosea the expression 'Canaan' could still be used both as an ethnic and as a sociological expression, whereas in the Psalms only ihe ethnic sense of the word survived. In the post-exilic wisdom literature, in the Book of Job and in Proverbs, however, Canaan finally lost the last traces of having been an ethnic term (although the ethnic interpretation of Canaan reemerges in the LXX translation of these passages). The double meaning of the word Canaan in the prophetic writings may, on the other hand, be used to explain the strange and obscure application of Canaan in Ezekiel 16 and 17, where the land of the Canaanites is seemingly placed in Mesopotamia. Furthermore, the ambiguity of the concept is also evident in Isa. 23.8, 11. In this passage the Canaanites are evidently 'merchants' (v. 8) while Canaan must at the same time be identified with Phoenicia (v. 11). In this connection it is of interest to note that the double meaning of the word lived on in the prophetic tradition, most likely until Hellenistic times, whereas there is no trace of it in the historical literature.

4 Here a comparison with the Greek is necessary. The original meaning of 'Phoenician' is likely to have been 'people who trade in purple'. However, the citation from *The Odyssey* above showed that the Greeks did not consider these Phoenicians to be particularly honest, and the reason may only have been that the Phoenician merchants were foreigners. No primitive ethnic or racist theory is needed here to support the idea that the Phoenicians were *de facto* dishonest people.

The history of the concept of Canaan in the historical literature must therefore have have been markedly different from the history of the concept in the prophetic tradition. The fact that the connotation of merchant never appears in this part of the Old Testament—not even the slightest hint—should be enough to demonstrate that the scope of this concept is totally different in the historical books. It is also obvious that the concept of Canaan in the historical books is interwoven with the Old Testament historians' description of the fate of Israel and plays no independent role of its own. In order to clarify the application of Canaan in this literature it was necessary to discuss which was the superior aim of the history writers; clearly this was to explain the troublesome character of Israel's relations with its land, before the settlement, after the settlement, and, finally, after the possession of the land was lost during the Exile. If the intentions of the history writers can be explained and furthermore, if the historical narratives can be dated with any certainty, then it should also be possible to ascertain why the expression 'the land of Canaan' was chosen as the name of Israel's land.

The history of Israel as told by the Old Testament history writers was hardly an old history, and at least as far as it concerns the earlier part of the period until the introduction of the Hebrew monarchy, it has little to do with what actually happened in Palestine.[5] Rather than writing history, the Israelite historians composed a *novel*, the theme of which was the origin of Israel and its ancient history. To ascertain the character of history writing in the Old Testament, it should at first be noted that the concept of scholarly reconstructions of the past, the only (or main) goal of which is to describe a historical development 'as it really happened', is a fairly modern invention of the European tradition. This kind of history writing hardly precedes the era of romanticism, and it has prospered in the last two centuries when history writing became part of the positivistic sciences, or so it was believed. However, if we characterize Old Testament history writing as *novelistic*, it should at the same time be acknowledged that

---

5   Today it may be an open question how old the reliable historical information in the Old Testament is. Some may be of the conviction that the oldest reliable information goes back to the Davidic and Solomonic eras, while other scholars will be more cautious and maintain that the first reliable sources in the Old Testament are among those dealing with Israelite history during the 9th century BCE.

two different kinds of novelistic treatments of history are possible.[6] In both cases authors of a historical novel will have as their aim to entertain their public. In order to do so the historians may choose to write a novel describing the past history of intended readers in such a way as to explain to them their present situation, and, perhaps, their own individuality and identity. The history writer may, however, also choose to tell the audience what is going to happen, and adopt a method of describing the past in such a way that the description of the historical development will at the same time promote a programme for the future direction of the society. We may say that it is by no means certain that the Old Testament historians only wanted to tell their readers, the early Jews, why their society was punished in such a harsh way and driven away from its land, although this land had been promised to the Jews by their God. It is just as feasible that the historians wanted to explain to their fellow citizens how they were to reconquer their former possessions and become a great nation again by not repeating the mistakes of the past.

Modern historians believe that the aim of history writing is to relate events which have happened in the past without political or moralistic aims. However, the Old Testament history writing has very little in common with modern history writing.[7] The act of writing history in the modern world is often nothing more than a scholarly pastime, for the stimulation of other scholars, or for the education of the layperson who wants to know 'what happened in the past'; and although the borders have sometimes becomed blurred because of the publication of historical novels, it is easy for most modern people to distinguish between the two literary genres of history writing and historical novels. Ancient Israelite—or rather early Jewish—society was hardly interested in a scholarly presentation of the hard historical

6　We may at the same time admit that the firm belief in the distinction which was current among the members of the positivistic school of historians between fictional literature and history writing is sometimes questioned by modern historians.

7　An analogous and even more remarkable example of this is history writing in the gospels. The gospels contain express reconstructions of the life and fate of Jesus, but they are at the same time also propaganda writings, intended for the Christian and pagan communities of their own times; the aim of the evangelists was evidently 'to promote the gospel'. Thus we may say that the gospels represent a history writing which deals with what is going to happen (the promotion of the kingdom of God). At the same time, in order to carry weight, they have to deal with past history and maintain that their message for the future is true because it has actually already happened.

facts; they understood history to contain a significant narrative in which their own fate in the past, in the present and also in the future would be exposed. History writers were therefore free to convey their message to their readers in the form they had themselves chosen and were not bound to present a true picture of what had actually happened. A narrative would be considered true and genuine if its message was understood and accepted by the audience, not because it was true to the facts of past history.[8]

It is unlikely that the message of the Old Testament history writers can be squeezed into one formula only. The narratives are too complicated and contain too many facets to be narrowed into one single sentence. Although this must be acknowledged, it should at the same time be possible to propose a theory concerning the elements of the narrative which are relevant to the theme of this study, namely the relationship between Israel and its land. The two entities, Israel and its land, have been described respectively as the 'anti-place' and the 'place', and it should be noted that the conflict between these two entities is never fully resolved. Although at the end of its early history Israel conquers its land, which was already promised to its ancestors and visited by them, Israel was not allowed to remain in its land, but just like the ancestors of the nation, it had to leave its land again after the destruction of Jerusalem.

The conflict between Israel and its land governs several of the compositional arrangements in the historical narratives. We may thus speak about a structural resemblance between the roles of the ancestors, who received a promise of ownership of the land, once they had settled in it, and of Israel, which could become master of the land if it was able to conquer it. When the ancestors received the promise of the land it was at the same time predicted that they would have to leave it again, whereas Israel in connection with the conclusion of its conquest of the land and the restatement of the covenant between Israel and its God, is informed of the danger of being expatriated should this covenant be broken again. Israel is, so to

8   Van Seters is seemingly of the opinion that history was written in ancient times only to amuse its readers. This at least is the impression which emerges from the introduction to his *In Search of History* (New Haven, 1983). In reality he should have said that the historical narratives were composed to broaden the horizons of their audience and thus they were likely to create a feeling of identity and social cohesion in a group of people who identified themselves with the fate of the heroes of the narratives.

speak, never allowed to dwell in its land without having to fear for the consequences of its doings.

Given the present state of Old Testament scholarship it should be quite evident that Old Testament history writing did not arise in the period of the united kingdom in the 10th century BCE. We can think of no situation so unlikely to provide the background for this narrative, according to which the relationship between Israel and its land must be considered highly problematic and likely to be broken off at any time, as the period of David and Solomon, when Israel was becoming one of the great powers of the day—at least this is the impression of this ge which the Old Testament history writers have left to us.[9]

The next period considered by many Old Testament scholars to be the period in which the historical writings of the Old Testament were composed is the time of the Babylonian Exile in the middle of the 1st millennium BCE. The following argument is still of fundamental importance in this connection. Irrespective of whether the historical narratives were composed in Palestine after 587 BCE or in Babylonia among the exiles, they only cover the period down to the destruction of Jerusalem and, with a single exception (2 Kgs 25.27-30), are totally silent as to what happened after 587 BCE. If the corpus of historical narratives was collected with a specific and ideological aim this would suit the situation of the Exile in an excellent way, because Israel had just then lost its country and had only a faint hope of returning after the crisis of 587 BCE.[10] We, however, have to present a couple of critical remarks about this dating of the historical narratives.

9   In this place we need not discuss the question of the historicity of the Old Testament description of the history of the united kingdom. This problem is yet to be solved, but is on the other hand not absolutely irrelevant to the argument in this book. If it could be proved that the Old Testament's description of the period of David and Solomon is based on fiction and not on facts, then this would deal a death-blow to the opinion that Israelite history writing goes back to the times of these two kings.

10 We can find some remarkable arguments in favour of an exilic date for the Israelite history writing in the work of the Danish scholar Heike Friis, notably 'Das Exil und die Geschichte', *DBAT* 18 (1984), pp. 63-84 (Danish original: *DTT* 38 [1975]), 'Die Mosebücher als Quellen für die älteste Geschichte Israels. Geschichtsschreibung als Legitimationsform', *DBAT* 21 (1985), pp. 5-27; cf. also her *Die Bedingungen für die Errichtung des Davidischen Reichs in Israel und seiner Umwelt* (DBAT Beiheft, 6; Heidelberg, 1986 [the original Danish version dates to 1969]). See esp. pp. 138-44.

First of all we have to consider the reason why the authors of these narratives wrote a work which seems to beg Israel to leave *Egypt* when the exiles actually stayed in Mesopotamia. The presupposition behind this question is of course that the historical narratives contain a programme for the future, in that they can be read as being a proposal and encouragement to the Jews to return to their country.[11]

The second question which is provoked by the proposal to date the historical narratives to the exilic period is concerned with the role of the Canaanites in these narratives. Now it can with certainty be ascertained that parts of the Old Testament were actually composed during the Babylonian Exile, whether in Palestine or in Mesopotamia. Thus the bulk of the prophecies contained in Deutero-Isaiah (Isaiah 40-55) evidently have to be seen in the light of the fate of the exiles in Babylonia. We do not have to discuss any of the specific problems which the prophecies of this anonymous prophet may cause, except for one peculiar fact: it may actually seem strange that this prophet, who lived during the Exile and most probably in Mesopotamia, expressed his view of the population which remained in Palestine in terms which are quite different from the ones found in the historical books, and furthermore, that his picture of the world (being rather universalistic in character) in connection with his idea of a new Exodus, from Babylonia, not from Egypt, has little to do with the arrangement of the world in the historical books, with its focus exclusively on the land of Israel. The argument may read: If it were known to Isaiah's contemporaries that their homeland was inhabited by Canaanites—the implication being that the Israelites, that is, the Jews, lived in Babylonia[12]—why does Deutero-Isaiah not mention

11 A traditio-historical evaluation of the emergence of the Pentateuch may confirm that the patriarchal narratives might after all derive from the exilic period in that they actually propose an emigration from Babylonia. The role of Egypt in these narratives should not, however, be overlooked: Egypt is the country where the patriarchs have to live in exile.

12 A qualified 'guess' would be that the 'Canaanites' embraced that part of the Palestinian population which did not convert to the *Jewish* religion of the exiles, the reason being that it had no part in the experience of exile and living in a foreign world which had been the fate of the Judaeans who were carried off to Babylonia in 587 BCE. The Palestinian—or rather old Israelite—population were not considered to be Jews because they were not ready to acknowledge the religious innovations of the exilic community, that Yahweh was the only god to be worshipped. Thus the real difference between the Canaanites and the Israelites would be a religious one and not the difference between two distinct nations.

these Canaanites by name?[13]

Although this last question may be disregarded as irrelevant and based on an *argumentum e silentio* and therefore from a logical point of view not correct to pose, it may nevertheless raise some doubt whether the exilic date of the historical narratives is, after all, self-evident. It is a correct observation that Deutero-Isaiah, when he proposes a new exodus to Israel, imagines this to be a reenactment of the old one, and he knows that the exodus of ancient time was from Egypt and not from Mesopotamia. This idea is already present in the prophecies of Hosea, who lived some 200 years before Deutero-Isaiah. Hosea, however, could speak about this part of Israel's early history without disclosing any knowledge of the reconstruction of the history of early Israel presented by the historical writings of the Old Testament.[14] It may therefore be possible that Deutero-Isaiah could have borrowed this idea of a new exodus from Hosea (who actually proposed that Israel return to Egypt, or to the desert in order to be purified of its false beliefs), without having been acquainted with the presentation of Israelite history in the Pentateuch or the Deuteronomistic History, or, at least, in some of the older strata comprising these works.

It has sometimes been argued that Deutero-Isaiah is dependent on the historical tradition of the Pentateuch and the Deuteronomistic History, which must thus predate this prophet. It could, however, equally well be maintained that Deutero-Isaiah created some of the preconditions for the appearance of the historical literature, and that

---

13 Cf. on this *Early Israel*, pp. 312-14 and 325-26.
14 It ought to be said that H. Friis in her article in *DBAT* 21, esp. p. 26, refers to the importance of endogamous marriage alliances in the ancestral narratives, an issue which she considers to speak in favour of an exilic date for these narratives. The discussion of mixed marriages in the books of Ezra and Nehemiah, however, shows that the problem of marriage alliances did not lose its importance in the post-exilic period; rather, it was sharpened because the differences which appeared between the Palestinian populations and the Jews who returned from Babylonia were not felt to be as important as the more conspicuous differences between the Jews and the Babylonians during the Exile. Moreover, the geographical horizon of the ancestral narratives is certainly Palestinian. After all, the patriarchs had to travel to Mesopotamia in order to obtain wives; the patriarchs were not leaving Mesopotamia. In a post-exilic context this would make sense because it might have told the Jews who had returned to Palestine that they eventually had to go to Mesopotamia to find suitable women for marriage, rather than marrying 'Canaanite' women.

for this reason he should be placed at the beginning of the process which led to the collection of historical memories in one more or less coherent corpus of narratives, while at the same time being in a position to elaborate in his own way on some of the themes which were already known from the tradition of Hosea.

In this connection it should be emphasized that there is no reason to believe that all historical information in the historical books must be late, even though the historical literature itself may be of a late date, either exilic or post-exilic. Present scholarship sometimes seems too ready to disregard any possibility of the survival of older sources in late literary works, although it should have been made clear by older traditio-historical research that such old sources are obviously present in the history books. This is not to say that such sources need to be five hundred years or a millennium older than their present literary context; my point is that the authors of the exilic and post-exilic period were of course free to use whatever sources they might have come across.

My own position here has sometimes been misunderstood, as if I were claiming that the Old Testament contains no sources for Israel's ancient history at all. The Old Testament certainly contains such sources; however, my intention is to emphasize that the late literary context makes these sources an unlikely starting point for historical analysis so long as we cannot with any certainty decide which tradition is old and which is not. In the case of Deutero-Isaiah, this prophet's use of pre-existing traditions, not only historical ones but also religious traditions, is very conspicuous. This fact does not make any of the possibly old traditions in Deutero-Isaiah historical in our sense of the word; it only says that he—like the authors of the historical narratives—was free to use whatever source, document or saying he chose. However, it is also true that he in his application of such material moulded it into a series of programmatic utterances which were meant to increase the interest of the exiles in returning home again.

The stereotypical way in which the concept of Canaan is used in the Pentateuch and in the Deuteronomistic History tells us that the authors of the historical narratives had very clear ideas about who the Cananites were supposed to be, as well as where their country was to be sought. The authors of these narratives evidently knew what to do with the Canaanites. Or, to be more exact, because the Canaanites are allowed only to act inside the framework of the historical reconstruction and cannot depart from the role allotted to them, we are entitled to say that the description of these Canaanites has little or nothing to do with the ancient pre-Israelite inhabitants of Palestine. On the contrary, the Canaanites may be considered a kind of ideological prototype of an ethnic phenomenon which was very much a reality in the period when the historical narratives were reduced to writing, and, furthermore, it is obvious that the Canaanites represented a phenomenon which was considered to be extraneous and hostile to the Israelites.

When we are confronted in the historical books with a total rejection of all manifestations of Canaanite culture—not least the religious beliefs of the Canaanites—this has hardly anything to do with religious-historical problems going back to the dark ages of Israel before the monarchy. On the contrary, such anti-Canaanite sentiments were nourished among the historians who wrote the Pentateuch and the Deuteronomistic History and concerned the religious, ethnic and political conditions of their own time.

The possibility of a pre-exilic date for the Pentateuch and the Deuteronomistic History can be ignored. Therefore the answer to the question, 'What problems existed when the historical literature was composed which could have provoked such a rejection of the Canaanites as presented by this literature?', must be looked for either in the exilic or the post-exilic period. In this connection it may be an important fact that Deutero-Isaiah never mentions the Canaanites, nor does he nourish any kind of hatred against foreigners (except, of course, against the Babylonians) which can be compared to the racist bias of the history writers. This may indicate that the grudge against the Canaanites in the historical books was not a part of the heritage of the exiles but originated in conditions which perhaps only arose after the official return of the Jews to Jerusalem after 538 BCE, and, furthermore, that the answer to the question, 'Who were the Canaanites?' should be looked for in the post-exilic period and not in either pre-exilic or exilic times.

Although it cannot be claimed with any kind of certainty, it is worth proposing that the Canaanites of the Old Testament historical literature were actually that part of the Palestinian population in the post-exilic period who were considered opponents of the official Jewry. Being a 'synonym' for such groups, the Canaanites were allowed no entry to the religious institutions of the Jews, nor were the members of the Jewish community permitted to intermarry with them. This view of the Canaanites may draw support from the narratives in the books of Ezra and Nehemiah, according to which the official representatives of official Jewry opposed mixed marriages between Jews and non-Jews. A marriage in ancient times represented far more than just an alliance between two individuals, male and female, because the marriage was actually the symbolic expression of a far-reaching alliance between two different families or lineages. Therefore the refusal of the right to marry with non-Jews can be interpreted as a total rejection of any person who was not a member of the Jewish community.[15]

How old these chapters in Ezra and Nehemiah are is difficult to say. The answer should, however, be sought in connection with the dating of the collections of historical narratives in the Pentateuch and the Deuteronomistic History, because Ezra 9-10 and Nehemiah 9 presuppose that this collection was known to the authors of Ezra and Nehemiah. If a post-exilic date for this collection is plausible, then Ezra 9-10 and Nehemiah 9 may be recollections dating from the Persian era, as indicated by the books themselves. However, it is not absolutely certain that the conditions described by these chapters only existed in the 5th century BCE. Could the date of the Pentateuch and the Deuteronomistic History be lowered, it might be equally possible that the opposition against mixed marriages belonged, perhaps, to the 4th century BCE or to an even later period.

It is of course less than certain whether such a late date for the composition of the historical literature in the Pentateuch and the Deuteronomistic literature is at all plausible. Certainly the so-called Priestly source of the Pentateuch, and accordingly the Pentateuch itself, are works of the post-exilic period. However, in favour of a post-exilic date for other strata of the historical literature may be that the focus of the account is put on the escape of the Israelites from Egypt and their entry to Canaan. Although this idea of an exodus from Egypt was no invention of the author of the book of Exodus, as was indicated above with a reference to the 'exodus traditions' in Hosea and Deutero-Isaiah, the emphasis on this event in the Pentateuch and in the Deuteronomistic History and its importance for the organization of the Pentateuchal material may have had as its back-

15 Cf. again the problem of mixed marriages in Ezra 9-10.

ground the presence of a Jewish diaspora in Egypt for whom the historical narratives about the escape from Egypt may have been composed.

There is actually no reason to present a paraphrase of the Old Testament narrative of the Exodus and to maintain that the conditions of the life of the Israelites in Egypt as described by the book of Exodus, or the Joseph novella, may reflect the actual conditions of life of the members of the Jewish diaspora in the post-exilic period. It is far more likely that the main theme of the Exodus narrative may have a kind of typological significance. In this way the historical narratives may contain a 'programme' which was not intended for the exilic Jewish community of Babylonia (because the history books were not yet in existence in the 6th century BCE), but rather that the programme of these narratives was directly aimed at the Jews of Egypt, the intention being to persuade these Jews to return to their own country. Just like Deutero-Isaiah, who tried to persuade his fellow countrymen to return to Jerusalem (and we now know that his endeavours were only partly successful, because the majority of the Jews evidently decided to stay in Babylonia even after 538 BCE), the authors of the historical literature tried to persuade other Jews to leave Egypt and return to reconquer their old country from the hands of the Canaanites. In this case there is no reason to ask why the Exodus had to take place from Egypt and not Babylon; this now seems self-evident.

Furthermore, a decision to date the collection of historical narratives in the Pentateuch and the Deuteronomistic History to the post-exilic period, and not only to the years following immediately after 538 BCE but also perhaps to the 5th or 4th centuries BCE, will present some additional clues to our interpretation of the historical narratives. Such a late date could possibly provide an explanation for the fact that the writers decided to make use of the two terms 'the land of Canaan' and 'the Canaanites' as second names for Palestine and the non-Jewish population of this country. These expressions may have been chosen because they made sense from an *Egyptian* point of view, while at the same time in the eyes of the Jews of Egypt it was unimportant whether these terms concurred with actual conditions in Palestine. The rejection of Canaanite culture in its totality could thus be understood to be the expression of religious and political disagreements which may have existed between the Jews living in the

Egyptian diaspora and the Jews of Jerusalem, or it could be taken as evidence that Egyptian Jewry understood itself to be the centre of the Jewish community.

Against a proposal like this one may argue—among other things—that we have no additional evidence of a state of disagreement between the part of the Jewish community which lived in Egypt and their Palestinian brothers. We are, accordingly, forced to discuss other possibilities for the place of origin of the historical literature, whether in Mesopotamia or in Jerusalem. Against Mesopotamia speak the same arguments which could be directed against the proposal to see Egypt as the home of the historical literature. In this literature the two geographical centres are evidently Egypt on one side and Palestine on the other, whereas Mesopotamia proper is only the ancient starting point for the migrations of the ancestors. In favour of Mesopotamia speaks the fact that, according to the ancestral narratives, Mesopotamia was still the right place for a law-abiding Jew to look for a wife.

The last point, that of correct Jewish marriages, that is, marriage alliances between Jews of Palestine (Jerusalem) and Jewish women from Mesopotamia, could, however, also be adduced in favour of a location of these narratives in Jerusalem and Palestine. It would thus be possible to maintain that the ancestral narratives show that in the eyes of the Jews of Palestine, their relatives in Mesopotamia were still and rightfully to be considered true members of the Jewish community, whereas the Jews of Egypt are, so to speak, 'ordered' to return home. In favour of a location of these narratives in Jerusalem, one may also argue that they express a view of the Canaanites that would equally well make sense in this community. In this case it should not be too difficult to make proposals as to the identity of these Canaanites: they were likely to have consituted that part of the Palestinian population which was thought to be the enemies of the Jews of Jerusalem. In the 4th century BCE (but perhaps as early as the latter part of the 5th century BCE) these opponents of the Jews could have been the predecessors of the Samaritans, that is, the population living north of Jerusalem. Additional material from the books of Ezra and Nehemiah which testifies to the growing antagonism between Jerusalem and Samaria in the Persian era may also be called in to support this idea. The main problem for such an evaluation of the place of origin of the historical literature may, however, be the fact that, as it stands, the narrative about Israel's conquest of the land only reaches its conclusion when David conquered *Jerusalem*, although this argument may also be turned upside-down and considered an argument which speaks in favour of Jerusalem as the home of the historical tradition, as the conquest of Jerusalem could with equal right be considered the climax in the narratives about the conquest of Israel's land, and the citizens of Jerualem therefore could truly be considered genuine Jews.

It is actually impossible to decide with certainty in which place, Egypt, Jerusalem or Mesopotamia, the historical books of the Old Testament were composed and edited. Important 'internal' arguments speak in favour of Egypt, but it is just as possible to point to Jerusalem and Palestine. Should Egypt, however, be the home of the great historical works of the Old Testament, then we certainly need to explain how and when the Egyptian diaspora obtained such a position that it could produce literary works which were to become normative for the whole Jewish community.

We will have to break off the discussion at this point. At the moment it is only possible to make proposals which may only count as postulates rather than proper theories. Here I have only indicated in which direction one may look for an answer to the problem of the emergence of the historical literature, should a post-exilic date be preferred.

Consequences

One could elaborate on a number of other important themes in connection with the discussion about the date of the historical literature of the Old Testament. One theme is the relationship between the history writing of the Greeks of the 6th to 4th centuries BCE and the Israelite—or rather Jewish—history writing which may belong to the post-exilic period and be more or less contemporary with the Greek. This question has already been dealt with in John Van Seters's *In Search of History* (1983). It may even be argued that instead of considering Old Testament history writing a unique feature of ancient Oriental society (which was formerly the opinion of many scholars), remotely related to so-called Hittite history writing,[16] it

---

16 On Hittite history writing, cf. H. Cancik, *Grundzüge der hethitischen und alt-testamentlichen Geschichtsschreibung* (Wiesbaden, 1976). Van Seters also tries

170 The Canaanites and Their Land

would be preferable to turn to the Greek historians and consider the older among them to be also the forefathers of the Jewish history writers of the post-exilic period. Thus the aim of the Greek historians to write universal history may form a very precise parallel to the biblical historians' description of the history of the world from the creation to the fall of Jerusalem.

Another potentially promising theme to discuss would be the relationship between the topics of the historical books of the Old Testament and the themes which were actually discussed in the early Jewish community. One such example was already referred to above, when I quoted Bernd Jørg Diebner's interpretation that the narrative about Dinah and Shechem in Genesis 34 originated in the post-exilic Jewish community of Jerusalem as a piece of propaganda directed against the Samaritans, whose religious centre should be sought in the environment of Shechem.[17]

Another theme that could be even more pertinent to the subject of this study would include an appraisal of the understanding of the land of Israel in the different parts of the Old Testament and in early Jewry.[18] It is possible to cite more topics for study, but the examples given here must suffice. What remains is to present some of the more general consequences of a study like the present one.

First of all this investigation should make it clear that it is incorrect to operate with a concept like 'the Canaanite religion', and use it to characterize the type of religion which existed in the land of Israel before the Babylonian exile and which may perhaps also be traceable in the exilic and post-exilic period. It would be preferable to use the terminology 'West-Semitic religion' instead of 'Canaanite religion', because the pre-exilic religion also counts as a manifestation of this West-Semitic religion.[19] Thus it makes sense that we never find

to characterize this history writing in his *In Search of History*, pp. 100-26, however, without drawing support from the two important studies on Hittite history writing by M. Liverani, 'Storiografia politica hittita–I: Šunaššura, ovvero: Della Reciprocità', *OA* 12 (1973), pp. 267-97, and 'Storiografia politica hittita–II: Telipinu, ovvero: Della Solidarità', *OA* 16 (1977), pp. 105-31.

17 Cf. above, p. 89.
18 On this discussion of the land of Israel in early Jewish society, cf. D. Mendels, *The Land of Israel as a Political Concept in Hasmonean Literature. Recourse to History in Second Century B.C. Claims to the Holy Land* (Texte und Studien zum Antiken Judentum, 15; Tübingen, 1987).
19 Cf. *Ancient Israel*, pp. 223-37.

a passage in the books attributed to pre-exilic prophets accusing the Israelites of worshipping the gods of Canaan, because no such 'gods of Canaan' ever existed. The accusations against the Israelites were invariably that they worshipped other gods or wrong manifestations of Yahweh, never that they worshipped the Baal or the El of the Canaanite peoples.[20] Only in the historical books, where the fixation of the concept of Canaan had already taken place, are the Israelites accused of religious abuses which include the worship of foreign and Canaanite deities.

Although Bernhard Lang in an inspiring study a few years ago tried to show that Yahwistic monotheism was a new religion which appeared in the 9th and 8th centuries BCE outside the great religious centres of the two Israelite states, and was promoted by a zealous religious minority which included the classical prophets of Israel's pre-exilic history,[21] we feel compelled to question his idea that the 'monoyahwistic' faith was actually a religious innovation, the reason for which was the religious policy and religious aspirations of the Israelite and Judaean kings. In my opinion, the Old Testament description of Israelite religion cannot be used as the starting point of an analysis of the religious history of the Israelites. I think it is far more reasonable to place the Old Testament description of Israelite religion at the end of a long religious development: it is the description of pre-exilic Israelite religion which emerged in the Jewish society of the exilic and post-exilic eras.

Finally, and this will be my last point in this study, the rejection of the concept of 'Canaanite religion' in this monograph will have other consequences as well, since it is only natural also to reject the idea of specific 'Canaanite' cultural traits as being distinctly different from ancient Israelite ones. We may say that just as the Canaanites are almost invisible in the historical sources of the ancient Near East, so is the culture. Western Asia was in ancient times the home of Many peoples and nations and its ethnic composition was extra-

---

20 It is interesting to note that in a passage like Hos. 6.1-3, where the prophet expresses the hope that the Israelites will return to the correct worship of Yahweh, Hosea can only describe the blessings of Yahweh's rule with definitely 'Canaanite' terms (v. 3: the REB hardly pays justice to the wording of the Hebrew text).

21 'The Yahweh-Alone Movement and the Making of Jewish Monotheism', in his *Monotheism and the Prophetic Minority* (The Social World of Biblical Antiquity 1; Sheffield, 1983), pp. 13-59.

ordinarily complex. We know of a long series of ethnic designations for the inhabitants of this area. To consider a single cultural or religious trait to be specific to only one ethnos among this multitude of nations would be presumptuous.

In this case also we are misled by our understanding of 'ethnicity' because we are all too willing to combine, for example, mute archaeological remains with the presence of specific ethnic entities. We do not, however, know whether the material remains coincide with the ethnic distribution of peoples of the Orient in ancient times. Maybe in some quarters of the area such a procedure is feasible, but in Western Asia, in the homeland of the 'Canaanites', this is certainly not possible. It would be preferable to operate with 'neutral' ethnic designations only, like 'Western Asiatic peoples' or 'Western Asiatic cultural features' and at the same time to stop using the ancient ethnic terms as a basis for scholarly analyses of the societies of the Western Asiatic world.

In this sense the present study examines only one facet of a more comprehensive issue. That is, the 'disappearance' of the Canaanites of the Old Testament can be seen as an indication of a problem which has been endemic to the study of the ancient Oriental world, namely, the application of modern ethnic concepts in oriental studies.[22]

22 The article by Karen Engelken, 'Kanaan als nicht-territorialer Terminus', *BN* 52 (1990), pp. 47-63, appeared too late for inclusion in this study. It is the thesis of her article that the name of Canaan as well as the Canaanites was without importance for the Israelites since the period of the Hebrew kings. Later, in the P-traditions, כנען and כנעני are endowed with new and different connotations (p. 50). According to Engelken, the Biblical narrators understand the Canaanites to represent a specific social group, in fact, the early urban population whose way of life was rejected by the early Israelites. (Later, in parts of the Biblical tradition, these 'Canaanites' developed into 'merchants', another group whom the Israelites clearly despised [p. 62].)

Although it is commendable that Engelken thus stresses the ideological content of the description of the Canaanites in the Old Testament, it is also evident that her analysis is based on a number of questionable premises. First, she seems to accept an interpretation of the origin of Israel which looks very much like a variant of the revolution hypothesis of Mendenhall and Gottwald (cf. p. 55). Secondly, she subscribes to the usual German tradition of Old Testament studies, which divides between very old Pentateuchal strata and very young ones (it is not obvious which variant of this scholarly tradition she actually follows), since she reckons with old sources (or at least narratives), such as Genesis 38, which may reflect early views of the Canaanites held by the Israelite non-urban population of the mountains and secondary developments of these notions in later strata. Thirdly, she clearly ackowledges a dichotomy to exist between urban and rural societies in the Middle East; this forms the very basis of her theory. Although she mentions my *Early Israel*, she seems not to have understood the argument in this book, that this funda- mental antagonism between the various sectors of the society represents a Eurocentric stereotype in early social-anthropological research and simply does not conform with the impression which several studies of traditional Near Eastern society have provided.

The result is that her theory depends on one hand on the outcome of the ongoing debate concerning the making of the Pentateuch. A modern view as represented by, e.g., John Van Seters and Erhard Blum, will deal a death-blow to her theorizing. Furthermore, her sociological basis is just as weak as the fundamentals of the revolution hypothesis itself.

BIBLIOGRAPHY

Aharoni, Y., *The Land of the Bible* (2nd edn; London, 1979).

Aḥituv, S., *Canaanite Toponyms in Ancient Egyptian Documents* (Jerusalem-Leiden, 1984).

Ahlström, G.W., 'Judges 5:20f. and History', *JNES* 36 (1977), pp. 287-88.

—*Who Were the Israelites?* (Winona Lake, 1986).

Ahlström, G.W. and Edelman, D., 'Merneptah's Israel', *JNES* 44 (1985), pp. 59-61.

Albrektson, B., *History and the Gods. An Essay on the Idea of Historical Events as Divine Manifestations in the Ancient Near and in Israel* (CBO, 1; Lund, 1967).

Albright, W.F., 'The Role of the Canaanites in the History of Civilization' (1942), *The Bible and the Ancient Near East* (ed. G.E. Wright; London, 1961), pp. 328-62.

—*Yahweh and the Gods of Canaan. A Historical Analysis of Two Contrasting Faiths* (London, 1968).

—'The Amarna Letters from Palestine' *CAH³*, II, 1 (Cambridge, 1975), pp. 98-116.

Aldred, C., 'Egypt: The Amarna Period and the End of the Eighteenth Dynasty', *CAH³*, II, 1 (Cambridge, 1975), pp. 49-97.

Alt, A., 'Die Landnahme der Israeliten in Palästina' (1925), *Kleine Schriften zur Geschichte Israels*, I (München, 1953), pp. 89-125.

—'Erwägungen über die Landnahme der Israeliten in Palästina' (1930), *Kleine Schriften zur Geschichte Israels*, I (München, 1953), pp. 126-75.

—'Ägyptische Tempel in Palästina und die Landnahme der Philister' (1944), *Kleine Schriften zur Geschichte des Volkes Israel*, I (München, 1953), pp. 216-30.

—'Ein Gesandter aus Philistäa in Ägypten', *BO* 9 (1952), pp. 163-64.

—'Kanaan — II. Geschichtlich', *RGG*, III, pp. 1109-11.

Andersen, F.I. and Freedman, D.N., *Hosea* (AB, 24; New York, 1980).

Astour, M.C., 'The Origin of the Terms 'Canaan', 'Phoenician', and 'purple'', *JNES* 24 (1965), pp. 346-50.

Attridge, H.W. and Oden, R.A., *Philo of Byblus. The Phoenician History. Introduction, Critical Text, Translation Notes* (CBQMS, 9; Washington, DC, 1981).

Barth, H., *Die Jesaja-Worte in der Josiazeit* (WMANT, 48; Neukirchen, 1977).

Bertholet, A., *Hezekiel* (HAT, I, 13; Tübingen, 1936).

Blum, E., *Die Komposition der Vätergeschichte* (WMANT, 57; Neukirchen, 1984).

Boling, R.G., *Judges* (AB, 6A; New York, 1975).

Bottéro, J., *Le problème des ḫabiru à la 4ᵉ rencontre assyriologique internationale* (Cahiers de la Société asiatique, 12; Paris, 1954).

Buccellati, G., *Cities and Nations of Ancient Syria* (Studi Semitici, 26; Rome, 1967).

Budde, K., *Das Buch der Richter* (KHCAT, 7; Freiburg i. B., 1897).

Buhl, F., *Jesaja oversat og fortolket* (2nd edn, Copenhagen, 1912).

Caminos, R.A., *Late Egyptian Miscellanies* (Oxford, 1954).

Campbell, E.F., 'Shechem in the Amarna Archive', Appendix 2 in G.E. Wright, *Shechem. The Biography of a Biblical City* (London, 1965), pp. 191-207.

Cancik, H., *Grundzüge der hethitischen und alttestamentlichen Geschichtsschreibung* (Wiesbaden, 1976).

Carroll, R.P., *From Chaos to Covenant* (London, 1981).

—*Jeremiah. A Commentary* (OTL; London, 1986).

Chassinat, É., 'Un interprète égyptien pour les pays chananéens', *BIFAO* 1 (1901), pp. 98-100.

Childs, B.S., *Exodus* (OTL; London, 1974 [5th edn, 1984]).

Cross, F.M., *Canaanite Myth and Hebrew Epic* (Cambridge, MA, 1973).

Day, J., *God's Conflict with the Dragon and the Sea. Echoes of a Canaanite Myth in the Old Testament* (Cambridge, 1985).

Diebner, B.J., 'Gen 34 und Dinas Rolle bei der Definition 'Israels'', *DBAT* 19 (1984), pp. 59-76.

Diepold, P., *Israels Land* (BWANT, 95; Stuttgart, 1972).

Dietrich, M., and Loretz, O., 'Die soziale Struktur von Alalaḫ und Ugarit (II)', *WO* 5, 1 (1969), pp. 56-93.

—'Die Inschrift der Statue des Königs Idrimi von Alalaḫ', *Ugarit-Forschungen* 13 (1981), pp. 199-269.

Dietrich, W., *Israel und Kanaan. Vom Ringen zweier Gesellschaftssysteme* (Stuttgarter Bibelstudien, 94; Stuttgart, 1979).

Donner, H., *Geschichte des Volkes Israel und seiner Nachbarn in Grundzügen* (ATD Ergänzungsreihe, 4/1; Göttingen, 1984).

Donner, H. and Röllig, W., *Kanaanäische und aramäische Inschriften*, I-III (Wiesbaden, 1962-1964).

Dossin, G., 'Une mention de cananéens dans une lettre de Mari', *Syria* 50 (1973), pp. 277-82.

Drower, M.S., 'Syria c. 1550-1400 B.C.', *CAH³*, II, 1 (Cambridge, 1973), pp. 417-525.

Duhm, B., *Das Buch Jesaia* (GHKAT, III/1; 4th edn, 1922 [repr. Göttingen, 1968]).

Edel, E., 'KBo I 15 + 19, ein Brief Ramses' II. mit einer Schilderung der Ḳadeš-schlacht', *ZA* 49 (1950), pp. 195-212.

—'Die Stelen Amenophis' II. aus Karnak und Memphis', *ZDPV* 69 (1953), pp. 97-176.

—'Weitere Briefe aus der Heiratskorrespondenz Ramses' II.: KUB III 37'; *Geschichte und Altes Testament. Festschrift Alt* (Tübingen, 1953), pp. 29-63.

Eissfeldt, O., *Sanchunjathon von Berut und Ilumilku von Ugarit* (Beiträge zur Religionsgeschichte des Altertums, 5; Halle, 1952).

Emerton, J.A., 'Judah and Tamar', *VT* 29 (1979), pp. 403-15.

Engel, H., 'Die Siegesstele des Merenptah', *Biblica* 60 (1979), pp. 373-99.

Engelken, K. 'Kanaan als nicht-territorialer Terminus', *BN* 52 (1990), pp. 47-63.

Evans-Pritchard, E.E., *The Nuer* (Oxford, 1940).

Faulkner, R.O. 'Egypt: From the Inception of the Nineteenth Dynasty to the Death of Ramesses III', CAH^3, II, 2 (Cambridge, 1975), pp. 217-51.

Flanagan, J.W., *David's Social Drama. A Hologram of Israel's Early Iron Age* (The Social World of Biblical Antiquity, 7/JSOTSup, 73; Sheffield, 1988).

Fohrer, G., *Ezekiel* (HAT, I, 13; Tübingen, 1955).

Friis, H., 'Das Exil und die Geschichte', *DBAT* 18 (1984), pp. 63-84.

—'Die Mosebücher als Quellen für die älteste Geschichte Israels. Geschichtsschreibung als Legitimationsform', *DBAT* 21 (1985), pp. 5-27.

—*Die Bedingungen für die Errichtung des Davidischen Reichs in Israel und seiner Umwelt* (DBAT Beiheft, 6; Heidelberg, 1986).

Garelli, P. (ed.), *Le palais et la royauté* (XIXᵉ rencontre assyriologique internationale; Paris, 1974).

Garbini, G., 'Il Cantico di Debora', *La Parola del Passato* 33 (1978), pp. 5-31

—*History and Ideology in Ancient Israel* (London, 1988).

Geus, C.H.J. de, *The Tribes of Israel* (Studia Neerlandica Semitica, 18; Assen, 1976).

Gibson, J.C.L., *Canaanite Myths and Legends* (Edinburgh, 1978).

Giveon, R., 'Toponymes ouest-asiatiques à Soleb', *VT* 14 (1964), pp. 239-55.

—*Les bedouins Shosou des documents égyptiens* (Documenta et monumenta Orientis Antiqui, 18; Leiden, 1971).

Görg, M., 'Der Name 'Kanaan' in ägyptischer Wiedergabe', *BN* 18 (1982), pp. 26-27.

Goetze, A., 'The Struggle for the Dominion of Syria (1400-1300)', CAH^3, II, 2 (Cambridge, 1975), pp. 1-20.

—'Anatolia from Shuppiluliumash to the Egyptian War of Muwatallish', CAH^3, II, 2 (Cambridge, 1975), pp. 117-29.

—'The Hittites and Syria (1300-1200 B.C.)', CAH^3, II, 2 (Cambridge, 1975), pp. 252-73.

Gottwald, N.K., 'Domain Assumptions and Societal Models in the Study of Pre-Monarchic Israel' (SVT, 28; Leiden 1975), pp. 89-100.

—*The Tribes of Yahweh. A Sociology of the Religion of Liberated Israel, 1250-1050 B.C.E.* (New York, 1979).

Greenberg, M., *Ezekiel 1-20* (AB, 22; New York, 1983).

Gurney, O.R. *The Hittites* (Harmondsworth, 1952; rev. edn, 1964).

—'Anatolia c. 1600-1380 B.C.', CAH^3, II, 1 (Cambridge, 1973), pp. 659-82.

Hallbäck, G., 'Sted og Anti-sted. Om forholdet mellem person og lokalitet i Markus-evangeliet', *Religionsvidenskabeligt Tidsskrift* 11 (1987), pp. 55-73.

Halpern, B., *The First Historians. The Hebrew Bible and History* (San Francisco, 1988).

Hammershaimb, E., 'On the Ethics of the Prophets' (1959), reprinted in E. Hammershaimb, *Some Aspects of Old Testament Prophecy from Isaiah to Malachi* (Copenhagen, 1966), pp. 63-90.

Helck, W., *Die Beziehungen Ägyptens zu Vorderasien im 3. und 2. Jahrtausend v. Chr.* (Ägyptologische Abhandlungen, 5; Wiesbaden, 1962).

—'Kanaan', *LÄ*, V (1977), p. 310.

Hempel, J., 'Kanaan' and 'Kanaaniter', *BHH*, II, pp. 926-30.

Holladay, W.L., *Jeremiah*, I-II (Hermeneia; Philadelphia, 1986-1989).

Holm-Nielsen, S., *Tolvprofetbogen fortolket* (Copenhagen, 1985).

Holm-Nielsen, S., *et al.* (eds), *Tolvprofetbogen. Det gamle Testamente i ny oversættelse* (Copenhagen, 1985).

Hurvitz, A., 'Dating the Priestly Source in Light of the Historical Study of Biblical Hebrew. A Century after Wellhausen', *ZAW* 100, *Supplement* (1988), pp. 88-100.

Hvidberg, F.F., *Graad og Latter i Det gamle Testamente. En Studie i kanaanæisk-israelitisk Religion* (Copenhagen, 1938). English Translation: *Weeping and Laughter in the Old Testament. A Study of Canaanite-Israelite Religion* (ed. F. Løkkegaard; Copenhagen, 1962).

Høgenhaven, J., *Gott und Volk bei Jesaja* (Acta Theologica Danica, 24; Leiden, 1988).

Jacob, E., *Ras Shamra et l'Ancien Testament* (Neuchâtel, 1960).

Jaroš, K., *Die Stellung des Elohisten zur kanaanäischen Religion* (Orbis Biblicus et Orientalis, 4; Freiburg, Schweiz, 1974).

Jeppesen, K., *Græder ikke saa saare. Studier i Mikabogens sigte*, I-II (Århus, 1987).

Kaiser, O., *Isaiah 1-12* (OTL; London, 1983 [German original 1981]).

—*Der Prophet Jesaja. Kapitel 13-39* (ATD, 18, 3rd edn; Göttingen, 1983).

Kapelrud, A.S., *The Ras Shamra Discoveries and the Old Testament* (Oxford, 1965).

Kaufmann, Y., *The Biblical Account of the Conquest of Palestine* (Jerusalem, 1953).

Kenyon, K.M., *Amorites and Canaanites* (The Schweich Lectures, 1963; London, 1966).

Kissane, E.J., *The Book of Isaiah*, I (Dublin, 1960).

Kitchen, K.A., *Ramesside Inscriptions Historical and Biographical*, I (Oxford, 1968-75).

Klengel, H., 'Aziru von Amurru und seine Rolle in der Geschichte der Amärnazeit', *MIO* 10 (1964), pp. 57-83.

—*Geschichte Syriens im 2. Jahrtausend v.u.Z.* II, *Mittel- und Südsyrien* (Deutsche Akademie der Wissenschaften zu Berlin. Institut für Orientforschung. Veröffentlichung, 70; Berlin, 1969).

Kloos, C., *Yhwh's Combat with the Sea. A Canaanite Tradition in the Religion of Ancient Israel* (Leiden, 1986).

Knudtzon, J.A., *Die el-Amarna Tafeln*, I-II (Vorderasiatische Bibliothek, 2,1-2; Leipzig, 1915).

Lang, B., 'The Yahweh-Alone Movement and the Making of Jewish Monotheism', in *Monotheism and the Prophetic Minority* (The Social World of Biblical Antiquity, 1; Sheffield, 1983), pp. 13-59.

Lemche, N.P., "Hebrew' as a National Name for Israel', *Studia Theologica* 33 (1979), pp. 1-23.

—*Early Israel. Anthropological and Historical Studies on the Israelite Society before the Monarchy* (SVT, 37; Leiden, 1985).

—*Ancient Israel. A New History of Israelite Society* (The Biblical Seminar, 5; Sheffield, 1988).

—'The Development of the Israelite Religion in Light of Recent Studies on the Early History of Israel' (to be published in *Congress Volume Leuven* 1989; SVT).

Liverani, M., *Storia di Ugarit nell'età degli archivi politici* (Studi Semitici, 6; Rome, 1962).

—'Contrasti e confluenze di concezioni politiche nell'età di El-Amarna', *RA* 61 (1967), pp. 1-18.

—'Per una considerazione storica del problemo Amorreo', *Oriens Antiquus* 9 (1970), pp. 5-27.

—'Le lettere del Faraone a Rib-Adda', *OA* 10 (1971), 253-68 (English transl. 'Pharaoh's Letters to Rib-Adda', *Three Amarna Essays* [Sources and Monographs on the Ancient Near East. 1/5; Malibu, 1979], pp. 3-13).

—'The Amorites', in D.J. Wiseman (ed.), *Peoples of Old Testament Times* (Oxford, 1973), pp. 100-33.

—'Storiografia politica hittita–I: Šunaššura, ovvero: Della Reciprocità', *OA* 12 (1973), pp. 267-97.

—'Partire sul carro, per il deserto', *AIUON* ns 22 (1972), pp. 403-15.

—'La royauté syrienne de l'âge du bronze récent' in P. Garelli (1974), pp. 329-56.

—'Rib-Adda, giusto sofferente', *Altorientalische Forschungen* 1 (1974), pp. 175-205.

—'Il modo di produzione', in S. Moscati (ed.), *L'alba della civiltà*, II (Torino, 1976), pp. 1-126.

—'Storiografia politica hittita–II: Telipinu, ovvero: Della Solidarità', *OA* 16 (1977), pp. 105-31.

—'Economia delle fattorie palatine ugaritiche', *Dialoghi di Archeologia* n.s. 1 (1979), pp. 57-72.

—'Farsi ḫabiru', *Vicino Oriente* 2 (1979), pp. 65-77.

—*Three Amarna Essays* (Sources and Monographs on the Ancient Near East. Monographs, 1/5 (Malibu, 1979).

—'Political Lexicon and Political Ideologies in the Amarna Letters', *Berytus* 31 (1983), pp. 41-56.

–'Aziru, servitore di due padroni', *Studia Mediterranea* 4 (*Studi Orientalistici in Ricordo di Franco Pintore*, ed. O. Carruba, M. Liverani and C. Zaccagnini; Pavia, 1983), pp. 93-121.

Luther, M., *Die gantze heilige Schrifft Deudsch* (Wittenberg, 1545).

McKane, W., *A Critical and Exegetical Commentary on Jeremiah*, I (ICC; Edinburgh, 1986).

Maisler, B. (Mazar, B.), *Untersuchungen zur alten Geschichte und Ethnographie Syriens und Palästinas* I (Arbeiten aus dem Orientalischen Seminar der Universität Gießen; Gießen, 1930).

–'Canaan and the Canaanites', *BASOR* 102 (1946), pp. 7-12.

Margalit, B., *A Matter of 'Life' and 'Death'. A Study of the Baal-Mot Epic (CTA 4-5-6)* (AOAT, 206; Kevelaer/Neukirchen, 1980).

Marti, K., *Das Dodekapropheton* (KHCAT, 13; Tübingen, 1904).

Mayes, A.D.H., 'The Historical Context of the Battle against Sisera', *VT* 19 (1969), pp. 353-60.

–*Israel in the Period of the Judges* (Studies in Biblical Theology, II/29; London, 1974).

Mazar, B., 'Lebo-hamath and the Northern Border of Canaan', in his *The Early Biblical Period. Historical Studies* (ed. S. Aḥituv and B.A. Levine; Jerusalem, 1986), pp. 189-202.

Mendels, D., *The Land of Israel as a Political Concept in Hasmonean Literature. Recourse to History in Second Century B.C. Claims to the Holy Land* (Texte und Studien zum Antiken Judentum, 15; Tübingen, 1987).

Mendenhall, G.E., *The Tenth Generation* (Baltimore, 1973).

Meyer, E., *Geschichte des Altertums*, I.2, (3rd edn, Berlin, 1913 [repr. Darmstadt, 1965]).

Miller, J.M., 'Jebus and Jerusalem: A Case of Mistaken Identity', *ZDPV* 90 (1974), pp. 115-27.

Moor, J.C. de, *New Year with Cananites and Israelites*, I-II (Kampen, 1972).

–*An Anthology of Religious Texts from Ugarit* (Religious Texts Translation Series Niṣaba, 16; Leiden, 1987).

Moran, W.L., 'Rib-Adda: Job at Byblos?', in Ann Kort and S. Morschalker (eds.), *Biblical and Related Studies Presented to Samuel Iwry* (Winona Lake, 1985), pp. 173-81.

–*Les lettres d'el-Amarna. Correspondance diplomatique du pharaon* (Littératures ancienne du Proche-Orient, 13; Paris, 1987).

Mowinckel, S., *Psalmenstudien.* II. *Das Thronbesteigungsfest Jahwäs und der Ursprung der Eschatologie* (Oslo, 1922 [reprint Amsterdam, 1966]).

Mullen, E.T., *The Assembly of the Gods. The Divine Council in Canaanite and Early Hebrew Literature* (HSM, 24; Chico, 1980).

Nielsen, E., *Shechem. A Traditio-Historical Investigation* (2nd edn; Copenhagen, 1959).

–'Historical Perspectives and Geographical Horizons. On the Question of North-Israelite Elements in Deuteronomy', *ASTI* 11 (1978), pp. 77-89, reprinted in

E. Nielsen, *Law, History and Tradition. Selected Essays by Eduard Nielsen* (Copenhagen, 1983), pp. 82-93.

Noth, M., *Die Welt des Alten Testaments* (4th edn; Berlin, 1962).

—*Geschichte Israels* (Göttingen, 1950).

—*Das Buch Josua* (HAT, I, 7; 2nd edn; Tübingen, 1953).

—*Die Welt des Alten Testaments* (4th edn; Berlin, 1962).

—*Das zweite Buch Mose. Exodus* (ATD, 5; 3rd edn; Göttingen, 1966).

—*Das vierte Buch Mose. Numeri.* (ATD, 7; Göttingen, 1966).

Nowack, W., *Die kleinen Propheten* (GHKAT, III/4; 3rd edn; Göttingen, 1922).

Otto, E., *Jakob in Sichem* (BWANT, 110; Stuttgart, 1979).

Otzen, B., *Studien über Deuterosacharja* (Acta Theologica Danica, 6; Copenhagen, 1964).

Rad, G. von, *Das formgeschichtliche Problem des Hexateuch* (1938), reprinted in *Gesammelte Studien zum Alten Testament* (Theologische Bücherei, 8; München, 1958), pp. 9-86.

—*Das erste Buch Mose. Genesis* (ATD, 2/4; 7th edn, Göttingen, 1964).

Rainey, A.F., *The Social Stratification of Ugarit* (Diss. Brandeis University, 1962).

—'A Canaanite at Ugarit', *IEJ* 13 (1963), pp. 43-5.

—'Ugarit and the Canaanites Again', *IEJ* 14 (1964), p. 101.

—*El Amarna Tablets 359-379* (AOAT, 8; Neukirchen-Kevelaer, 1970).

Redford, D.B., *A Study of the Biblical Story of Joseph (Genesis 37-50)* (SVT, 20; Leiden, 1970).

Rendtorff, R., *Das überlieferungsgeschichtliche Problem des Pentateuch* (BZAW, 147; Berlin, 1977).

Robinson, T.H. and Horst, F., *Die zwölf kleinen Propheten* (HAT, I, 14, 3rd edn; Tübingen, 1964).

Rose, M., *Deuteronomist und Jahwist. Untersuchungen zu den Berührungspunkten beider Literaturwerke* (AThANT, 67; Zürich, 1981).

Rost, L., *Die Überlieferung von der Thronnachfolge Davids* (BWANT, III/6; Stuttgart, 1926), reprinted in L. Rost, *Das kleine Credo und andere Studien zum Alten Testament* (Heidelberg, 1965), pp. 119-253.

Roussel, P., 'Laodicée de Phénicie', *Bulletin de Correspondance Hellénique* 35 (1911), pp. 433-40.

Rudoiph, W., 'Jesaja 23,1-14' (*Festschrift F. Baumgärtel*, ed. L. Rost; Erlangen, 1959), pp. 166-74.

—*Hosea* (KAT, 13, 1; Gütersloh, 1966).

Schmid, H.H., *Gerechtigkeit als Weltordnung. Hintergrund und Geschichte des alttestamentlichen Gerechtigkeitsbegriffes* (BHTh, 40; Tübingen, 1968).

Schmidt, W.H., *Alttestamentlicher Glaube und seine Umwelt* (Neukirchen, 1968).

Schmitt, H.C., *Die nichtpriesterliche Josephgeschichte* (BZAW, 154; Berlin, 1980).

Selms, A. van, 'The Canaanites in the Book of Genesis', *OTS* 12 (1958), pp. 182-213.

Smend, R., *Jahwekrieg und Stämmebund* (FRLANT, 84; 2nd edn, Göttingen, 1966).

182   *The Canaanites and Their Land*

Smith, S., *The Statue of Idri-mi* (Occasional Publications of the British Institute of Archaeology in Ankara, 1; London, 1949).

Soden, W. von, *Akkadisches Handwörterbuch*, II (Wiesbaden, 1972).

Soggin, J.A., *Le livre de Josué* (Commentaire de l'Ancien Testament, Va; Neuchâtel, 1970).

—*A History of Israel* (London, 1984).

Speiser, E.A., 'The Name Phoinikes', *Language* 12 (1936), pp. 121-26.

—*Genesis* (AB, 1; New York, 1964).

Stager, L.E., 'Mernephtah, Israel and the Sea Peoples', *Eretz Israel* 18 (1985), pp. 56*-64*.

Steindorff, G., 'The Statuette of an Egyptian Commissioner in Syria', *JEA* 25 (1939), pp. 30-33 and pl. VII.

Strange, J., *Caphtor/Keftiu. A New Investigation* (Acta Theologica Danica, 14; Leiden, 1980).

Thompson, T.L., *The Historicity of the Patriarchal Narratives. The Quest for the Historical Abraham* (BZAW, 133; Berlin, 1974).

—*The Origin Tradition of Ancient Israel. I. The Literary Formation of Genesis and Exodus 1-23* (JSOTSup, 55; Sheffield, 1987).

Tångberg, K.A., 'Eblaite. An Introduction to the State of Research on the Cuneiform Tablets of Ebla', *SJOT* 1/1 (1987), pp. 110-20.

Uehlinger, C., 'Der Amun-Tempel Ramses' III. in p3-Knᶜn, seine südpalästinischen Tempelgüter und der Übergang von der Ägypter- zur Philisterherrschaft: ein Hinweis auf einige wenig beachtete Skarabäen', *ZDPV* 104 (1989), pp. 6-25.

Van Seters, J., 'The Terms 'Amorite' and 'Hittite' in the Old Testament', *VT* 22 (1972), pp. 64-81.

—'The Conquest of Sihon's Kingdom: A Literary Examination', *JBL* 91 (1972), pp. 181-97.

—*Abraham in History and Tradition* (New Haven, 1975).

—*In Search of History* (New Haven, 1983).

Vaux, R. de, 'Le pays de Canaan', *JAOS* 88 (1968), pp. 23-30.

—'Palestine in the Early Bronze Age', *CAH³*, I, 2 (Cambridge, 1971), pp. 208-37.

Weippert, M., 'Canaan, Conquest and Settlement of', *IDBS*, pp. 125-30.

—'Kanaaan', *RLA*, V, pp. 352-55.

—'Semitische Nomaden des zweiten Jahrtausends. Über die š3šw der ägyptischen Quellen', *Biblica* 55 (1974), pp. 265-80, 427-33.

Weiser, A., 'Das Deboralied. Eine Gattungs- und traditionsgeschichtliche Studie', *ZAW* 71 (1959), pp. 67-97.

Wellhausen, J., *Die Composition des Hexateuchs und der historischen Bücher des Alten Testaments* (4th edn; Berlin, 1963).

Westermann, C., *Genesis*, I (BKAT, I/1; Neukirchen, 1974).

—*Genesis*, II (BKAT, I/3; Neukirchen, 1982).

Wildberger, H., *Jesaja*, II (BKAT, X/2; Neukirchen, 1978).

Wiseman, D.J., *The Alalakh Tablets* (Occasional Publications of the British Institute of Archaeology at Ankara, 2; London, 1953).

—'Supplementary Copies of Alalakh Tablets' *JCS* 8 (1954), pp. 1-30.

Wolff, H.W., *Hosea. Dodekapropheton*, I (BKAT, XIV/1; 2nd edn; Neukirchen, 1965).

Würthwein, E., *et al., Die fünf Megilloth* (HAT, I, 18; Tübingen, 1969).

Young, G.D. (ed.), *Ugarit in Retrospect* (Winona Lake, 1981)

Zimmerli, W., *Ezechiel 1-24. Ezechiel*, I (BKAT, XIII/1, 2nd edn; Neukirchen, 1970).

Zobel, H.-J., 'כְּנַעַן, כְּנַעֲנִי', *TWAT*, IV, cols. 224-43.

INDEX

INDEX OF BIBLICAL REFERENCES

INDEX OF AUTHORS